Rethinking Taxation for Growth in Latin America and the Caribbean

Rethinking Taxation for Growth in Latin America and the Caribbean

Objectives, Behavioral Responses, and Technological Advances

Guillermo Vuletin

WORLD BANK GROUP

Contents

Boxes

Figures

Maps

Tables

Foreword

Three perennial challenges facing countries in Latin America and the Caribbean (LAC)—an absence of fiscal space, persistent inequality, and low growth and job creation—converge at the ostensibly jejune subject of taxation policy. US Supreme Court Justice Oliver Wendell Holmes's observation that "taxes are the price we pay for a civilized society" applies in all capital letters to LAC: the revenues to remedy the region's shortfalls in education, infrastructure, innovation, and transfers are critical to advancing development and the well-being of its citizens. Yet the way states raise revenue is critical, and identifying the optimal combination of instruments to reach societal goals has merited more study in the developing world. Much of the debate to date has narrowly focused on trade-offs between collection efficiency and equity for the various tax instruments.

Rethinking Taxation for Growth in Latin America and the Caribbean: Objectives, Behavioral Responses, and Technological Advances is an invitation to revisit these trade-offs in light of newly available technologies and redistributional mechanisms and, more generally, to take a more holistic view of the entire portfolio of tax instruments and other transfer mechanisms available. For instance, better monitoring technologies and a proven track record of conditional tax transfers ease the equity concerns of tax policy per se. Perhaps more critically, it moves LAC's disappointing growth squarely to the center of the discussion of trade-offs and brings to the fore the possible disincentives of current systems to greater dynamism.

To these ends, the volume brings new data, empirical evidence, and conceptual frameworks to bear. It establishes the stylized facts around the mix of tax instruments used in the region, their incidence across income groups, and, most novelly, the behavioral responses of the taxed and their impacts on collection and growth. This overlooked issue surfaced centrally in discussions of the proposal of Brazil's President Lula for wealth taxes. Given the fluidity with which agents can move funds across borders, careful consideration of what forms of wealth are least open to evasion is essential. More subtly, it shows that the present extraordinarily progressive personal income tax has negative impacts on entrepreneurship and investment and that, as a result, actual taxes take (and likely growth) are substantially below what is intended. Similarly, although prospects for nearshoring are cloudier than several years ago, regional policy makers do need to consider the disincentive effects of some of the highest statutory corporate tax rates in the world on both domestic and foreign investment. The volume also revisits the role of value added tax, arguing that its perceived regressivity has been overstated; hence, it can play a more prominent and efficient role as a cornerstone of tax collection in the region.

The region, as with most developing countries, faces an urgent parallel agenda in making government more efficient and responsive. In this sense, the World Bank's work on government analytics and reports such as *Data for Better Governance: Building Government Analytics Ecosystems in Latin America and the Caribbean*, as well as the recent *Public Spending Policies in Latin America and the Caribbean: When Cyclicality Meets Rigidities*, are vital complements to this work. Indeed, the argument in the volume is not necessarily to increase revenues, although in several countries of the region that is appropriate, but rather how to readjust the portfolio to better optimize the collection of whatever level is deemed optimal across the three objectives.

Rethinking Taxation aims to build a bridge from novel research findings to practical and actionable guidance for policy makers. The debates it engenders will be important to engage in not only in LAC, but also wherever raising revenues is a central policy concern.

William F. Maloney
Regional Chief Economist
Latin America and the Caribbean Region
World Bank

Acknowledgments

This study was led and authored by Guillermo Vuletin, Senior Economist at the World Bank, under the overall guidance of William F. Maloney, Chief Economist for the Latin America and the Caribbean Region. It benefited from contributions from a dedicated team, including Pablo Garriga (Economist, World Bank), Daniel Riera-Crichton (Professor, Bates College), and Lucila Venturi (Research Fellow, Growth Lab–Harvard University), as well as the following team of consultants and researchers: Ivana Benzaquen (World Bank), Jessica Bracco (World Bank), Jose Andree Camarena Fonseca (World Bank), Fernando Castano (World Bank), Matías Ciaschi (Universidad Nacional de La Plata), Guillermo Falcone (World Bank), Isidro Guardarucci (Universidad Nacional de La Plata), Gaston Marinelli (World Bank), and Pilar Ruiz Orrico (World Bank).

We are grateful to the distinguished peer reviewers whose insights greatly enriched the report. Carlos Castelan, Doerte Doemeland, Ayhan Kose, and Thiago Scot—all at the World Bank—provided thoughtful guidance and detailed feedback on the concept note and decision drafts. We also benefited from the expertise and support of many colleagues and collaborators, including Anne Brockmeyer (World Bank), Hugo Ñopo (World Bank), Carola Pessino (Inter-American Development Bank), Dario Tortarolo (World Bank), and Oscar Valencia (Inter-American Development Bank), as well as several editors and anonymous referees who reviewed background papers submitted to academic journals. Thanks also go to Guillermo Beylis, Vicenzo Di Maro, Nathalie Gonzalez-Prieto, Marcela Melendez Arjona, Valeria Anne Mercer Blackman, Daniel Navia, and Ayat Soliman for their valuable comments and insights along the way.

During the final stages of the study, we received helpful feedback from participants at the launch event held during the 2024 Latin American and Caribbean Economic Association conference in Montevideo, Uruguay, as well as from other international and regional conferences. The report also benefited from valuable insights shared by policy makers and participants in several regional policy meetings, including the XXVII Workshop in International Economics and Finance in Paraguay, held May 28–30, 2025, as well as presentations at the Banco de España, Universidad de San Andrés, Universidad Católica, and Universidad de Belgrano in Argentina.

Cindy Fisher, Patricia Katayama, and Mark McClure of the World Bank's publishing program oversaw the report's publication. Bill Pragluski designed the book cover. The World Bank's Cartography Unit prepared the final versions of several maps featured in the report. We are also grateful to Jacqueline Larrabure Rivero for her excellent administrative support.

Although reviewers, advisers, and collaborators provided valuable input, any errors or omissions are solely the author's responsibility.

About the Author

Guillermo Vuletin is a Senior Economist in the Office of the Chief Economist for Latin America and the Caribbean Region of the World Bank. He is also an associate editor of the *Economía LACEA Journal*. He was previously a lead economist in the Research Department of the Inter-American Development Bank, a fellow at the Brookings Institution, a lecturer at Johns Hopkins University, and a professor at Colby College (United States).

His research focuses on fiscal and monetary policies with a particular interest in macroeconomic policy in emerging and developing countries. His work has been published in the *American Economic Journal: Economic Policy*, *Journal of Development Economics*, *Journal of International Economics*, and *Journal of Monetary Economics*, as well as in other journals. His research has been featured in prominent media outlets, such as *The Economist*, *The Financial Times*, *The Wall Street Journal*, and *The Washington Post*, and other international and regional newspapers. He holds a PhD in economics from the University of Maryland and an undergraduate degree and an MA in economics from the Universidad Nacional de La Plata, Buenos Aires, Argentina.

Executive Summary

Introduction

Governments tax to raise revenue to fund public spending and the provision of social services to their citizens. In selecting the optimal set of tax instruments to achieve this objective, tax policy has traditionally focused on the trade-off between collection efficiency and the pursuit of equity. This report aims to enrich the debate in two key ways. First, it examines how the behavioral responses of those who are taxed and recent technological advances may affect this traditionally viewed trade-off. Second, it introduces a previously understressed trade-off with a third critical goal—economic growth—in which the Latin America and the Caribbean (LAC) region persistently underperforms.

The importance of core taxes for government revenue. Governments use a diverse set of tax instruments; value added tax (VAT), personal income tax (PIT), corporate income tax (CIT), and wealth tax (WT) typically constitute 70–80 percent of total government revenue. VAT and CIT are particularly significant revenue sources for most emerging and developing economies (EMDEs), including those in the LAC region, compared with advanced economies, which tend to rely more heavily on PIT and WT.

Traditional view of core taxes: main objectives and instruments. When evaluating the main advantages and disadvantages of each type of tax instrument, the tax policy literature traditionally focuses on two key objectives: collection efficiency and income redistribution incidence. Each of the core taxes has strengths and weaknesses along these dimensions (refer to table O.1). On the one hand, VAT and CIT (especially VAT) are conventionally considered easier to collect than PIT and WT, primarily because of the higher levels of evasion and avoidance associated with the latter. On the other hand, PIT and WT are often supported as prime instruments for achieving tax progressivity, in contrast to the VAT, which is generally considered regressive. This is because low-income earners typically consume a larger portion of their income, whereas high-income earners tend to save more, reducing their exposure to VAT. Precisely for this reason, most countries in the world implement reduced VAT rates on essential goods and services, such as food and basic necessities, to mitigate its regressive impact.

Table O.1   **Traditional view of core taxes**

Tax	Collection efficiency	Redistribution incidence
Value added tax	High	Regressive
Corporate income tax	Moderate	Moderate progressive
Personal income tax	Low	Progressive
Wealth tax	Super low	Super progressive

Source: Original table for this publication.

This objective trade-off is acutely felt in EMDEs. Weak enforcement, a large informal sector, and resource constraints hinder effective tax collection. Consequently, EMDEs often prioritize revenue generation, relying heavily on VAT and CIT, even if it means accepting higher regressivity. This second-best equilibrium is particularly problematic given the high levels of poverty and inequality prevalent in these regions.

Rethinking taxation in LAC: Objectives, behavioral responses, and technological advances. This report reevaluates the traditional view of tax policy by examining how the understudied impact of behavioral responses and the emergence of recent technological advances affect the objectives of collection efficiency and equity as well as their trade-off. It also brings attention to a previously overlooked trade-off linked to a third vital goal—economic growth—an area in which the LAC region persistently falls short.

The behavioral responses of the taxed lead us to consider tax evasion and avoidance in a fiscal environment characterized by weak enforcement, compounded by the erosion of tax morale because of corruption and inefficiencies. We must also consider tax base mobility in an increasingly interconnected global economy and the behavioral responses of labor and investment to taxation in the context of the generally unfriendly business environment in LAC. This underscores the critical point that theoretically sound tax policies or reforms can prove less appealing in practice if significant and heterogeneous behavioral responses emerge across various dimensions.

Technological advances are remaking the fiscal landscape. We examine the emergence of new fiscal instruments, such as targeted cash transfers (TCTs), to shift the landscape of redistribution, as well as how modern digital tools and increased firm interconnectivity can both assist governments in strengthening tax enforcement and administration (for example, through better property valuation and firms acting as tax collectors) and present new challenges (for example, by facilitating the hiding of financial assets). Consequently, the inherent impact of these technological shifts on fiscal instruments fundamentally reconfigures their benefits and costs, ultimately defining the new spectrum of opportunities and challenges for fiscal authorities.

Central to this report is the explicit integration of economic growth as a primary objective in tax policy design for LAC, an understressed dimension in traditional discussions that often prioritize revenue and equity. This analysis moves beyond the conventional static focus and delves into the dynamic behavioral responses of economic agents to taxation, particularly in the context of LAC's unique business environment. By examining how different tax instruments affect investment, entrepreneurship, labor supply, and capital flows, this report offers novel insights into designing tax systems that minimize growth-inhibiting distortions and instead foster a more dynamic and competitive regional economy. This perspective underscores the critical need to evaluate tax policies not only on their immediate revenue and distributional effects but also on their long-term implications for sustainable economic expansion in LAC.

Given the extensive body of work on taxation, the intent of this report is not to be comprehensive in the treatment of each tax. Rather, the central goal is to offer novel perspectives on main taxes across the relevant dimensions of behavioral responses, evolving fiscal instruments, technological advancements, and growth implications. Following is a synopsis of the content covered in each chapter.

TCTs: The "new" instrument to deal with equity objectives. This chapter examines the transformative impact of TCTs on income redistribution, a goal traditionally pursued through progressive taxation. Although progressive taxes on wealth, income, and corporations have historically been favored for promoting equity, TCTs offer a distinct and precisely targeted mechanism to achieve this goal. These direct payments to eligible individuals, based on criteria such as income, ensure resources reach those most in need, as demonstrated by programs such as Brazil's Bolsa Familia.

The increasing prevalence of TCT programs fundamentally alters policy considerations, potentially reducing the sole emphasis on highly progressive tax systems. This shift allows policy makers to prioritize maximizing overall government revenue, even through more neutral taxes, because redistributive goals can be effectively addressed through TCTs. For example, eliminating reduced VAT rates could increase revenue to fund more generous TCTs, potentially making even seemingly regressive taxes contribute to progressive outcomes. Beyond traditional conditional cash transfers, instruments such as negative income taxes can further expand the reach of social support to low- to moderate-income individuals.

Furthermore, TCTs may offer a way to mitigate behavioral responses linked to aggressive progressive taxation, such as tax evasion, avoidance, and disincentives to work or invest. Although progressive taxes remain important, well-designed TCTs lessen the pressure to rely solely on maximizing tax progressivity, particularly when facing significant behavioral responses. The emergence of large-scale TCTs, particularly in LAC since the mid-1990s, provides policy makers with a more precise tool to address income inequality and potentially rebalance traditional tax policy trade-offs. This evolution necessitates improved targeting mechanisms, such as the integration of geographic information systems and administrative data, to minimize inclusion and exclusion errors and enhance program efficiency.

Demystifying VAT regressivity and the pitfalls of high standard rates.
This chapter reframes the debate on VAT, a critical revenue source in LAC, by challenging the conventional view of its inherent regressivity. It highlights the limitations of traditional income-based analyses, especially in informal economies, where consumption offers a more stable measure of long-run well-being. Analyzing VAT incidence through consumption reveals it to be less regressive, or even progressive. As demonstrated by Bachas, Gadenne, and Jensen (2020), substantial VAT-exempt informal consumption among lower-income households leads standard analyses to overstate the tax burden on the poor.

However, this chapter underscores a key policy dilemma: balancing equity and growth. Although reduced VAT rates on essentials aim to achieve equity, they can necessitate higher standard VAT rates, which Gunter et al. (2021) show may have nonlinear and detrimental growth effects, particularly above a 16 percent threshold.

To reconcile these competing objectives, the chapter suggests a potential policy shift: reevaluating reduced VAT rates (which can disproportionately benefit the rich) and decreasing reliance on high standard VAT rates. This could create fiscal space for a more progressive overall fiscal structure, minimize distortions, and promote growth.

To address the political challenges of VAT reform, the chapter stresses strategic management: clear communication, phased implementation, and strengthened institutional capacity, particularly for TCTs. Given that many LAC countries already possess well-developed social transfer systems, as demonstrated by Mexico's successful shift from generalized subsidies to targeted transfers, this provides a significant advantage. Experiences such as the global shift to targeted transfers post–COVID-19 further highlight the adaptability and scalability of these interventions.

CIT: from chasing butterflies to drawing bees. LAC now contends with some of the highest CIT rates globally, a consequence of a relative lack of downward adjustment since the 1980s, while the rest of the world significantly reduced their rates. This high tax burden exacerbates an already challenging business environment marked by excessive regulation, a poorly skilled workforce, inadequate infrastructure, and significant institutional rigidities.

Consistent with trends in other EMDEs, LAC firms demonstrate a greater sensitivity to CIT changes than their counterparts in advanced nations. This heightened responsiveness arises from both weak enforcement, enabling strategic tax evasion and profit manipulation, and firms' actual responses, including relocation to favorable jurisdictions, a shift toward the informal sector, curtailing labor hiring as a cost-saving measure (because of greater capital mobility and labor cost pressures), discouraging investment, and stifling innovation.

Instead of ineffectively chasing easily evasive "butterflies" with high CIT rates that hinder growth, policy makers should strategically reduce these rates to improve competitiveness with other EMDEs. This should be combined with increased reliance on less distortionary and more easily collected taxes. Within the CIT framework, bolstering enforcement and fostering innovative public-private partnerships, such as leveraging firms for tax collection, are essential. This comprehensive approach seeks to cultivate a business-friendly environment, stimulate economic growth, and ultimately attract productive "bees" that generate jobs and flourish in a prosperous and dynamic LAC economy.

PIT beyond top income earners. Despite boasting significantly high top marginal PIT rates, LAC suffers from a remarkably narrow tax base, hindering its fiscal capacity and potentially stifling economic growth. New evidence shows that top earners in LAC exhibit a higher sensitivity to tax changes than upper-middle-income earners, who actually show little behavioral response—a finding consistent with US studies. This larger behavioral response at the top is driven by increased tax evasion and avoidance, as well as adjustments in labor supply. In particular, the fact that most entrepreneurs and firm owners are concentrated at the most highly taxed part of the distribution suggests that the current PIT structure penalizes the entrepreneurship that would drive faster growth. Consequently, the chapter argues for moderately broadening the tax base as opposed to further increasing the rates on the very highest earners, which, in some cases, are already at US levels.

This approach, supported by US historical precedent, offers a better way to boost LAC's fiscal capacity while remaining progressive. Before the mid-20th century, the United States had high top tax rates on a narrow base, which yielded low average tax rates. World War II necessitated a shift toward a broader base, significantly increasing government revenue. Moderately expanding the tax base in LAC, excluding vulnerable and informal populations, offers a more effective strategy for increasing efficiency in revenue collection without harming economic activity or growth.

Taxing the tangible and immobile wealth. This chapter argues that although WTs, particularly on billionaires, are gaining global attention, policies need to be tailored to the different types of wealth for them to be effective. Financial assets, inherently easy to hide and move, face even fewer constraints in an increasingly digital and technologically advanced world. However, in LAC, most wealth, even among the highest income earners, is held in the form of property, and hence property taxes have potential to generate significant revenue. Furthermore, property is far easier to identify and less mobile, and it arguably induces fewer growth-discouraging distortions. Property is often more a store of value than a productive asset; hence, shifting away from CIT or PIT may have fewer adverse effects on growth through behavioral offsets in investment or entrepreneurship. Given these attractive characteristics, it is somewhat paradoxical that property taxes are currently underused in the region. Unlike WTs on billionaires, which may be difficult to implement and enforce because of the limited number of ultra-wealthy individuals, their high mobility, and the significant challenges of taxing financial assets (requiring near-perfect global coordination), property taxes offer a practical and effective solution, further enhanced by the fact that digital platforms such as real estate websites like Zillow and Trulia are rapidly making accurate and cost-effective property valuation a more readily achievable goal.

Rethinking taxation in LAC: distilling the new insights for taxation in LAC. This report has undertaken a critical reevaluation of taxation in LAC, moving beyond conventional frameworks by explicitly incorporating the significant influence of behavioral responses, the transformative potential of technological advancements, and the imperative of fostering sustained economic growth. This analysis of core tax instruments reveals several key insights that challenge traditional views, as briefly summarized in table O.2. TCTs emerge as a powerful tool for achieving equity, offering new possibilities for the design of the broader tax system. The inclusion of TCTs as a new fiscal tool challenges the traditional view by alleviating the trade-off between collection efficiency and redistribution, thereby shifting the focus of taxation policy toward more effective revenue collection alongside, rather than solely through, achieving progressivity. The perceived regressivity of the VAT in LAC is called into question by emerging evidence, suggesting avenues for revenue mobilization with less adverse distributional effects. Furthermore, novel growth evidence suggests that the reduction of high standard VAT rates can boost economic growth. This potential revenue decline could be offset by eliminating reduced VAT rates and broadening the tax base, which would also enhance revenue collection from higher-income individuals. The experience with the CIT underscores the critical need for competitive tax rates to prevent capital flight and stimulate investment. The PIT, characterized by high top rates and a narrow base, highlights the importance of broadening participation to enhance revenue and minimize disincentives for entrepreneurship and evasion. Finally, although the taxation of billionaires and financial assets may hold popular appeal, its practical implementation faces significant hurdles because of the high mobility of these tax bases, potentially necessitating near-perfect international tax coordination. The concentration of wealth in tangible assets within the region positions property taxes as a practical and underused mechanism for wealth taxation, particularly as technological solutions for valuation become increasingly accessible.

Table O.2   New insights on core taxes

| Tax | Collection efficiency | Redistribution incidence | | Growth | Main implications |
		Without considering TCTs	Considering TCTs		
VAT	High	Neutral or moderate progressive	Super progressive	Neutral if moderately taxed, negative if highly taxed	Expand the tax base (eliminating reduced rates) and avoid high VAT rates
CIT	Moderate	Moderate progressive	Super progressive	Negative	Reduce high CIT rates (in line with other EMDEs), improve business environment, and use firms as tax collectors
PIT	Low on top earners, yet moderate (or high) on upper-middle income earners	Progressive	Super progressive	Neutral on upper-middle income earners, yet negative on top earners	Expand the tax base, while avoiding encroachment on middle- and low-income earners
WT	Super low on financial assets, yet high on properties	Super progressive	Super progressive	Weakly negative, especially on properties	Tax property as opposed to financial assets

Source: Original table for this publication.

Note: CIT = corporate income tax; EMDEs = emerging markets and developing economies; PIT = personal income tax; TCTs = targeted cash transfers; VAT = value added tax; WT = wealth tax.

The insights presented in this report suggest a promising recalibration of LAC's tax systems. Rather than solely relying on potentially distortionary high rates on narrow bases or on difficult-to-tax assets, a more strategic blend emerges to simultaneously enhance revenue, promote equity, and foster growth: leveraging the broad base of the VAT and reducing standard VAT rates, provided that their current level is excessively high; moderately expanding the reach of the PIT; implementing intelligent property taxation (as opposed to challenging financial assets); fostering corporate dynamism through a more competitive CIT regime; and strategically deploying TCTs to address equity concerns more effectively.

These new insights collectively point to a nuanced and context-specific approach to tax policy in LAC. Moving beyond the traditional trade-offs between collection efficiency and equity, policy makers must embrace a more dynamic perspective that considers both how individuals and firms respond to taxation and the increasingly interconnected and digital world we live in. The strategic deployment of new fiscal instruments such as TCTs significantly reshapes the traditional view of the collection efficiency and equity trade-off. This, coupled with a willingness to reexamine long-held beliefs about the incidence and impact of core taxes, offers a pathway toward building more effective, equitable, and growth-enhancing tax systems in the LAC region, as well as in other EMDEs. Ultimately, by embracing the understanding of these evolving realities, LAC countries can move forward in their efforts to harness the power of taxation for sustainable development and improved lives, with this report contributing valuable perspectives to that complex challenge.

References

Bachas, P., L. Gadenne, and A. Jensen. 2020. "Informality, Consumption Taxes, and Redistribution." Policy Research Working Paper 9267, World Bank, Washington, DC.

Gunter, S., D. Riera-Crichton, C.A. Vegh, and G. Vuletin. 2021. "Non-Linear Effects of Tax Changes on Output: The Role of the Initial Level of Taxation." *Journal of International Economics* 131: 103450.

Abbreviations

AMPITR	average marginal PIT rates
A*STAR	Agency for Science, Technology, and Research
CAs	collection agents
CABA	city of Buenos Aires
CCTs	conditional cash transfers
CBO	Congressional Budget Office
CEQ	Commitment to Equity Institute
CIT	corporate income tax
CONASUPO	Compañía Nacional de Subsistencias Populares
CV	coefficient of variation
DiD	difference-in-differences
EDB	Economic Development Board
EMDEs	emerging markets and developing economies
ETI	elasticity of taxable income
EU	European Union
FDI	foreign direct investment
G&S	goods and services
GDP	gross domestic product
GIPS	Greece, Italy, Portugal, Spain
GIS	geographic information systems
ICA	Immigration and Checkpoints Authority
IFI	*Impôt sur la Fortune Immobilière*
ISF	*Impôt de Solidarité sur la Fortune*
ITR	*Imposto sobre a Propriedade Territorial Rural*
LAC	Latin America and the Caribbean
Max	maximum

Min	minimum
MNCs	multinational corporations
OECD	Organisation for Economic Co-operation and Development
PBA	province of Buenos Aires
PIT	personal income tax
PROGRESA	Programa de Educación, Salud y Alimentación
PUT	payments under the table
PwC	PricewaterhouseCoopers
R&D	research and development
SAR	special administrative region
SINIRUBE	Sistema Nacional de Información y Registro Único de Beneficiarios del Estado
t	quarter
TCTs	targeted cash transfers
TT	trade taxes
UNCTAD	United Nations Conference on Trade and Development
VAT	value added tax
VAT+	value added tax plus other taxes on consumption
WT	wealth tax

1

Tax Policy: Foundations, Traditional Views, and Evolving Strategies

Introduction

Taxes provide governments with the revenue needed to fund public spending, such as national defense; police and fire departments; the court system; transport infrastructure, such as roads and bridges; education; health care; and transfers to individuals through a variety of social and welfare programs. A surprisingly large share of tax inflows, roughly 20 percent, goes toward interest on the national debt and, occasionally, paying it down.

How much government should spend is beyond the scope of this report: there is no magic formula or one-size-fits-all answer. It is a complex issue influenced by a multitude of factors. Economic development plays a crucial role, as evidenced by Wagner's law, which suggests that government spending tends to increase as a proportion of gross domestic product (GDP) as economies develop and demand for public services such as education, health care, and social safety nets grows. Moreover, societal preferences strongly influence the extent to which citizens desire government involvement. For instance, citizens of societies with a higher degree of risk aversion may favor greater government involvement in areas such as social security and unemployment insurance, whereas those of societies with a stronger emphasis on individual responsibility may prefer less involvement.

Equally as important for balancing fiscal accounts is the efficient use of public funds. Studies by Izquierdo, Pessino, and Vuletin (2018) suggest that approximately 4 percent of GDP, or 12 percent of total spending, could be saved by preventing transfer leakages and eliminating wasteful expenditures. Therefore, alongside efforts to raise revenue efficiently, there should be a parallel focus on improving the state's operational efficiency, a point emphasized in Rogger and Schuster (2023). This increased efficiency can also positively influence tax morale—that is, people's willingness to pay taxes. When citizens are confident that their hard-earned income is being used effectively and this view is widely shared, tax evasion tends to decrease, and tax collection efficiency improves.

Importance of Core Taxes for Government Revenue

Governments rely on a mix of taxes to collect revenue, only a handful of which typically represent the main bulk of revenue collection in most countries. Value added tax (VAT), personal income tax (PIT), corporate income tax (CIT), and wealth tax (WT) are the core taxes and some of the most important for government revenue collection (refer to figure 1.1, panel a). For example, in the case of Latin America and the Caribbean (LAC), VAT, PIT, CIT, and WT account for about 70 percent of total tax revenues (refer to figure 1.1, panels b and c). In terms of tax structure, emerging markets and developing economies (EMDEs, such as LAC) rely more heavily on VAT and CIT than their advanced counterparts, which tend to rely more on PIT and, in some cases, WT.

Figure 1.1   Tax revenue composition across regions and by LAC country

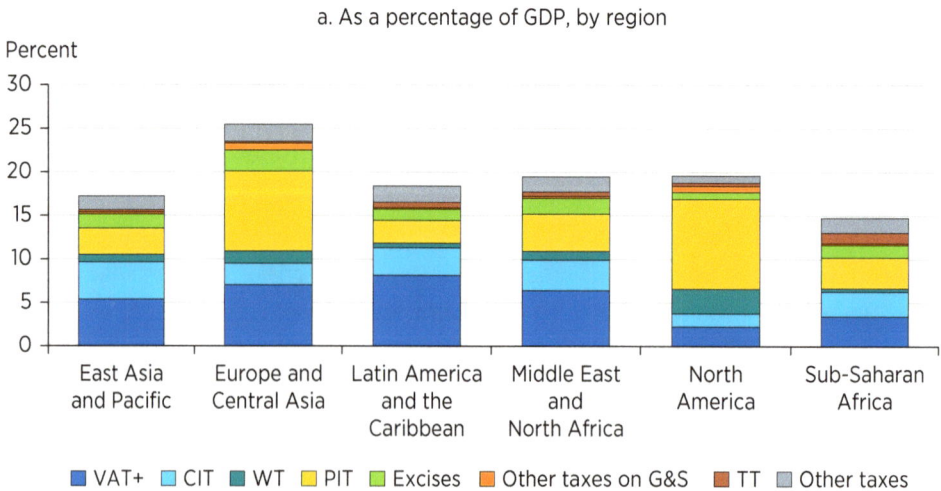

a. As a percentage of GDP, by region

figure continued next page

Figure 1.1   Tax revenue composition across regions and by LAC country *(continued)*

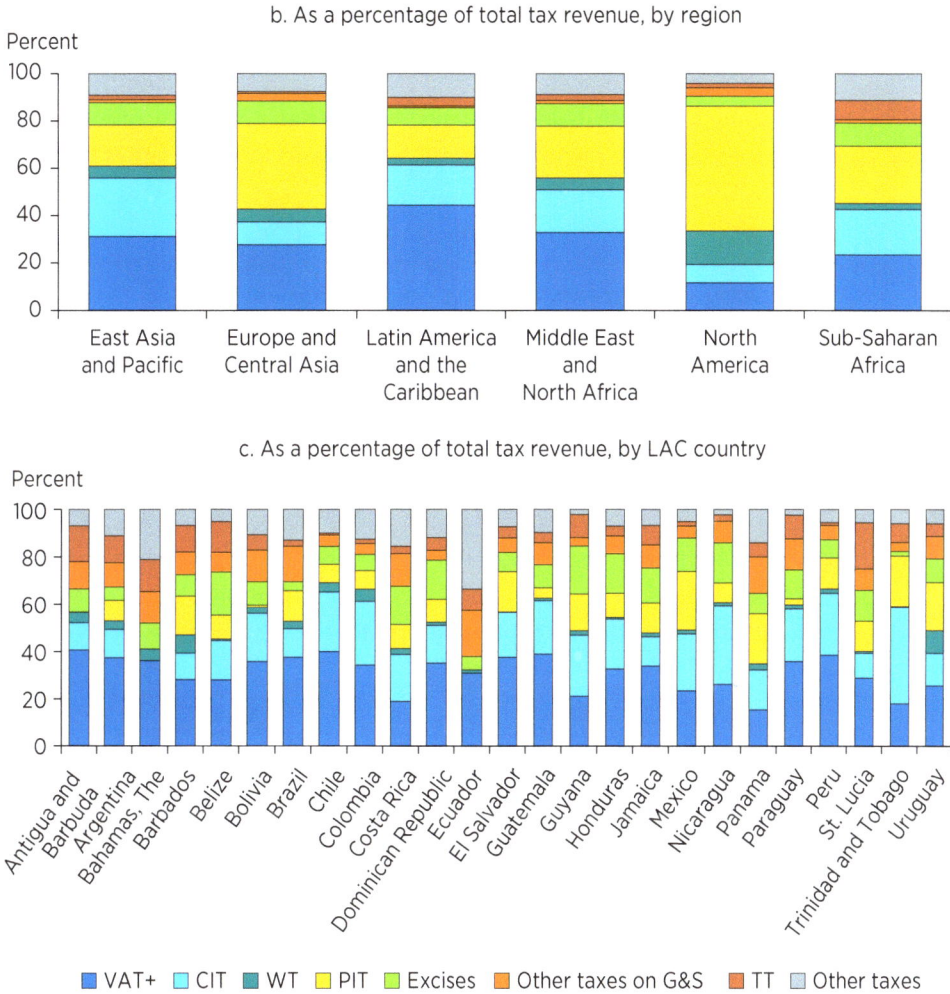

b. As a percentage of total tax revenue, by region

c. As a percentage of total tax revenue, by LAC country

■ VAT+   □ CIT   ■ WT   ■ PIT   □ Excises   ■ Other taxes on G&S   ■ TT   □ Other taxes

Source: Original calculations for this publication using data from the OECD's Global Tax Revenue Statistics Database (https://www.oecd.org/en/data/datasets/global-revenue -statistics-database.html) and the World Bank.

Note: Consolidated government statistics. CIT = corporate income tax; G&S = goods and services; GDP = gross domestic product; LAC = Latin America and the Caribbean; PIT = personal income tax; TT = trade taxes; VAT+ = value added tax plus other taxes on consumption (for example, sales tax); WT = wealth tax.

Traditional View of Core Taxes

When evaluating the main advantages and disadvantages of each type of core tax, the fiscal policy literature traditionally centers on two key dimensions: collection efficiency and redistribution incidence. *Collection efficiency* refers to the ability of a tax system to maximize tax revenue while minimizing tax evasion and avoidance. It involves efficient and effective tax administration, including robust enforcement mechanisms to deter and detect illegal tax practices.

Redistribution incidence refers to the distribution of tax payments across different income groups. This can be regressive, where lower-income individuals bear a disproportionately larger tax burden, or progressive, where higher-income individuals pay a greater share of their income in taxes.

Table 1.1 summarizes the main takeaways from the traditional view of core taxes, and what follows is a discussion of the main arguments for each type of tax.

VAT: Easily Collected Yet Regressive

VAT's multistage implementation is designed for efficient collection. Unlike a sales tax, which is levied only at the final point of purchase, VAT is collected at each stage of production and distribution. Businesses add the tax to the value they contribute, and they can reclaim the VAT they have paid on their own inputs. This self-policing mechanism, in which businesses have an incentive to track and report VAT to claim refunds, minimizes evasion. Furthermore, because the tax is spread across numerous transactions, the risk of large-scale revenue loss from a single point of failure is reduced. This structure, along with standardized rates and clear documentation requirements, simplifies administration and ensures a relatively consistent flow of revenue for governments.

However, because VAT is applied to the final price, it can have a disproportionate impact on low-income earners who spend a larger portion of their income on essentials with VAT. High-income earners have more disposable income (for example, for savings and investments) and are less affected by VAT. Consequently, VAT has typically been viewed as a regressive tax, meaning that the effective tax rate (that is, the portion of income paid in taxes) decreases as income increases. For this reason, most countries use a standard VAT rate along with reduced rates or even exemptions for essential goods and services—especially basic foodstuffs and medicine. Reducing VAT rates on necessities, which make up a large

Table 1.1 Main takeaways from the traditional view of core taxes

Tax type	Collection efficiency	Redistribution incidence
VAT	High	Regressive
CIT	Moderate	Moderate progressive
PIT	Low	Progressive
WT	Super low	Super progressive

Source: Original elaboration for this publication based on literature review.

Note: CIT = corporate income tax; PIT = personal income tax; VAT = value added tax; WT = wealth tax.

proportion of the budget of low-income earners, is aimed at lessening the total tax burden of low-income earners in relation to high-income earners. In essence, reduced rates aim to mitigate the VAT's inherent regressivity. However, this is an imperfect adjustment, so some degree of regressivity always remains.

CIT: Chasing Butterflies

The CIT, although a direct tax on profits, has moderate collection efficiency because of its inherent complexities. Corporations often maintain detailed accounting records, facilitating some aspects of tax filing, but they also possess numerous avenues to minimize their tax liabilities. Companies frequently use legitimate deductions and tax credits, but they may also engage in more problematic practices, such as inflating costs or underreporting revenues, obscuring their true taxable income (OECD 2021a). These practices make it challenging for tax authorities to accurately assess and collect taxes owed. Multinational corporations (MNCs) further exacerbate these difficulties. Their intricate global structure and cross-border transactions provide fertile ground for tax avoidance through profit shifting, transfer pricing manipulation, and exploitation of international tax loopholes, significantly complicating collection efforts and reducing their effective tax rate (CBO 2023). Most countries rely on a flat CIT rate applied to corporate profits, meaning that the tax burden is independent of the profit size.

Despite collection challenges, the CIT enhances progressivity because corporate profits are a significant source of income for wealthy shareholders. Taxing these profits at a higher rate than PIT on dividends increases the progressivity of the tax system (Marr et al. 2021).

PIT: Tailored to Tax High-Income Earners

The PIT, a direct tax levied on an individual's taxable income (for example, wages, salaries, interest, and dividends), is often seen as the prime example of a progressive tax targeting high-income earners. Its inherent progressive structure increases the tax rate as taxable income rises. However, as a result of incremental lawmaking over time, PIT has become complex (Guenther 2024), with numerous intricate rules, loopholes, and exceptions (Ferriere et al. 2022; Wamhoff 2024). In fact, this complexity, coupled with high enforcement costs, typically leads to lower efficiency in tax collection.

WT: In Theory, Progressivity on Steroids

WTs are typically levied on an individual's net worth (assets minus liabilities). Typical assets include real estate (for example, houses, apartments, land), financial investments (for example, stocks, bonds, mutual funds), business ownership, funds in banks or cash, and luxury goods (for example, yachts, art collections, jewelry). In theory, WTs can be more transparent than PIT, especially when coupled with robust asset valuation methods. However, they can be complex to administer, requiring accurate valuations of often-illiquid assets such as real estate or private businesses. Additionally, the ease with which wealthy individuals can move liquid assets across borders to jurisdictions with lower tax rates further undermines the effectiveness of WTs. This complexity can lead to inefficiencies in collection and potentially higher administrative costs (Saez and Zucman 2019). Proponents argue that WTs are more progressive than PIT, because wealthy individuals often have a significant share of their wealth in assets that generate low or no taxable income.

Objective Trade-Offs

The traditional view points to a clear trade-off between ease of collection (where VAT and CIT have advantages over PIT and WT, which are often characterized by high levels of evasion and avoidance) and the impact of income redistribution (where PIT and WT have distinct advantages in supporting high tax progressivity). This dilemma is exacerbated in EMDEs because of their weaker fiscal enforcement environment resulting from limited resources, including understaffed tax authorities, inadequate infrastructure, and widespread corruption. Furthermore, tax enforcement and collection in these countries is further complicated by a pervasive informal, or shadow, economy that relies on cash, lacks formal records, and operates outside of the tax system (that is, it is hidden from authorities by evasion, regulation, or institutional factors). Consequently, EMDEs primarily rely on VAT and CIT to generate revenue, accepting a higher degree of regressivity to ensure sufficient tax revenue. Unfortunately, this second-best type of equilibrium, in which ease of collection is prioritized over equity concerns, is particularly troublesome in EMDEs, given their higher levels of poverty and income inequality.

Rethinking Taxation in Latin America and the Caribbean

This report reevaluates traditional tax policy perspectives, delving into the often-overlooked influence of behavioral responses. Specifically, it examines how tax evasion and avoidance, prevalent in fiscal environments marked by weak enforcement, and the increased mobility of tax bases in the interconnected global economy, as well as the sensitivity of labor and investment to taxation amid the LAC region's challenging business climate, significantly affect tax policy outcomes. Moreover, the report explores the transformative potential of recent technological advances, such as targeted cash transfers, in reshaping redistribution strategies. It also investigates how digital innovations can empower governments to address enforcement shortcomings and enhance tax administration. Critically, the analysis reveals a previously underappreciated trade-off with economic growth, a crucial area in which the LAC region consistently struggles, underscoring the need for a more holistic approach to tax policy design.

Behavioral Responses of Taxpayers

The reality of taxpayer behavior compels governments to confront the challenges posed by tax evasion and avoidance and the critical issue of diminished tax morale arising from corruption and inefficiencies in weak fiscal systems. Furthermore, the increasing fluidity of tax bases in a globalized economy, coupled with the sensitivity of labor and investment to taxation in the LAC region's often adverse business landscape, adds significant complexity. This highlights a fundamental concern: that even well-designed tax policies and reforms may fall short of their intended outcomes if they do not adequately account for the diverse and substantial behavioral adaptations that arise in practice.

Tax Evasion and Avoidance

As discussed earlier, the traditional view emphasizes the issues of tax evasion and avoidance, which is even more pressing in EMDEs. Although raising taxes can increase government revenue, it can also incentivize tax evasion and avoidance. When taxes rise, some people might be tempted to evade them by shifting their taxable activities toward areas in which taxes are harder to enforce. For example, a handyman with a full-time job might consider taking more cash-only jobs to avoid paying taxes on those earnings. Legal loopholes and deductions could also be used to reduce their tax burden. For example, a wealthy individual might exploit loopholes in the tax code by donating a large sum of money to a charitable foundation they control, effectively reducing their taxable income while still maintaining control over the funds.

Weak revenue institutions and low tax enforcement create fertile ground for both tax evasion and tax avoidance. When the chances of getting caught for evasion and avoidance are minimal because of lax or low enforcement or an opaque tax system, the temptation to cheat becomes stronger. Moreover, honest taxpayers may feel that their diligent contributions are in vain, further eroding their trust in the system and discouraging honest compliance by a larger margin. Citizens' perception of government corruption, and of wasteful and inefficient public spending, can significantly reduce tax morale. In turn, this erosion of trust weakens the social contract in which citizens pay taxes to the government in exchange for the provision of public goods and services. Unfortunately, these issues tend to be more prevalent in EMDEs, creating a clear challenge for policy makers. Figure 1.2, panel a, illustrates that estimates of the shadow economy, expressed as a percentage of GDP, are higher in EMDEs than in their advanced counterparts. Within LAC, Guatemala and Bolivia have the largest shadow economies, skyrocketing to 50 percent (refer to figure 1.2, panel b). Conversely, Chile boasts the smallest shadow economy at around 13 percent, aligning with levels found in advanced economies.

Figure 1.2   Estimates of the shadow economy as a percentage of GDP, 2010–15 average

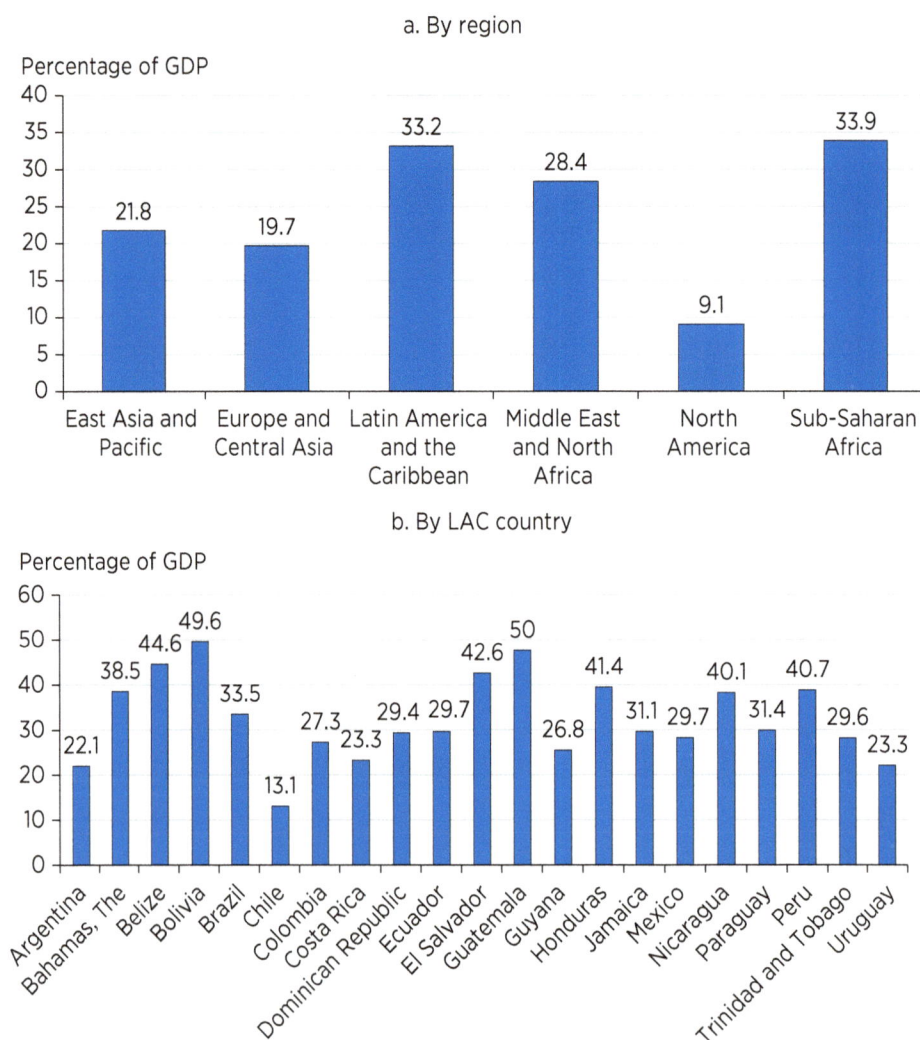

a. By region

Percentage of GDP

b. By LAC country

Percentage of GDP

Source: Original calculations for this publication using data from Medina and Schneider 2019.

Note: GDP = gross domestic product; LAC = Latin America and the Caribbean.

A Lengthy Undertaking

Policy makers can deter further increases in tax evasion and avoidance by implementing several strategies. In addition to increasing transparency, so that citizens can better understand how their tax dollars are being used, policy makers should also focus on improving the effectiveness and efficiency of public spending, particularly on infrastructure and social programs. Strengthening anticorruption measures is also crucial. For example, box 1.1 presents Spain's experience in the 1980s and demonstrates the importance of transparency in boosting tax morale. However, as illustrated in box 1.1, achieving these goals, particularly enhancing transparency and improving public spending, can be a protracted process. Spain's tax transformation demonstrates that significant improvements in tax morale often require sustained efforts over an extended period, potentially spanning several decades. Therefore, although these strategies are undoubtedly necessary, they unfortunately involve a long-term commitment to reforms and patience in their implementation.

Box 1.1

From tax rebels to responsible contributors: The Spanish tax transformation of the 1980s

Spain's relationship with taxation has been a roller-coaster ride. The pre-1980s era was particularly bumpy, marked by a thriving black market and rampant tax evasion. Estimates suggest that more than 40 percent of taxes went unpaid, crippling the government's ability to fund essential services. This culture of noncompliance had deep historical roots. However, the Spanish government managed to turn things around. Its success offers valuable insights into the types of reforms that increase tax morale.

A legacy of distrust

Spain's long history of authoritarian rule fostered a deep distrust in central government authorities. During the oppressive Franco regime (1939–75), taxes were seen as a tool of repression rather than a means to improve public services. Additionally, the complex and bureaucratic tax system was rife with loopholes, creating fertile ground for evasion. Ordinary citizens felt that their tax contributions were mismanaged, further eroding tax morale.

box continued next page

Box 1.1

From tax rebels to responsible contributors: The Spanish tax transformation of the 1980s *(continued)*

A booming black market

The economic strains of the 1970s also fueled tax evasion. High inflation and unemployment pushed many Spaniards toward the informal economy. The combination of economic hardship and a lack of faith in the government's use of tax funds incentivized individuals and businesses to operate outside the formal economy, avoiding taxation altogether in an attempt to survive or maximize profits. A thriving black market emerged, offering goods and services at lower prices but depriving the government of much-needed revenue. The lack of effective enforcement also allowed this black market to grow unchecked. This cycle of tax evasion and stunted economic growth threatened Spain's future.

The winds of change

The death of Francisco Franco in 1975 ushered in a period of democratic transition. The newly formed government recognized the urgent need to address the nation's fiscal woes. A series of bold reforms were implemented in the 1980s, aimed at tackling tax evasion and fostering a culture of responsible citizenship. Several specific reforms boosted tax morale:

- *Targeting evasion, not the evaders.* Instead of mass audits that could be seen as harassment, Spain focused on strengthening enforcement capabilities. This included better data analysis to identify potential evaders and increased collaboration with international tax authorities. The message was clear: tax evasion would not be tolerated, but the focus was not on punishing the little guy.

- *Simplification is key.* The notoriously complex tax code underwent a major overhaul. Loopholes were closed, and procedures were streamlined. The government also invested in public education campaigns, explaining the tax system in clear and concise language. Citizens could more readily understand how their taxes were being used, which fostered a sense of control and purpose.

- *Visible improvements.* The government prioritized efficiency in the use of tax revenue. Public services such as health care, education, and

box continued next page

Box 1.1

From tax rebels to responsible contributors: The Spanish tax transformation of the 1980s *(continued)*

infrastructure were significantly improved. Citizens witnessed a direct correlation between their tax contributions and a better quality of life. This transparency and visible investment in public goods bolstered trust and encouraged compliance.

Increase in tax morale

These reforms, implemented throughout the 1980s and 1990s, yielded remarkable results. Studies documented a significant rise in voluntary tax compliance (Martinez-Vazquez and Torgler 2009). Crucially, tax authorities aggressively pursued high-profile evasion cases, demonstrating that no one was above the law and reinforcing the message that the rules applied to everyone. This unwavering enforcement, combined with systemic improvements and increased transparency, fostered a widespread perception of fairness. Spanish citizens, now confident that their contributions were being used effectively and fairly, embraced their civic duty to pay taxes. Consequently, the black market shrunk as the formal economy flourished, reflecting a fundamental shift in the national culture.

Lessons learned

The Spanish experience offers valuable insights for other nations grappling with tax evasion:

- *Building trust is paramount.* Focusing on targeted enforcement, clear communication, and efficient use of tax revenue can rebuild public trust in government. When everyone feels they are playing by the same rules, compliance increases.

- *Transparency matters.* A complex and opaque tax system breeds suspicion. Streamlining procedures, making tax information readily available, and investing in public education all contribute to a more transparent system that encourages responsible behavior.

- *Growth is a powerful ally.* A robust economy makes paying taxes less of a burden and empowers citizens to invest in their nation's future. The Spanish government's focus on economic growth strategies played a crucial role in improving tax morale.

box continued next page

Box 1.1

From tax rebels to responsible contributors: The Spanish tax transformation of the 1980s *(continued)*

Conclusion

Spain's transformation from a nation plagued by tax evasion to one with a higher level of tax morale is a testament to the power of well-designed reforms. By tackling historical distrust, simplifying the system, fostering economic growth, and implementing a fair tax structure, Spain created a sustainable tax system built on a foundation of civic responsibility. This case study offers valuable lessons for policy makers around the world, demonstrating that a well-functioning tax system is not just about collecting revenue but also about fostering a sense of shared purpose and national progress.

Mobility of the Tax Base

The mobility of people and firms, particularly MNCs, creates a challenge for governments. High taxes can incentivize people and firms to move to other countries. Highly skilled workers and wealthy individuals have more options when it comes to where they live. If a country imposes a high PIT, high earners might choose to relocate to a country with a lower tax rate, draining the government of revenue from these people. Businesses, particularly MNCs, are also mobile and could relocate operations to countries with lower CIT.

VAT, however, demonstrates a limited susceptibility to relocation in comparison with other taxes, primarily because of the destination principle used in most VAT systems. The destination principle dictates that VAT revenue is collected in the country in which the final consumption of the good or service occurs. Although the rise of online shopping has played a role in eroding some tax bases, VAT retains its relative stability. Unlike with CIT, where businesses might relocate operations to avoid high rates, moving production facilities or distribution centers solely to avoid VAT is a complex and expensive undertaking for most companies. This logistical complexity, coupled with the potential loss of established markets and supply chains, creates a significant deterrent. As a result, VAT boasts a higher degree of tax base immobility compared with other options. This characteristic, along with VAT's ability to generate a consistent revenue stream, is a key reason why EMDEs and advanced economies have heavily relied on it as a source of indirect taxation.

WTs levied on financial assets, such as stocks, bonds, and investment accounts, result in a high degree of tax base mobility because they exist electronically and can be readily transferred to different countries. But WTs specifically levied on real estate are likely those least susceptible to tax base mobility for two key reasons. First, real estate is inherently immobile. Unlike financial assets or businesses, land and buildings cannot be relocated to jurisdictions with lower tax rates. Second, property taxes often directly fund essential services, such as schools, hospitals, road maintenance, and public safety initiatives, at the local and provincial or state levels, creating a strong connection between the taxes paid and the benefits received by property owners.

International Coordination Can Play a Crucial Role in Mitigating This Problem

Typical measures to address the potential mobility of the tax base include, for example, profit allocation rules, which determine how profits are distributed among different jurisdictions. This, in turn, can disincentivize companies from artificially inflating expenses in high-tax countries to lower their taxable income. Other measures include the establishment of a shared minimum corporate tax rate, which makes it less attractive for companies to shift profits to tax havens. For instance, the European Union's (EU's) 2021 agreement on a 15 percent minimum corporate tax rate aims to make tax havens with rates below 15 percent less attractive (OECD 2021b). This discourages companies from shifting profits solely to avoid taxes. The agreement also includes a "top-up" tax provision: if an EU-based company has subsidiaries in low-tax jurisdictions, the parent company may be required to pay the difference between the local tax rate and the 15 percent minimum threshold. This ensures a minimum level of taxation occurs within the EU.

Challenge of Achieving a Global Consensus on Taxes

Effective global cooperation on taxation requires near-universal participation. This is because the mobility of capital, goods, people, and services allows individuals and entities to exploit tax differentials across jurisdictions. The "$N - 1$" problem underscores this challenge: as long as even a single country deviates from agreed-upon tax policies, loopholes are created that can be exploited by taxpayers worldwide.

These challenges are particularly acute for developing economies. Limited resources, lack of influence in international tax negotiations, and dependence on larger economies can significantly constrain their ability to effectively participate in and benefit from global tax cooperation. Developing economies may lack the capacity to effectively monitor and enforce tax laws, address tax evasion, and counter harmful tax practices. Moreover, the complexity of international tax rules and the sophistication of tax avoidance schemes can make it difficult for developing economies to effectively navigate the global tax landscape and ensure their tax systems remain competitive and sustainable. Some developing economies may even be tempted to deviate from global tax cooperation, potentially seeking to become tax havens themselves, attracting capital inflows by offering lower tax rates and fewer regulations. This can create a race to the bottom in global taxation, further undermining the efforts of countries striving to implement fair and equitable tax systems.

Role of Low Taxes in a Holistic Development Strategy for EMDEs

In addition to being tax havens, some EMDEs have strategically used low taxes—for example, low corporate tax rates—as a tool within a broader development policy tool kit. This approach recognizes that attracting foreign direct investment can be a powerful engine for economic growth (UNCTAD 2023). By offering competitive tax rates, EMDEs can incentivize multinational corporations to establish regional headquarters, manufacturing facilities, or other operations within their borders. This influx of investment not only brings capital but also facilitates valuable knowledge transfers, technological advancements, and access to international markets (Maloney et al. 2023). However, it is crucial to remember that low tax rates are just one piece of the puzzle. Successful EMDEs have typically combined this strategy with investments in other areas, such as infrastructure development (for example, modern transportation networks, reliable electricity grids), education, skills training (that is, creating a workforce that meets the needs of MNCs), and fostering a business-friendly environment (for example, with streamlined regulations, political stability, and a transparent legal system). This multipronged approach creates fertile ground for economic activity, innovation, and, ultimately, sustainable development for EMDEs. For a concrete example of how this multipronged approach can work in practice, consider the case of Singapore, which provides a compelling example of this successful approach (refer to box 1.2). By combining a business-friendly environment, including competitive tax rates, with substantial investments in education, infrastructure, and a skilled workforce, Singapore has transformed itself into a global economic powerhouse.

Box 1.2

Singapore: A case study in balancing tax rates and investment attraction

Singapore's use of low corporate tax rates to attract foreign investment is a well-studied example. It offers valuable insights into the potential benefits of and challenges for emerging markets and developing economies (EMDEs). In this box, we provide a deeper look at Singapore's strategy.

box continued next page

Singapore: A case study in balancing tax rates and investment attraction *(continued)*

From humble beginnings to global hub

After independence in 1965, Singapore lacked natural resources and a domestic market. The newly formed nation needed a plan to jumpstart its economy. The Economic Development Board (EDB) was established and tasked with attracting foreign investment. One of its key strategies was establishing a pro-business environment (EDB 2023), which included highly competitive corporate tax rates. Singapore began with a rock-bottom corporate tax rate of 4 percent in the 1960s, gradually increasing it to the current rate of 17 percent. This low tax rate signaled Singapore's openness to foreign investment and offered significant cost advantages to companies compared with high-tax jurisdictions (PwC Singapore 2023). Singapore also recognized that tax rates alone would not be enough. It invested heavily in education and training, infrastructure development, and political stability and the rule of law.

Singapore prioritized building a skilled workforce capable of meeting the demands of foreign companies. This included establishing world-class universities, technical schools, and vocational training programs (Birdsall et al. 1993). It also embarked on ambitious infrastructure projects, creating a modern and efficient transportation network (airports, seaports, highways) and a robust telecommunications infrastructure. This made Singapore a strategic location for international trade and logistics (Maloney et al. 2023). Finally, Singapore established a reputation for political stability, a transparent legal system, and a corruption-free environment. This instilled confidence among foreign investors and fostered a predictable business climate (Transparency International 2023).

The fruits of a multipronged approach

These combined efforts yielded significant results. There was a surge in foreign direct investment (FDI). The low tax rate, coupled with the skilled workforce and excellent infrastructure, made Singapore highly attractive to multinational corporations (MNCs). Global giants such as Shell, ExxonMobil, and Nestlé established regional headquarters in Singapore, bringing in billions of dollars in FDI (UNCTAD 2023). The influx of MNCs fueled rapid economic growth. Singapore transformed from a developing nation into a high-income, knowledge-based economy. The tax revenue generated from MNCs, even at a lower rate, provided funds for further infrastructure development, social programs,

box continued next page

Box 1.2

Singapore: A case study in balancing tax rates and investment attraction *(continued)*

and continued investments in education and training (Yusuf 2020). Recognizing the evolving global landscape, Singapore did not become complacent. It fostered a strong ecosystem for innovation and entrepreneurship. Initiatives such as the establishment of science and technology parks and generous start-up grants attracted innovative companies and talent (A*STAR 2023).

Challenges and the road ahead

With the rise of minimum tax rate initiatives, Singapore faces challenges. However, it continues to adapt its strategy:

- *Shifting focus.* Although tax rates remain competitive, Singapore is placing greater emphasis on attracting high-value industries such as biomedical sciences, artificial intelligence, and financial technology. This strategy leverages Singapore's existing strengths in research and development and positions it for future growth (EDB 2023).

- *Skilled talent acquisition.* To maintain a competitive edge, Singapore actively seeks and attracts top talent from around the world. This includes streamlined immigration policies and generous relocation packages for skilled professionals (ICA 2023).

Lessons for other EMDEs

Singapore's success story offers valuable takeaways for other EMDEs. Although competitive tax rates can be a starting point, a holistic approach that prioritizes infrastructure development, education, and fostering innovation is crucial for sustainable economic growth (Maloney et al. 2023). EMDEs should focus on long-term advantages and aim to build a strong, skilled workforce and a business-friendly environment that goes beyond tax breaks, thus creating long-term advantages that are less susceptible to changes in global tax policies. The global economic landscape is constantly evolving. EMDEs need to be adaptable and willing to adjust their strategies to remain attractive to foreign investment.

Singapore's experience highlights how low tax rates can be a strategic starting point to attract foreign investment. However, to achieve sustainable economic growth and become a global player, it is critical to foster a comprehensive and innovation-driven business environment. This broader ecosystem should encompass factors beyond taxes, such as strong infrastructure, a skilled workforce, and robust legal frameworks.

Behavioral Responses Beyond Evasion, Avoidance, and Mobility

Tax evasion and avoidance as well as tax base mobility are well-known strategies used by individuals and firms to minimize their tax burdens (Zucman 2015). However, these are not the only ways people and firms react to tax increases. Tax hikes can trigger a range of behavioral responses that can have significant economic consequences. Next we discuss some of the most well-known responses.

Work Less

Tax hikes can trigger a range of responses from individuals, and their impact on labor supply is a significant concern for policy makers. Here is a breakdown of how tax increases might influence the amount of work people are willing to do.

- *Cutbacks in overtime.* When after-tax earnings from overtime become less attractive because they result in higher taxes, employees might choose to work fewer overtime hours. This can lead to reduced productivity for businesses that rely heavily on overtime to meet production demands.

- *Early retirement.* Tax hikes can disincentivize continued work for individuals nearing retirement. If the take-home pay after taxes becomes less satisfying, they might opt for early retirement, potentially leading to a shortage of skilled workers in specific industries.

- *Shift to part-time work.* Individuals with flexible job options, such as those in freelance or gig-based economies, might choose to transition to part-time positions. This allows them to maintain some income while keeping their taxable income lower.

- *Leaving the labor force.* When taxes increase, the net amount of money people take home after taxes decreases. This can disincentivize work, particularly for those on the margins of the labor force. Whereas those living paycheck to paycheck might have less ability to reduce their work hours even with a tax increase, people at the top of the income distribution or those who are more vulnerable (that is, those making large efforts to work) could have larger behavioral responses. For example, a single parent working part time to supplement childcare costs might find that a tax hike on their earnings reduces the financial benefit of working enough hours to cover childcare, potentially leading them to leave the workforce entirely. Also, people with higher incomes or more wealth have more flexibility to adjust their work hours.

Entrepreneurship and Risk

Tax hikes can make people less interested in risky investments or encourage them to put more money into tax-advantaged accounts.

- *Discouraging risky ventures.* Tax hikes can make corporations less willing to invest in risky ventures such as start-ups and research and development (R&D) projects with uncertain returns. Higher capital gains taxes on potential profits from successful ventures can be a disincentive. The potential for higher capital gains taxes might make these options less attractive because of a smaller after-tax profit. If tax hikes significantly discourage investment and R&D, they can lead to slower economic growth. Reduced investment in innovation and new ventures can hinder long-term productivity gains.

- *Shifting investments.* Companies might react to tax increases by shifting their investments toward assets or projects with more favorable tax treatments.

- *Increased focus on depreciation.* Corporations might invest more heavily in assets with significant depreciation deductions, allowing them to lower their taxable income.

A deeper understanding of these behavioral responses is essential for crafting effective policies. This knowledge will empower policy makers to design tax structures that achieve revenue goals while minimizing disruptions to labor markets and investment.

LAC's Unfriendly Business Environment

A better understanding of the behavioral dimensions influencing how workers, people, and firms respond to taxes is particularly relevant for a region such as LAC. The persistence of low growth, stagnant labor market dynamics, and sluggish investment over decades points to an unfriendly business environment. It is crucial to design tax policies that minimize these distortions and foster a more conducive environment for growth and investment in LAC.

Of particular concern at this juncture is that the region's high effective average and marginal tax rates on firm profits are among the highest in the world. This is mainly because of relatively high corporate income tax statutory rates and tax provisions that are less generous than those in other jurisdictions (for example, allowances for corporate equity, half-year conventions, and inventory valuation methods; Hanappi et al. 2023). In fact, the average regional statutory corporate tax rate (25 percent) is the highest in the world, above that of Organisation for

Figure 1.3   Statutory corporate tax rates in LAC countries compared with the average of those in Asia and OECD countries

Percent

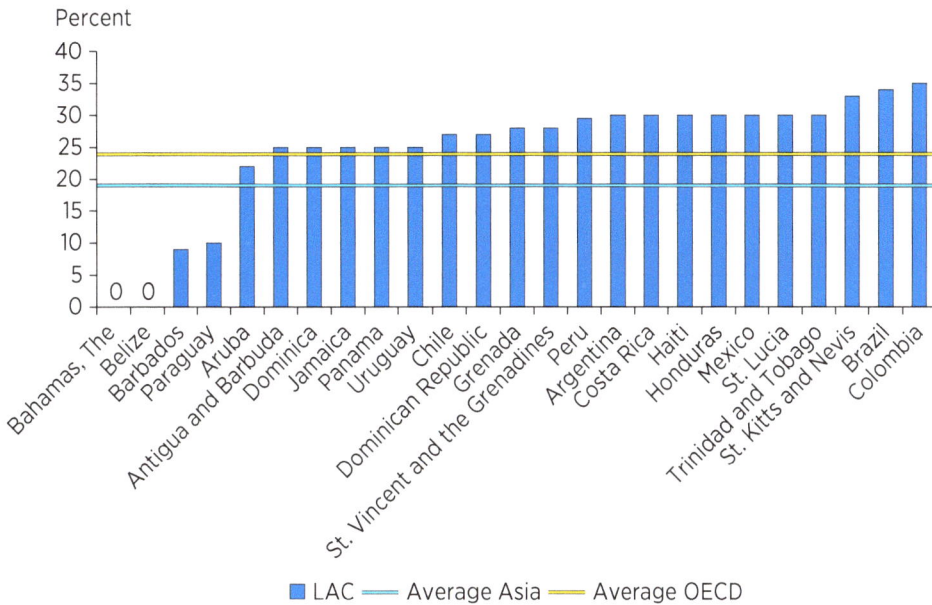

■ LAC —— Average Asia —— Average OECD

Source: OECD Corporate Tax Statistics (https://doi.org/10.1787/0959240d-en).

Note: LAC = Latin America and the Caribbean; OECD = Organisation for Economic Co-operation and Development.

Economic Co-operation and Development (OECD) countries (24 percent) and far above that of Asia (19 percent) (refer to figure 1.3). Adjusting for exemptions and other modifications, the average effective rates across all firms remain above those of OECD countries. As LAC seeks to attract links in global value chains, increase investment for the green transition, and raise growth above the mediocre levels of the recent past, these high tax rates are often pointed to as offsetting the advantage the region has developed in terms of wages or proximity to the United States. These tax rates also compound the region's relatively unfriendly business environment, as measured by excessive regulation, inefficient judiciary systems, complex trade and tax compliance procedures, and a shortage of skilled human capital (refer to figure 1.4), as well as rising crime and violence (Maloney et al. 2023).

Figure 1.4   LAC's rankings on Enterprise Survey business environment indicators

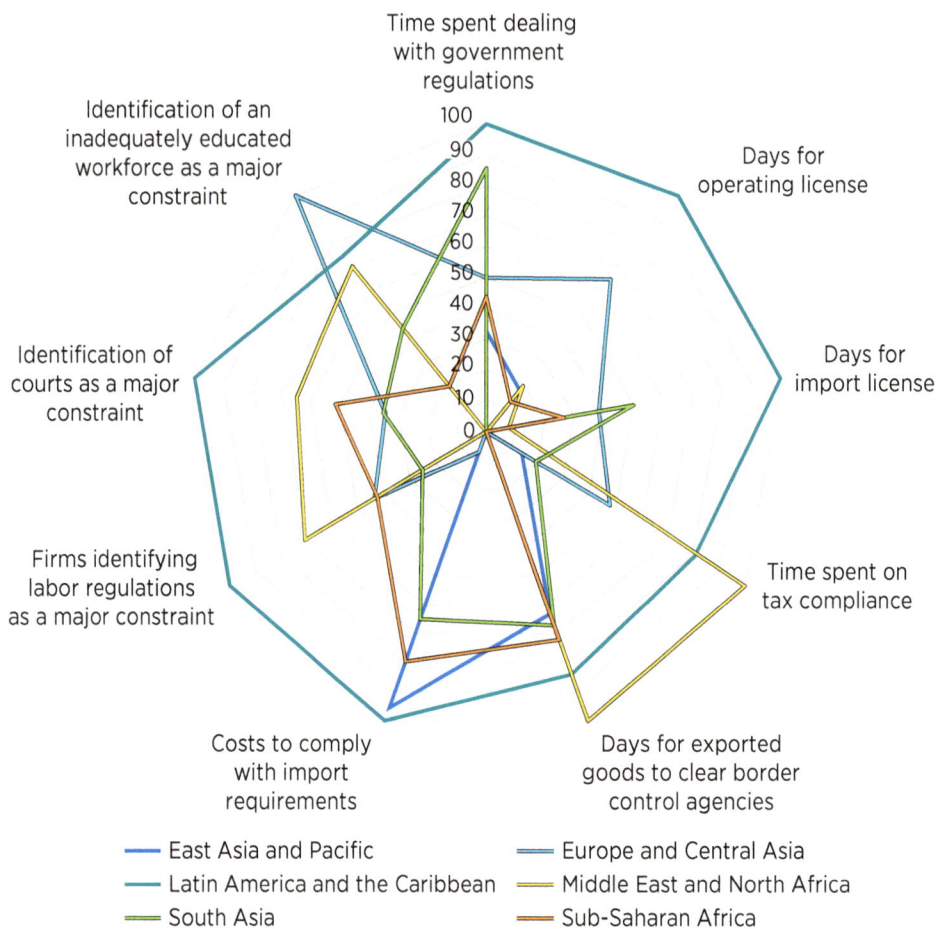

Source: World Bank Enterprise Surveys (www.enterprisesurveys.org).

Note: Indicators were normalized to range from 0 to 100, with 0 representing the best performance and 100 the worst. LAC = Latin America and the Caribbean.

Leveraging Innovation: New Technology and Fiscal Tools

Technological advancements are reshaping fiscal policy, notably through targeted cash transfers (TCTs) and digital tools. TCTs offer a direct, efficient means to achieve equity, potentially reducing reliance on highly progressive taxes and allowing for revenue maximization through more neutral taxes. Meanwhile, digital tools improve tax administration but also create new challenges, such as asset concealment. These shifts redefine traditional trade-offs, emphasizing revenue generation alongside robust TCTs for effective redistribution.

TCTs: The Shifting Landscape of Redistribution

To address different policy objectives, governments use a toolbox of fiscal instruments, each with varying impacts and potential trade-offs. Traditionally, addressing income inequality has relied heavily on the principle of tax progressivity (Pessino et al. 2023). In fact, current global political discourse, including in LAC, generally favors WT, PIT, and CIT over VAT for promoting a progressive agenda. As discussed previously, most VAT systems worldwide use reduced rates to mitigate their inherent regressive effects.

However, taxes are not the sole policy tool for addressing income inequality, and the available policy tools are not static. The introduction of targeted transfers in the mid-1990s significantly bolstered efforts in this area. Targeted cash transfers are direct payments from the government to individuals or families who meet specific criteria, typically income level. They ensure that resources go directly to those who need them the most. For example, Brazil's Bolsa Familia program provides monthly payments to low-income families with children, conditional on school attendance and health checkups.

Digital Revolution

LAC, grappling with the long-standing challenge of tax collection inefficiency stemming from, among other structural limitations, outdated systems, is poised for transformation. A new era is dawning, powered by the transformative potential of digitization. The development of new digital tools can revolutionize tax collection in LAC, boosting efficiency, curbing evasion, and fostering a more equitable tax system.

Recognizing these challenges, some LAC nations began exploring digital solutions in the late 20th century. These efforts included early electronic filing (pioneering countries such as Argentina and Chile introduced electronic filing systems for select tax forms in the 1990s) and data-sharing agreements between tax authorities and financial institutions to improve information exchange.

The digital revolution, which gained significant momentum in the late 20th and early 21st centuries, presents a unique opportunity for LAC to transform its tax collection landscape. By embracing digitization, governments can address the challenges of the analog age and unlock a new era of tax administration.

E-Invoicing on the Rise

Countries such as Brazil and Mexico have successfully implemented e-invoicing systems, mandating electronic invoices for all business transactions. This allows tax authorities to track economic activity in real time and significantly reduce tax evasion (Barreix and Zambrano 2018). In 2008, Brazil introduced a mandatory e-invoicing system with a unique digital signature for each invoice. This not only reduced tax evasion but also simplified compliance for businesses. The success of this program is attributed to a strong public-private partnership and a focus on user-friendly technology (Barreix and Zambrano 2018).

Simplifying Tax Codes and Digital Filing

Several countries are focusing on simplifying tax codes and reducing loopholes. This strategy, combined with a digital filing system, can make compliance easier and less time-consuming for taxpayers (Schlotterbeck 2017). For example, Colombia undertook a tax code reform in 2019, streamlining procedures and reducing tax rates for some businesses. This, coupled with the launch of a digital tax platform for filing and payments, has increased voluntary compliance and boosted revenue collection (Reyes-Tagle, Dimitropoulou, and Rodríguez Peña 2023).

Data-Driven Audits

Digital systems allow tax authorities to leverage big data analytics to identify anomalies and target audits more effectively. This frees up resources for investigating complex tax evasion schemes. For example, Mexico's tax authority, Servicio de Administración Tributaria, implemented a sophisticated data analytics platform that can identify suspicious tax returns and patterns of tax avoidance. This allows it to target audits more strategically and deter potential evaders (OECD 2022).

Automation

Governments are developing mobile applications that allow taxpayers to easily file taxes, access information, and communicate with tax authorities. This promotes inclusivity, especially for those with limited access to a traditional computer. For example, Peru's tax authority, Superintendencia Nacional de Aduanas y de Administración Tributaria, launched a mobile app called "Sunat Operaciones en Línea" that allows taxpayers to file tax returns, generate receipts, and pay taxes electronically (PwC Peru 2023). This initiative has been particularly beneficial for small businesses and individuals in remote areas, promoting financial inclusion and simplifying tax compliance.

Leveraging Real Estate Digital Platforms

Traditional methods of property valuation relying on cadastre systems struggle to keep pace with the dynamic nature of real estate markets. Fortunately, technological advancements offer powerful tools to address this challenge. By leveraging digital platforms, such as the real estate websites Zillow and Trulia, and modernizing cadastre systems, governments can unlock the untapped potential of property valuation.

The digital revolution offers LAC a golden opportunity to transform its tax collection system. By embracing digitization, governments can overcome the limitations of the past and create a more efficient, fair, and sustainable system. Building trust, investing in cybersecurity and infrastructure, and ensuring digital inclusion are key to maximizing the benefits of this transformation. Automation can free up tax authorities' resources, allowing them to focus on more complex tasks such as tax policy development and targeted enforcement activities.

Growth Reimagined: Beyond Static Paradigms

This report fundamentally shifts the tax policy discourse in LAC by explicitly integrating economic growth as a primary objective, moving beyond the traditionally dominant focus on revenue and equity. We challenge the conventional static analysis by delving into the dynamic behavioral responses of economic agents to taxation, particularly within LAC's unique and often challenging business environment. Recognizing that the high CIT rates prevalent in the region can stifle investment and innovation—critical drivers of growth— we advocate for strategic reductions to enhance competitiveness, coupled with improved enforcement and public-private partnerships. Similarly, PIT, characterized by high top rates and a narrow base, demands a recalibration. We propose moderately broadening the tax base, excluding vulnerable populations, to increase revenue without discouraging entrepreneurship. Furthermore, we explore the growth implications of the VAT, suggesting a shift away from high standard rates and reduced rates on specific goods, which often benefit wealthy individuals. Instead, we propose leveraging the VAT's broad base to fund TCTs, thus achieving equity goals more efficiently. This approach not only mitigates the regressive effects of the VAT but also minimizes economic distortions. Recognizing the concentration of wealth in tangible assets within LAC, we advocate for the strategic use of property taxes, which are less distortionary and more easily administered than taxes on highly mobile financial assets. By incorporating these dynamic considerations—the impact of tax policies on investment, entrepreneurship, labor supply, and capital flows—we offer novel insights into designing tax systems that foster a more competitive and sustainable regional economy, moving beyond short-term revenue gains to long-term economic expansion.

References

A*STAR (Agency for Science, Technology, and Research). 2023. *Annual Report April 2022–March 2023: Creating Growth, Enhancing Lives*. Singapore: Agency for Science, Technology, and Research.

Barreix, A., and R. Zambrano. 2018. *Electronic Invoicing in Latin America.* Washington, DC: Inter-American Development Bank and Inter-American Center of Tax Administrations.

Birdsall, Nancy M., Jose Edgardo L. Campos, Chang-Shik Kim, W. Max Corden, Lawrence MacDonald (editor), Howard Pack, John Page, Richard Sabor, and Joseph Eugene Stiglitz. 1993. *The East Asian Miracle: Economic Growth and Public Policy.* Vol. 1 of 2. World Bank Policy Research Report. New York: Oxford University Press. http://documents.worldbank.org/curated/en/975081468244550798.

CBO (Congressional Budget Office). 2023. *Trends in Corporate Economic Profits and Tax Payments, 1998 to 2017.* Washington, DC: CBO.

EDB (Economic Development Board). 2023. "2023 in Review: Singapore's Incentives and Schemes for Global Businesses and Local Enterprises." Dec. 27, 2023. https://www.edb .gov.sg/en/business-insights/insights/2023-in-review-singapores-incentives-and -schemes-for-global-businesses-and-local-enterprises.html.

Ferriere, A., P. Grübener, G. Navarro, and O. Vardishvili. 2022. "On the Optimal Design of Transfers and Income-Tax Progressivity." International Finance Discussion Paper 1350, Board of Governors of the Federal Reserve System, Washington, DC.

Guenther, Gary. 2024. *Federal Individual Income Tax Brackets, Standard Deduction, and Personal Exemption: 1988 to 2024.* CRS Report RL34498. Washington, DC: Congressional Research Service.

Hanappi, T., S. Nieto Parra, J. Orozco, and A. Rasteletti. 2023. "Corporate Effective Tax Rates in Latin America and the Caribbean." Technical Note IDB-TN-2782. Washington, DC: Inter-American Development Bank.

ICA (Immigration and Checkpoints Authority). 2023. *ICA Annual Statistics Report 2023.* Singapore: Immigration and Checkpoints Authority.

Izquierdo, A., C. Pessino, and G. Vuletin. 2018. *Better Spending for Better Lives: How Latin America and the Caribbean Can Do More with Less.* Washington, DC: Inter-American Development Bank.

Maloney, W.F., D. Riera-Crichton, E. Ianchovichina, G. Vuletin, and G. Beylis. 2023. *The Promise of* Integration: *Opportunities in a Changing Global Economy.* Latin America and the Caribbean Economic Review (April 2023). Washington, DC: World Bank. https://doi .org/10.1596/978-1-4648-1987.

Marr, C., S. Jacoby, G. Fenton, and S. Washington. 2021. "Corporate Rate Increase Would Make Taxes Fairer, Help Fund Equitable Recovery." Center on Budget and Policy Priorities, Washington, DC. https://www.cbpp.org/research/federal-tax/corporate -rate-increase-would-make-taxes-fairer-help-fund-equitable-recovery.

Martinez-Vazquez, J., and B. Torgler. 2009. "The Evolution of Tax Morale in Modern Spain." *Journal of Economic Issues* 43 (1): 1–28.

Medina, Leandro, and Friedrich Schneider. 2019. "Shedding Light on the Shadow Economy: A Global Database and the Interaction with the Official One." CESifo Working Paper Series 7981. Center for Economic Studies and Ifo Institute for Economic Research (CESifo), Munich, Germany.

OECD (Organisation for Economic Co-operation and Development). 2021a. *Corporate Tax Statistics—Third Edition.* Paris: OECD Publishing.

OECD (Organisation for Economic Co-operation and Development). 2021b. "Statement on a Two-Pillar Solution to Address the Tax Challenges Arising from the Digitalisation of the Economy—8 October 2021." Paris: OECD. https://www.oecd.org/tax/beps /statement-on-a-two-pillar-solution-to-address-the-tax-challenges-arising-from-the -digitalisation-of-the-economy-october-2021.htm.

OECD (Organisation for Economic Co-operation and Development). 2022. "Housing Taxation in OECD Countries." OECD Tax Policy Studies 29, OECD Publishing, Paris.

Pessino, C., A. Rasteletti, D. Artana, and N. Lustig. 2023. "Distributional Effects of Taxation in Latin America." Working Paper Series IDB-WP-01534, Inter-American Development Bank, Washington, DC.

PwC Peru (PricewaterhouseCoopers Peru). 2023. *Worldwide Tax Summaries—Peru*. Lima: PwC Peru.

PwC Singapore (PricewaterhouseCoopers Singapore). 2023. *Worldwide Tax Summaries—Singapore*. Singapore: PwC Singapore.

Reyes-Tagle, G., C. Dimitropoulou, and C. C. Rodríguez Peña. 2023. *Digitalization of Tax Administration in Latin America and the Caribbean: Best-Practice Framework for Improving E-Services to Taxpayers*. Washington, DC: Inter-American Development Bank.

Rogger, D., and C. Schuster. 2023. *The Government Analytics Handbook*. Washington, DC: World Bank.

Saez, E., and G. Zucman. 2019. "Progressive Wealth Taxation." *Brookings Papers on Economic Activity,* 2019 (Fall): 437–511.

Schlotterbeck, S. 2017. "Tax Administration Reforms in the Caribbean: Challenges, Achievements, and Next Steps." Working Paper WP/17/88, International Monetary Fund, Washington, DC.

Transparency International. 2023. *Corruption Perceptions Index*. Berlin: Transparency International. https://www.transparency.org/en/cpi/2023.

UNCTAD (United Nations Conference on Trade and Development). 2023. *World Investment Report 2023: Investing in Sustainable Energy for All*. New York: United Nations Publications.

Wamhoff, S. 2024. *Who Pays Taxes in America in 2024*. Washington, DC: Institute on Taxation and Economic Policy.

Yusuf, S. 2020. *Building Human Capital: Lessons from Country Experiences—How Singapore Does It*. Washington, DC: World Bank. http://documents.worldbank.org/curated/en /960921595409441570.

Zucman, Y. 2015. *The Hidden Wealth of Nations: The Scourge of Tax Havens*. Chicago: University of Chicago Press.

2

Targeted Cash Transfers: The "New" Instrument to Deal with Equity Objectives

Introduction

The concept of providing support to poor individuals has a long and varied history, with societies worldwide developing mechanisms to assist their most vulnerable members. These efforts, although diverse in form and scope, reflect a persistent societal concern for addressing destitution and promoting a degree of equity. Throughout history, support systems have evolved in response to changing economic conditions, social structures, and political philosophies. From ancient systems of charity and religious almsgiving to more formalized state-led interventions, the underlying motivation has often been to redistribute resources and provide a safety net for those who are unable to support themselves. This historical perspective provides a crucial backdrop for understanding the modern role of targeted cash transfers (TCTs) as a contemporary tool in the ongoing effort to achieve equity.

A Long History of Supporting the Poor

Early forms of poor relief frequently emphasized the provision of in-kind assistance. A notable example is the Elizabethan Poor Law of 1601, which established a system of poor relief in England (Slack 1995). This system provided tangible goods and services to those deemed unable to support themselves. Support included essential items such as food and clothing, materials for work, and housing in almshouses or poorhouses. Apprenticeships were also offered to provide training and skills for employment. These forms of in-kind support were aimed at directly addressing the immediate needs of poor individuals, providing the basic necessities for survival and, in some cases, the means to achieve self-sufficiency.

The transition from in-kind assistance to cash assistance represents a significant development in the history of poverty alleviation. In the United States, mothers' pensions, which began around 1911, are an early example of cash transfer programs (Aizer et al. 2024). These programs provided regular cash payments to poor mothers with dependent children who had lost their primary breadwinner.

The significance of the mothers' pensions lies in their recognition of the specific needs of vulnerable families and the empowerment of recipients through the provision of cash. The cash payments, equivalent to approximately US$500 per month in today's currency, allowed mothers to make decisions about how best to allocate resources to meet their family's needs. This approach contrasts with in-kind assistance, which can be limited in scope and may not always align with the specific priorities of recipients. Mothers' pensions represent an early step toward the modern understanding of cash transfers as a tool for promoting both equity and individual agency.

Development of Targeted Transfers in Latin America and the Caribbean

Similar to global trends, initial efforts to support poor individuals in Latin America and the Caribbean (LAC) often involved the provision of in-kind assistance. These programs sought to directly address immediate needs by distributing essential goods and services to vulnerable populations. Although specific examples may vary across countries, common forms of in-kind support included food rations, clothing distribution, and the provision of basic health care services (Mesa-Lago 1980). For example, Mexico's Compañía Nacional de Subsistencias Populares (CONASUPO), established in 1961, aimed to stabilize prices and distribute basic goods. These interventions provided crucial short-term relief, but they often faced challenges related to logistical inefficiencies, targeting accuracy, and the potential to create dependency (McMichael 1995).

Around the 1990s, many LAC countries began to popularize conditional cash transfers (CCTs) and other forms of TCTs. These programs represented a shift toward providing direct financial assistance to individuals and families, with a focus on empowering beneficiaries and promoting the development of human capital. CCTs, in particular, are designed to provide cash payments to recipients contingent on meeting specific requirements. For example, Brazil's Bolsa Familia, a prominent CCT program in LAC, provides monthly payments to low-income families with children, conditional on school attendance and health checkups. This conditionality aims to address the root causes of poverty and promote long-term social mobility. Mexico also shifted away from generalized subsidies, such as those provided by CONASUPO, and embraced targeted interventions through its Programa de Educacion, Salud y Alimentacion (PROGRESA) in the late 1990s.

The conceptual logic behind CCTs and TCTs lies in their ability to provide a safety net while simultaneously incentivizing investments in education, health, and nutrition. By providing cash directly, these programs offer beneficiaries greater autonomy in managing their resources and addressing their specific needs. Examples of prominent TCT programs in LAC include Brazil's Bolsa Familia and Mexico's PROGRESA. These programs demonstrate the potential of TCTs to effectively address poverty and inequality in the region. For example, evaluations of PROGRESA have shown significant reductions in poverty and improvements in key social indicators, including increased school enrollment rates, better child health and nutritional outcomes, and improved household consumption patterns. The program's success is attributed to its rigorous targeting methodologies and relatively low administrative costs.

Impact of the New TCT Instrument on Taxation

The emergence of effective TCT programs has significantly altered the traditional reliance on tax policy as the primary tool for achieving equity. Previously, progressive tax systems, with higher tax rates for higher-income individuals and corporations, were considered essential for redistributing wealth and reducing income inequality. However, TCTs offer a direct and precisely targeted mechanism for transferring resources to vulnerable populations. This is particularly relevant in situations in which progressive taxation is difficult to implement because of low collection efficiency or when it leads to significant behavioral responses that negatively affect economic activity. Such responses can include tax evasion, tax avoidance, and disincentives to work or invest. By addressing equity through TCTs, policy makers can potentially reduce the need for aggressive tax progressivity. The traditional view of tax policy often involves a trade-off between collection efficiency and equity. Taxes that are easier to collect, such as value added tax (VAT) and corporate income tax, may be less progressive, whereas more progressive taxes, such as personal income tax and wealth taxes, can be more complex to administer and are prone to evasion. TCTs can help reduce this trade-off. By effectively addressing equity through direct transfers, policy makers gain more flexibility to prioritize revenue generation through efficient tax instruments, even if those instruments are not inherently highly progressive.

The emergence of effective TCT programs significantly diminishes the emphasis on the importance of highly progressive tax systems. Efficient TCTs that effectively reach low-income citizens alter the policy focus. Instead of prioritizing tax progressivity, the emphasis shifts toward maximizing overall government revenue, regardless of whether this is achieved through progressive taxes or a more neutral tax system. A prominent example of this reassessment is highlighted by the debate surrounding the elimination of reduced VAT rates. Proponents argue that by removing these reduced rates, the government could increase overall tax revenue. Moreover, the extra revenue generated would primarily come from higher-income individuals who consume more because of their higher income. This additional revenue could then be used to fund more generous TCTs, directly supporting low-income earners. In other words, even regressive taxes such as the VAT can, when combined with highly targeted and progressive cash transfer programs, result in overall progressive fiscal policy.

Improved Targeting via Geographic Information Systems and Administrative Data

CCT programs, although crucial for poverty alleviation, often face the challenge of targeting accuracy. Two common errors arise: inclusion errors, in which benefits reach households above the poverty line, and exclusion errors, in which eligible poor households are left out. These errors can undermine the effectiveness and efficiency of CCTs. Inclusion errors dilute the impact of the program, diverting resources from those most in need, and exclusion errors perpetuate poverty and inequality by failing to provide support to vulnerable populations.

In LAC, targeting challenges are particularly salient. Studies have shown that a significant proportion of TCT beneficiaries are not poor, indicating inclusion errors. For example, Robles, Rubio, and Stampini (2015) found that, on average, 39.2 percent of CCT beneficiaries and 48.6 percent of noncontributory pension beneficiaries in LAC were not poor. At the same time, many eligible poor households remain uncovered by these programs, highlighting exclusion errors. Stampini, Medellin, and Ibarraran (2023) highlight that in the median country in the region, only 55 percent of the population in poverty lived in a household that received a transfer. These errors suggest a need for improved targeting mechanisms to enhance the redistributive power of TCTs.

Improving the Targeting of CCTs

One promising avenue for reducing inclusion errors in TCTs involves combining administrative data with geographic information systems (GISs). Administrative data, such as tax records, social security information, and property registries, can provide detailed information on household income and assets. GIS technology allows for the spatial visualization and analysis of these data, enabling policy makers to identify areas with a high concentration of poverty and to map the distribution of beneficiaries in relation to socioeconomic indicators.

Costa Rica's Sistema Nacional de Información y Registro Único de Beneficiarios del Estado (SINIRUBE) offers a compelling example of how administrative data and GIS can be integrated to improve targeting. SINIRUBE integrates and stores standardized data from various sources, including a social inclusion form, enabling a more precise identification of vulnerable populations. Monge and Tejerina (2023) highlight how SINIRUBE facilitates the development of precise social policies.

By combining SINIRUBE data with GIS, Costa Rica can conduct spatial analyses to identify areas in which inclusion errors are prevalent. For instance, map 2.1 illustrates how GIS mapping can reveal instances in which beneficiaries reside in relatively affluent areas, indicating potential inclusion errors. This visual representation allows policy makers to refine targeting criteria and implement strategies to reduce leakage.

Map 2.1   Potential inclusion errors in beneficiary distribution, Costa Rica, 2022

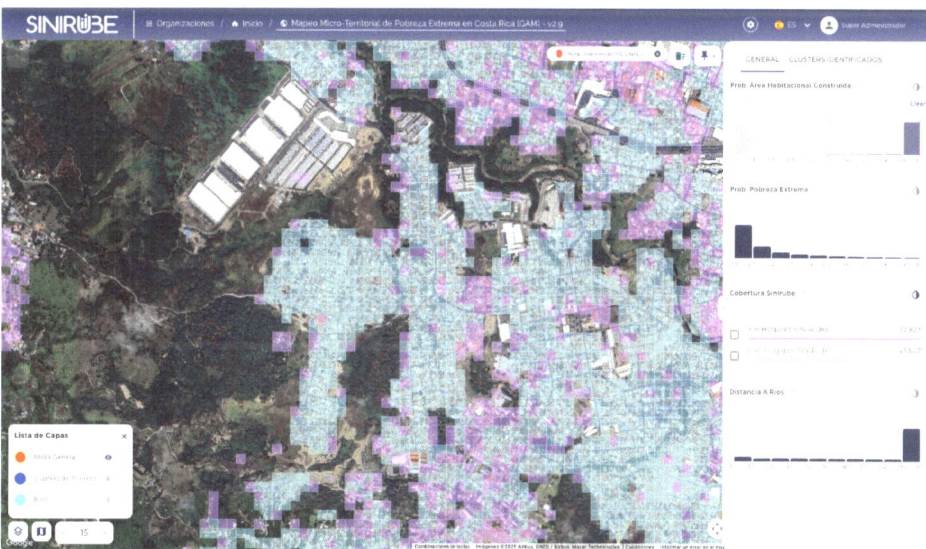

Source: Monge and Tejerina 2023.

Note: SINIRUBE = Sistema Nacional de Información y Registro Único de Beneficiarios del Estado.

The integration of GIS and administrative data offers several benefits. It enhances the accuracy of targeting, ensuring that benefits reach the intended beneficiaries. It also improves the efficiency of TCT programs by reducing leakage and maximizing the impact of public resources. Furthermore, this approach can strengthen program accountability and transparency because it provides a robust framework for monitoring and evaluation.

Targeting Beyond CCTs

Although CCTs are primarily focused on vulnerable populations, including those in the informal sector, a negative income tax, such as the earned income tax credit in the United States, can complement these efforts by targeting individuals and families with low to moderate incomes, including those who fall above the traditional poverty line.

A negative income tax operates by providing cash payments to individuals or families whose income falls below a certain threshold. Unlike traditional income taxes, in which earnings above a threshold are taxed, a negative income tax effectively subsidizes earnings below that threshold. As income increases, the subsidy decreases until it is phased out entirely. This mechanism aims to incentivize work and supplement earnings, particularly for low-wage workers.

Negative income tax programs can expand the reach of social support beyond those typically targeted by CCTs. By including individuals and families with slightly higher incomes, these programs can address the needs of the working poor and reduce income inequality across a broader spectrum of society. This is particularly relevant in contexts in which many individuals and families struggle to make ends meet despite being employed.

In addition to providing income support, negative income tax programs may also increase incentives for formal employment. By rewarding participation in the formal labor market with income supplements, these programs can encourage individuals to transition from the informal sector, thereby expanding the tax base and strengthening social security systems.

Butterfly Effect of TCTs on Taxation

It is intriguing to speculate how the landscape of taxation might have evolved had TCTs been widely implemented earlier in the development of modern tax systems. The butterfly effect analogy is apt: a seemingly small difference in initial conditions—the earlier availability of TCTs—could have led to significantly different outcomes in the design and structure of tax policies.

Given that TCTs became a prominent policy tool in the 1990s, well after the establishment of many key taxes, including the VAT with its reduced rates, it is fair to ask whether certain tax structures, such as the widespread use of reduced VAT rates, have become as entrenched. The discourse on revenue collection and progressivity might have diverged, with a potentially reduced emphasis on achieving equity solely through progressive taxation.

With effective TCTs in place, policy makers might have been more inclined to prioritize overall economic effects and efficiency in taxation, potentially favoring broader-based taxes with fewer exemptions and special rates. For instance, the debate surrounding the elimination of reduced VAT rates to increase revenue to funding more generous TCTs reflects this counterfactual scenario.

Tax policy objectives and means are in a constant state of adaptation, with policy makers continuously reevaluating the most effective ways to achieve their goals as new fiscal tools emerge. This dynamic process ensures that tax systems can adapt to the evolving needs of societies and economies in an efficient and fair manner.

Conclusion

Over time, social transfers have evolved from in-kind assistance to cash transfers, with the latter proving to be more efficient in alleviating poverty and, additionally, serving as key tools for promoting equity. Their strong targeting capacity allows public resources to be directed precisely to vulnerable populations, thereby reducing the traditional trade-off between progressivity and revenue collection. In this way, taxes such as the VAT—typically seen as regressive—can become part of a progressive fiscal system when their revenues are redistributed through well-targeted TCTs. Thus, the focus shifts from designing purely progressive taxes to strategically using public spending to achieve equity.

However, the redistributive effectiveness of these policies depends heavily on the quality of targeting. Inclusion and exclusion errors remain a major challenge, but tools exist today to substantially improve accuracy. The combination of comprehensive administrative data and geospatial technologies (such as GIS) offers a concrete opportunity to refine eligibility criteria and enhance the efficiency of social spending.

Finally, to move toward a more integrated and equitable system, cash transfers could be complemented with instruments such as a negative income tax, particularly aimed at low-income formal workers. Doing this will extend the redistributive reach to groups who, although not living in extreme poverty, still face significant economic hardship. Together, these tools form a new paradigm of fiscal policy—more flexible, efficient, and capable of adapting to the diverse forms of vulnerability in contemporary societies.

References

Aizer, A., S. Cho, S. Eli, and A. Lleras-Muney. 2024. "The Impact of Cash Transfers to Poor Mothers on Family Structure and Maternal Well-Being." *American Economic Journal: Applied Economics* 16 (2): 492–529.

McMichael, P. 1995. *Food and Agrarian Orders in the World-Economy*. Westport, CT: Praeger.

Mesa-Lago, C. 1980. *Social Security in Latin America: Pressure Groups, Stratification, and Inequality*. Pittsburgh, PA: University of Pittsburgh Press Digital Editions.

Monge, K. A., and L. Tejerina. 2023. *EL SINIRUBE: habilitador de política social de precisión en Costa Rica*. Washington, DC: Inter-American Development Bank. https://doi .org/10.18235/0004806.

Robles, M., M. G. Rubio, and M. Stampini. 2015. "Have Cash Transfers Succeeded in Reaching the Poor in Latin America and the Caribbean?" Policy Brief 246, Inter-American Development Bank, Washington, DC.

Slack, P. 1995. *The English Poor Law, 1531–1782*. Cambridge: Cambridge University Press.

Stampini, M., N. Medellin, and P. Ibarraran. 2023. "Cash Transfers, Poverty, and Inequality in Latin America and the Caribbean." Working Paper 01531, Inter-American Development Bank, Washington, DC.

3

Value Added Tax: Demystifying Its Regressivity and the Pitfalls of High Standard Rates

Introduction

The value added tax (VAT) is a cornerstone of public finance, particularly in Latin America and the Caribbean (LAC), where it contributes substantially to government revenue. About one-third of revenues in LAC countries rely on VAT (refer to figure 3.1). This consumption tax, applied at each stage of the production and distribution of goods and services, possesses a unique mechanism: businesses pay VAT only on the value they add, not on the total cost, because of their ability to reclaim VAT paid on purchases. Although this design makes VAT a potent tool for revenue generation, it is widely perceived as regressive, which often makes it a contentious issue for policy makers.

The crux of the regressivity debate lies in the observation that low-income households typically allocate a larger share of their spending to essential goods and services that are subject to VAT. The VAT thus consumes a larger percentage of their income compared with higher-income earners. This can create the impression that the VAT disproportionately burdens those with fewer resources. To mitigate this inherent regressivity, many countries implement a standard VAT rate with a reduced rate or exemption for essential goods and services, particularly basic food items and medicine. By applying lower or zero VAT rates to necessities that constitute a larger share of low-income households' budgets, the overall tax burden on these households is lessened relative to higher-income earners. Thus, reduced rates serve as a key mechanism to address the regressive nature of VAT. However, this view is increasingly challenged by research suggesting that using consumption as a proxy for income and accounting for the prevalence of informal markets can significantly alter the understanding of VAT's distributional impact.

Figure 3.1   Share of value added tax revenue

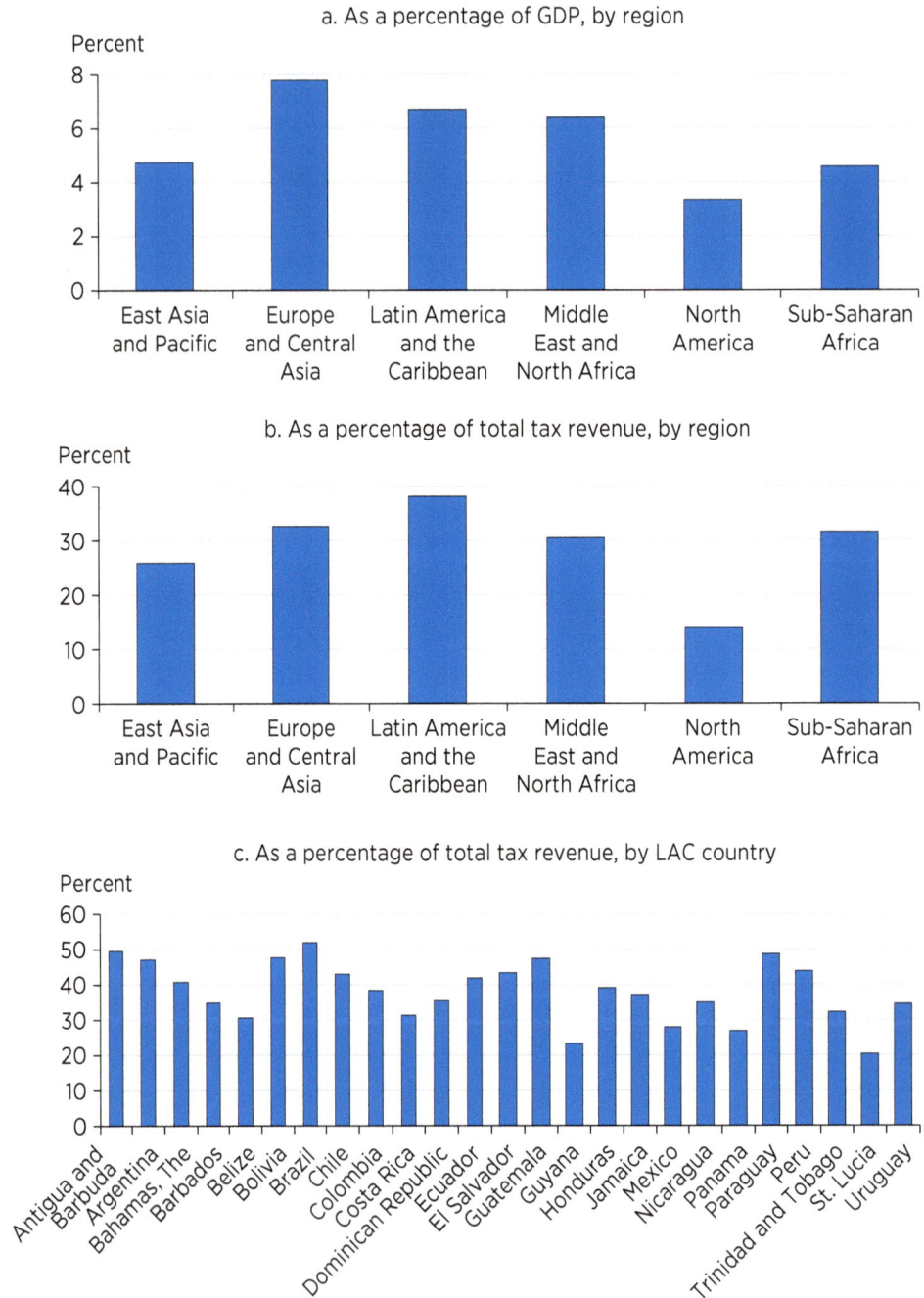

a. As a percentage of GDP, by region

Percent

b. As a percentage of total tax revenue, by region

Percent

c. As a percentage of total tax revenue, by LAC country

Percent

Source: Original calculations for this publication using the Organisation for Economic Co-operation and Development Global Revenue Statistics Database (https://www.oecd .org/en/data/datasets/global-revenue-statistics-database.html) and World Bank data.

Note: Consolidated government statistics. GDP = gross domestic product; LAC = Latin America and the Caribbean.

Furthermore, the balancing act between revenue needs and social equity concerns often leads to complex VAT structures. Policy makers often implement reduced VAT rates on essential goods such as food and medicine in an attempt to alleviate the burden on low-income households, but the need to compensate for revenue losses resulting from these reduced rates can sometimes push standard VAT rates higher, which, as we explore, may have negative consequences for economic growth.

This chapter delves into these complexities, aiming to provide a nuanced analysis of VAT in the LAC region. We explore the mechanics of VAT, dissect the debate on its regressivity, and examine the potential trade-offs among revenue generation, distributional equity, and economic growth.

Demystifying VAT Regressivity

In essence, two key mechanisms help to clarify the debate about the VAT's regressivity. First, the use of consumption, rather than current income, as a proxy for long-term income provides a more stable and accurate picture of a household's economic well-being. This is particularly important because current income can be highly volatile and may not accurately reflect a household's ability to pay taxes over the long term. Second, the existence of substantial informal markets, especially in developing economies, means that a significant portion of consumption, particularly that of lower-income households, may occur untaxed, thus reducing the overall burden of the VAT on these households.

VAT Regressivity Thesis and Income Measurement

VAT is a frequent subject of debate, particularly regarding its impact on income distribution. It is often argued that VAT is regressive. This view stems from traditional analyses that compare the tax burden with pretax or disposable income. These analyses indicate that lower-income households allocate a greater share of their income to consumption and, thus, appear to bear a disproportionately large share of the VAT burden. However, many economists contend that current income reported in surveys is not the most accurate measure of actual income. They suggest that consumption could be helpful because it is more closely aligned with long-term income (Poterba 1989).

The argument that consumption is a superior indicator of economic well-being is based on the observation that individuals tend to maintain a relatively stable pattern of spending over time. Although income can be highly volatile, especially for those with unstable employment, consumption tends to reflect a household's long-term resources and expectations. Therefore, assessments of the VAT's distributional impact that use consumption data may reach different conclusions. This perspective is consistent with the economic idea that consumption is linked to long-term expected income, rather than current income, and the view that individuals plan their spending and saving decisions throughout their lives. This is particularly relevant in contexts in which a significant portion of income is earned through informal channels and, therefore, is poorly measured in traditional income surveys.

When households are evaluated on the basis of their consumption rather than their income, the apparent regressivity of the VAT often diminishes. In some cases, it may even appear progressive. This is because consumption is less susceptible to short-term fluctuations and offers a clearer picture of a household's ability to pay taxes over an extended period. Specifically, although lower-income households do spend a larger proportion of their current income on consumption, that income may be highly variable. When viewed through the lens of consumption, their spending is more aligned with their long-term resources. Although higher-income households spend a smaller proportion of their current income on consumption, they also have a level of consumption that aligns with their long-term resources. This alignment of consumption with long-term resources for all income levels leads to the VAT appearing less regressive when analyzed through consumption.

Research, such as the work by Pessino et al. (2023), supports this perspective. Studies examining Latin American countries have compared the distribution of the VAT burden across income levels and consumption levels. These comparisons reveal a notable difference. When households are grouped by income, the tax burden tends to decrease as income increases, which aligns with the traditional view that VAT is regressive. However, when households are grouped by consumption, the tax burden is distributed more evenly, suggesting that the VAT is not necessarily regressive. This is because, as noted earlier, consumption provides a more stable measure of a household's long-term economic situation, smoothing out the short-term volatility that can make income a misleading indicator, especially for lower-income households.

Furthermore, analyses of tax progressivity in Latin America, as presented in Pessino et al. (2023), indicate a similar pattern (figure 3.2). When households are ranked by income, measures of tax progressivity often suggest that the VAT is regressive. However, when households are ranked by consumption, these measures tend to show a more neutral, or even progressive, impact of the VAT (figure 3.3). This occurs because the consumption-based analysis captures a household's ability to pay taxes over the long term, rather than being skewed by temporary income fluctuations.

Figure 3.2 Relative tax pressure from VAT by decile

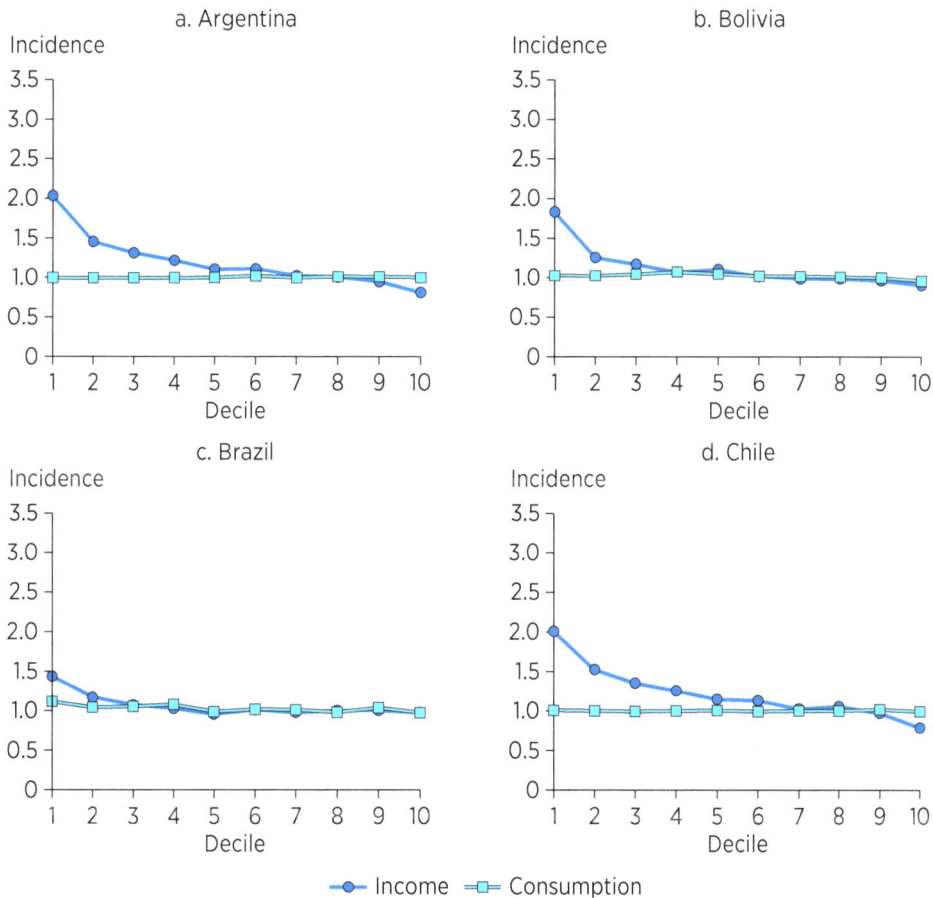

figure continued next page

Figure 3.2 Relative tax pressure from VAT by decile *(continued)*

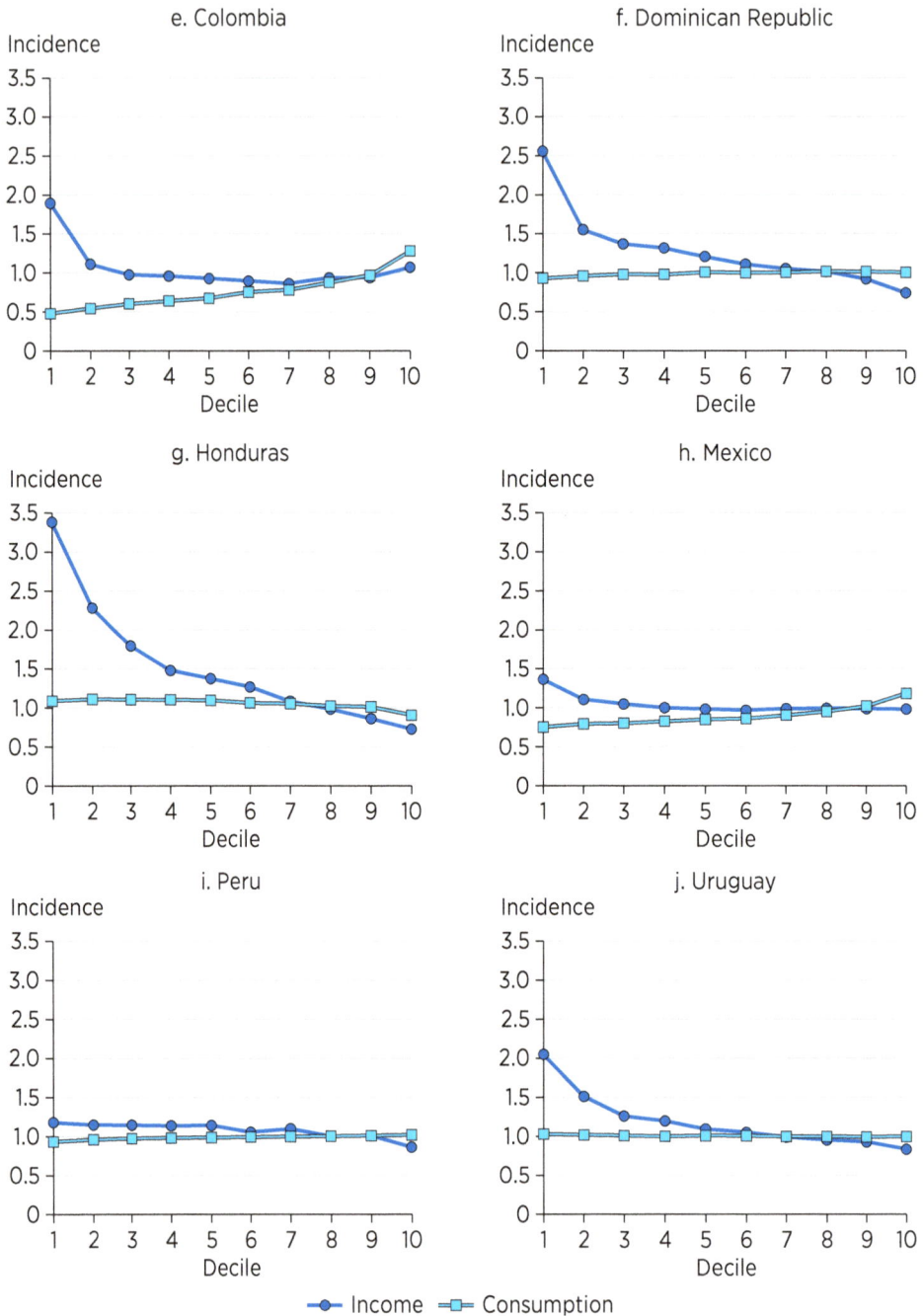

Source: Pessino et al. 2023.

Note: Tax pressure is measured by the ratio of the share of total VAT paid by decile with respect to total taxation by the share of the income or the consumption of the decile in total income or consumption. VAT = value added tax.

Figure 3.3 Kakwani index of VAT, ordered by disposable income and consumption deciles

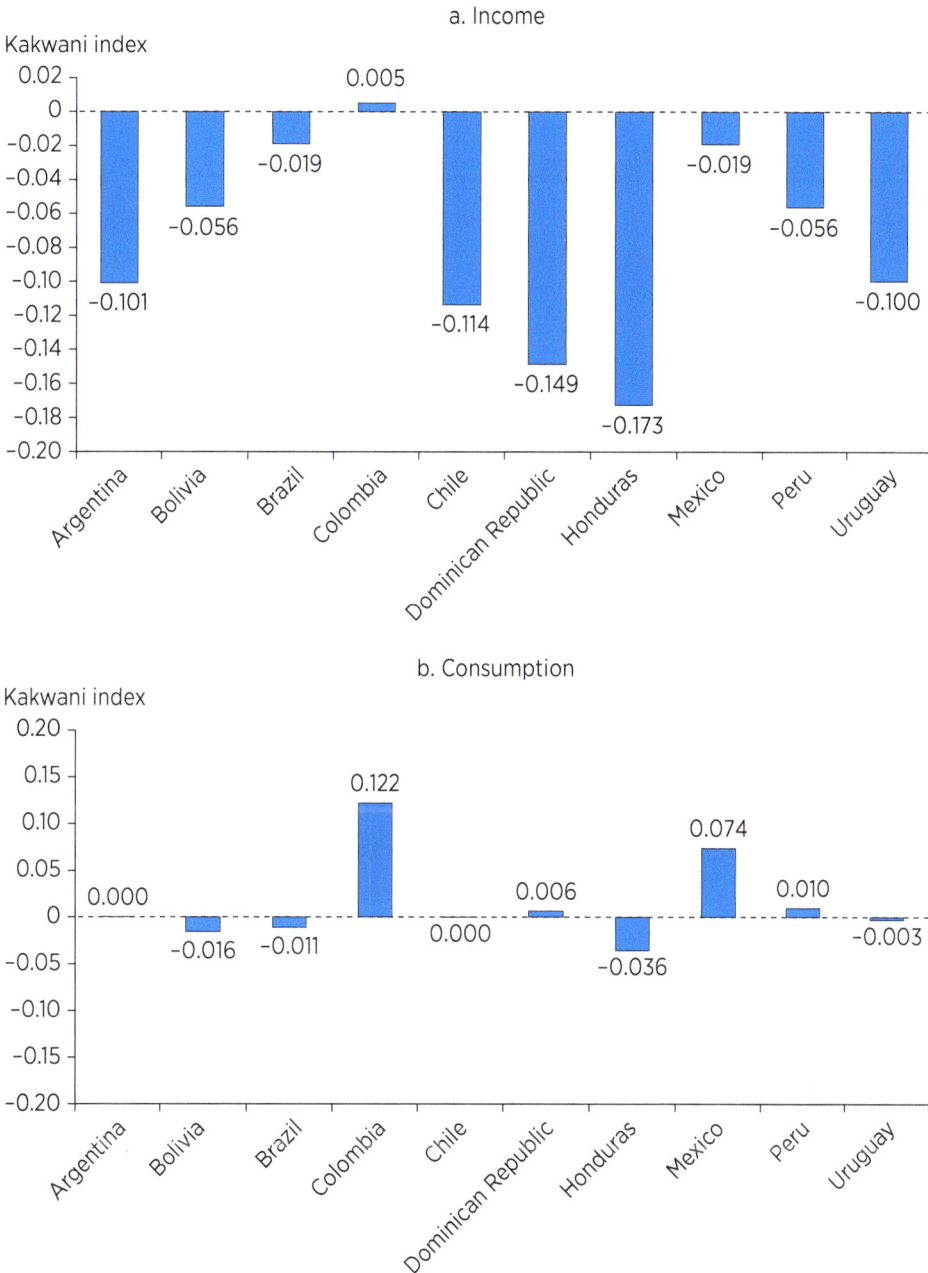

a. Income

Kakwani index

b. Consumption

Kakwani index

Source: Pessino et al. 2023.

Note: VAT = value added tax.

These findings indicate that the method used to measure household economic well-being significantly influences understanding of the VAT's distributional effects. The traditional view, which relies on income, may overstate the degree to which the VAT is regressive. By using consumption as a proxy for long-term income, researchers and policy makers can gain a more nuanced understanding of the VAT's impact and make more informed decisions regarding tax policy.

Although the distinction between income and consumption is important, it is also crucial to acknowledge that the debate about VAT regressivity is complex. Factors such as the specific goods and services that are taxed and the presence of exemptions or reduced rates also play a role in determining the VAT's distributional impact. Future research could explore these factors and their interaction with different measures of income in greater detail.

VAT Regressivity Thesis and Informality

Additionally, the impact of tax evasion, which is often more pronounced in developing economies, can influence the actual incidence of the VAT. In contrast to the traditional view of VAT regressivity in low-income countries, a recent and insightful study by Bachas, Gadenne, and Jensen (2020) suggests a more nuanced picture. Their examination of the significant role of informal purchases, particularly prevalent among low-income households, indicates that these transactions can substantially alter the distributional effects of the tax.

Poor Households Outsmart the Taxman in the Underground Economy

The Bachas, Gadenne, and Jensen (2020) study unveils a novel regularity: a downward-sloping informality Engel curve. This curve signifies a statistically significant decrease in the share of informal spending as household income rises across all studied countries. To identify informal purchases, these authors leverage data on household purchase locations from expenditure surveys, encompassing diverse settings such as home production and supermarkets. By analyzing these locations, they estimate the informal consumption proportion.

Bachas, Gadenne, and Jensen (2020) establish a microdatabase of expenditure surveys from 31 developing nations. These data include the place of purchase (for example, street stall or supermarket) for each transaction. Leveraging existing knowledge, they classify each purchase location as formal or informal based on the assumption that larger, modern retailers are more likely than smaller establishments to remit taxes (Kleven, Kreiner, and Saez 2016; Lagakos 2016).

This innovative approach yields novel insights into consumption patterns. Notably, Bachas, Gadenne, and Jensen (2020) document a consistent downward-sloping informality Engel curve. This curve signifies that, across all observed countries, the share of income spent in the informal sector declines significantly as household income increases. Figure 3.4 exemplifies this trend in Rwanda and Mexico, where the informal budget share plummets for higher income brackets.

Food Subsidies in Low-Income Countries Can Be a Miss

Bachas, Gadenne, and Jensen (2020) also show that consumption taxes are progressive because the informal sector is not taxed (de facto exemption). This means high-income people pay more in taxes. In fact, on average, the richest fifth (quintile) pays twice as much in taxes as the poorest fifth (refer to figure 3.5, blue line). This effect is stronger in poorer countries. Additionally, considering the informal sector, exempting food from taxes does not significantly affect redistribution (refer to figure 3.5, orange line).

Informal markets, where goods are bought and sold untaxed, complicate the design of consumption taxes and reduce tax collection efficiency. However, consumption taxes can still promote equity. Lower rates on necessities such as food benefit poor individuals, who rely on them more heavily, achieving progressive taxation. However, this effect weakens in very poor countries in which informal markets are widespread. Bachas, Gadenne, and Jensen's (2020) study highlights the challenge informal markets pose when crafting consumption tax policies that balance efficiency and equity in revenue collection.

Figure 3.4 Informality Engel curves in Rwanda and Mexico

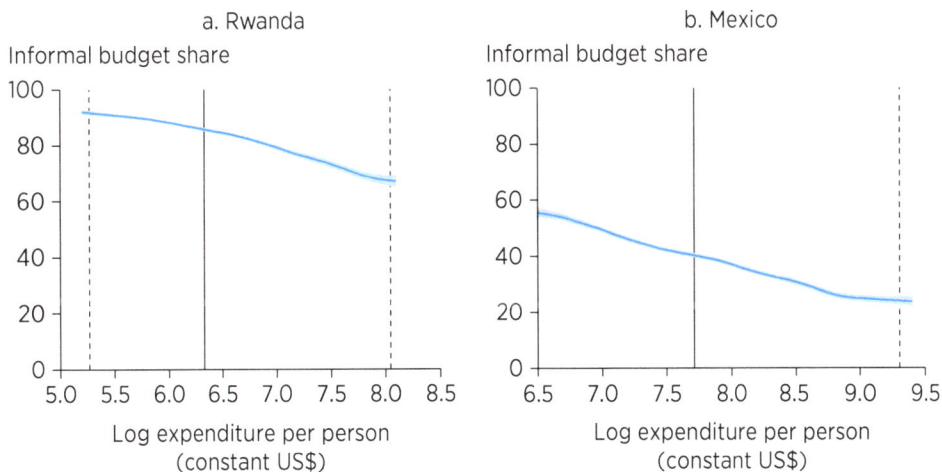

Source: Bachas, Gadenne, and Jensen 2020.

Note: These graphs plot the local polynomial fit of the informality Engel curves in Rwanda and Mexico. The shaded area around the polynomial fit corresponds to the 95 percent confidence interval. The solid line corresponds to the median of each country's expenditure distribution, and the dotted lines correspond to the 5th and 95th percentiles, respectively.

Figure 3.5 Taxed budget shares, average across all countries

Taxed budget share

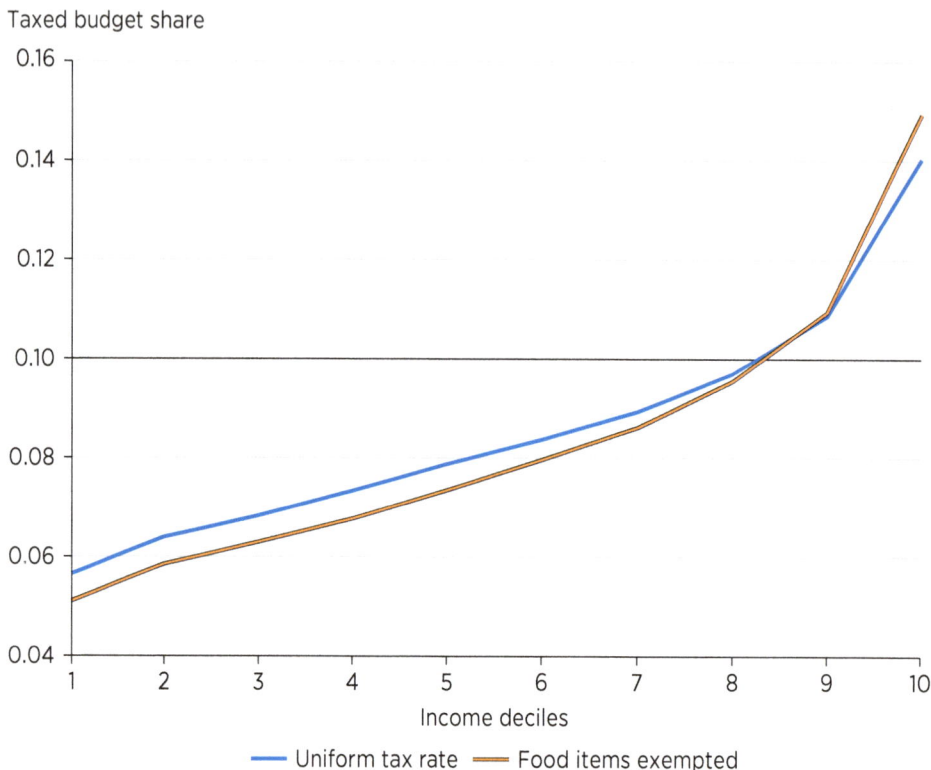

Income deciles

——— Uniform tax rate   ——— Food items exempted

Source: Bachas, Gadenne, and Jensen 2020.

Note: This figure plots the share of expenditures that is paid in taxes (effective tax rates), by decile, for each tax scenario. Both scenarios are simulated in all 31 countries in the sample; each point corresponds to the average effective tax rates of each decile across all countries. The blue line corresponds to a tax scenario in which a uniform tax is levied on all goods, but purchases in informal stores are de facto not taxed. The orange line corresponds to a tax scenario in which both a de facto informality exemption and a de jure food exemption are present.

Impact of VAT on Income Inequality: a Reassessment

Bachas, Gadenne, and Jensen (2020) examine the influence of consumption tax policies on income inequality, using tax rate data and household survey information (refer to figure 3.6). The authors use the percentage change in the Gini coefficient as the key metric for analyzing redistribution. A negative change signifies a reduction in inequality. The analysis reveals that when informal consumption is factored in, imposing a uniform and optimal tax rate on all formally recorded consumption leads to a significant decrease in income inequality (refer to figure 3.6, panel a, first row). This reduction is notably larger than previously established estimates of inequality reduction achieved through consumption tax policies in developing countries (refer to figure 3.6, panel b, first row).

These prior estimates often do not systematically account for the exemption of informal sector activity from taxation.

In fact, the Bachas, Gadenne, and Jensen (2020) study suggests that a uniform tax rate on formal consumption can achieve a level of inequality reduction comparable with that of current direct tax policies implemented in developing countries (refer to figure 3.6, panel b, second row). Furthermore, when informal consumption is considered, imposing a reduced tax rate on essential food items demonstrates a positive impact on inequality, although this marginal reduction is dwarfed by the effect of the informal sector (refer to figure 3.6, panel a, third row).

Bachas, Gadenne, and Jensen's (2020) study counters conventional wisdom, revealing consumption taxes to be far more progressive in developing economies. The secret weapon is large informal sectors, which are a haven for poor individuals. Conversely, efforts to tax food at a lower rate turn out to be weak tools for redistribution.

Figure 3.6 Estimated percentage of change in Gini from alternative policies

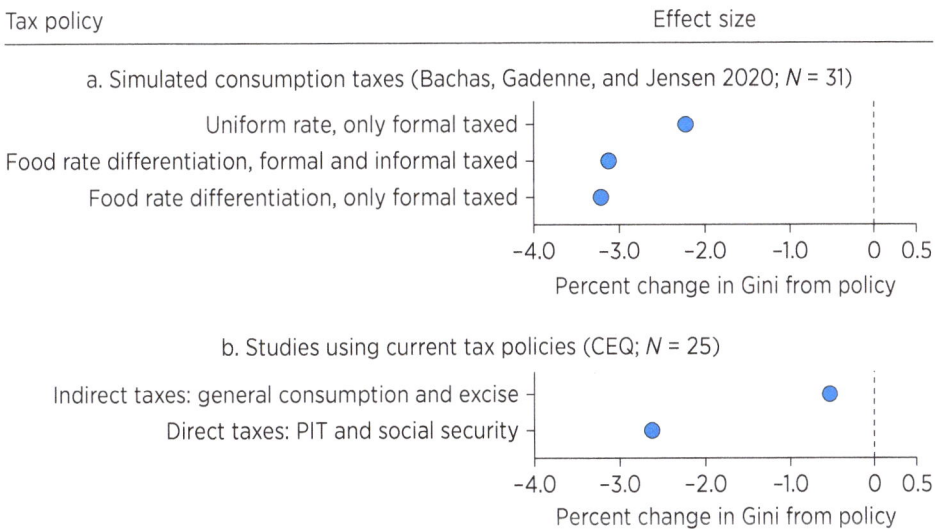

Tax policy   Effect size

a. Simulated consumption taxes (Bachas, Gadenne, and Jensen 2020; $N = 31$)

Uniform rate, only formal taxed
Food rate differentiation, formal and informal taxed
Food rate differentiation, only formal taxed

Percent change in Gini from policy

b. Studies using current tax policies (CEQ; $N = 25$)

Indirect taxes: general consumption and excise
Direct taxes: PIT and social security

Percent change in Gini from policy

Source: Bachas, Gadenne, and Jensen 2020.

Note: Panel a shows the average percentage change in Gini for different scenarios. In the first row, the dot represents the scenario in which a uniform rate is implemented, but only the formal sector is taxed. In the second row, the dot represents the scenario in which only nonfood items are taxed in both sectors. In the third row, the dot represents the scenario in which only nonfood items and only the formal sector are taxed. The reported effects reflect the change in Gini from the pretax income distribution to the posttax distribution. Panel b shows the percentage change in Gini using data from the CEQ. In the first row of panel b, actual general consumption and excise taxes are applied; in the second row, actual personal income taxes and compulsory social security contributions are applied. CEQ = Commitment to Equity Institute; PIT = personal income tax.

Pitfalls of High VAT Standard Rates

In recent years, a consensus has emerged among economists that tax hikes are contractionary, particularly in industrial European countries. Several individual and multicountry analyses (focusing solely on industrial economies, mostly European) have found tax multipliers—how gross domestic product (GDP) responds to tax changes—ranging from about −1.7 to −5.0 (Cloyne 2013; Gil et al. 2019; Hayo and Uhl 2014; Pereira and Wemans 2015). Such seemingly robust evidence has led to strong policy prescriptions. Alesina, Favero, and Giavazzi (2015, 1) concluded that "fiscal adjustments based upon spending cuts are much less costly, in terms of output losses, than tax-based ones."

In a recent study, Gunter et al. (2021a) investigated whether including a wider range of countries, particularly developing nations, would influence estimates of negative tax multipliers. To achieve this, they built a new dataset of standard VAT rates (henceforth, referred to simply as VAT rates) levied in 51 countries—a mix of 21 industrialized and 30 developing economies—spanning from 1970 onward. Their analysis revealed that the tax multiplier for the entire global sample peaked at −2.7 two years after the tax change. This falls within the lower range of previously reported tax multiplier estimates. Interestingly, when they divided the sample into industrial European economies and the rest of the world, they observed tax multipliers of −3.6 and −1.4, respectively. Although the multiplier in industrial European economies remained statistically significant and quite large (in absolute terms), aligning with recent research, the multiplier for the remaining countries was substantially weaker and roughly 2.5 times smaller in absolute value.

Nonlinear Effects of VAT Tax Changes on Output

Why would the tax multiplier vary so much? Theoretical distortionary and disincentive-based arguments (for example, Jaimovich and Rebelo 2017) imply that the effect of tax changes on output would be highly nonlinear: essentially zero under relatively low initial tax rate levels and more negative as the initial tax rate increases. As shown in figure 3.7, Gunter et al. (2021a) find that the effect of VAT tax changes on output is highly nonlinear. For example, the multiplier reaches −0.07 and is statistically zero when the initial tax rate is 8 percent, −1.6 and statistically zero when the initial tax rate is 14 percent, and −4.3 and statistically different from zero when the initial tax rate is 22 percent.

Figure 3.7 Nonlinear cumulative VAT tax multiplier after two years: role of the initial tax rate level

Tax multiplier

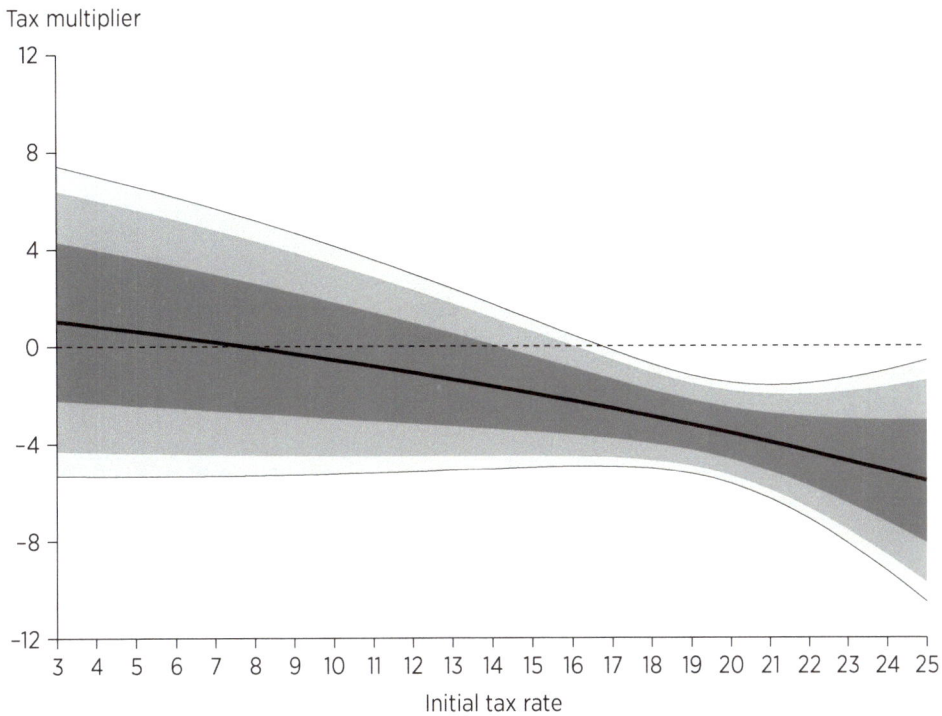

Initial tax rate

Source: Gunter et al. 2021a.

Note: The solid line represents the country fixed panel regression. Dark, medium, and light gray areas show 68, 90, and 95 percent confidence intervals, respectively. Standard errors are Driscoll-Kraay standard errors.

These nonlinear estimates suggest that a VAT rate of around 16 percent may be a critical threshold. Above this level, further VAT increases could increasingly harm economic activity. This finding suggests the existence of a tipping point at which the overall burden of the tax discourages economic activity. Businesses and consumers may become more responsive, leading to adjustments in behavior that ultimately reduce the tax base. These findings inform the traditional understanding of the Laffer curve, where there is a potential for tax revenue to fall even with a rising tax rate if economic activity weakens significantly.

This strongly suggests that the prevailing view of significant negative tax multipliers in industrialized countries, especially in Europe (for example, Alesina, Favero, and Giavazzi 2015), is mainly influenced by the high initial tax rates. Large negative tax multipliers are not a robust empirical regularity, especially in the developing world. The initial level of taxes varies greatly across countries, so it is natural that the potential output effect of changing tax rates varies too. Map 3.1, from a policy companion paper (Gunter et al. 2021b), shows that, given a country's current VAT rate, the tax multiplier could be statistically zero or moderate to high.

Map 3.1   VAT tax multipliers after two years, by country

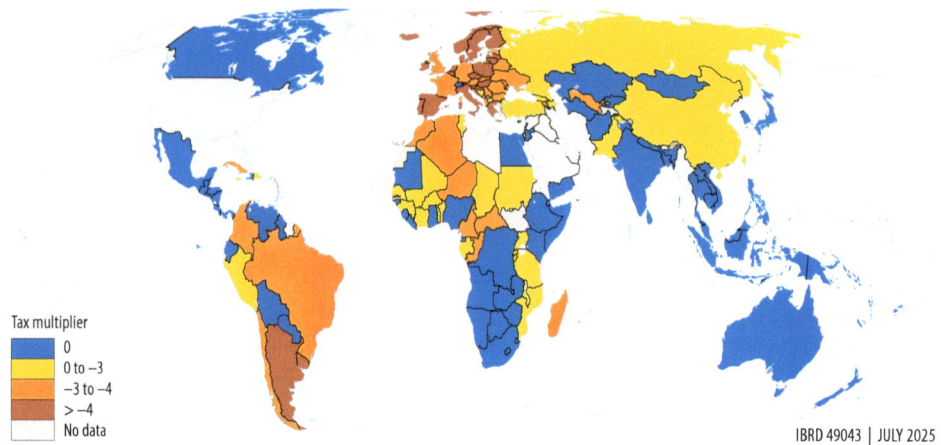

Tax multiplier
- 0
- 0 to −3
- −3 to −4
- > −4
- No data

IBRD 49043 | JULY 2025

Source: Gunter et al. 2021b.

Note: 0 indicates that the tax multiplier is not statistically significantly different from zero. VAT = value added tax.

As shown in map 3.1, for half the world (that is, 88 of 175 mapped countries) the tax multiplier is statistically zero. For example, tax changes would have virtually no effect on GDP in countries with low tax rates, such as Angola, Costa Rica, Ecuador, Guatemala, Nigeria, and Paraguay. In contrast, the same tax increase (or decrease) would cause output to fall (or increase) in countries with relatively high VAT rates, including emerging markets such as Argentina and Uruguay and especially many industrial European countries.

Policy Implications of Nonlinear Effects

In this section, we explore how the varying impact of tax changes on output can inform policy decisions. We examine how countries with low levels of provision of public goods, countries reliant on commodities, and the Laffer curve concept are all affected by these nonlinear effects.

Revenue Mobilization in Countries with Low Levels of Provision of Public Goods

Economists have long debated the ideal size and function of government. One theory, Wagner's law, suggests a link between economic development and government spending. As a nation's income grows, so does government spending, often in two ways: by taking on new activities (that is, extensive margin) and by expanding existing responsibilities (that is, intensive margin). This well-documented and strongly supported empirical regularity is shown in figure 3.8.

Figure 3.8 Relationship between GDP per capita and size of government spending relative to GDP

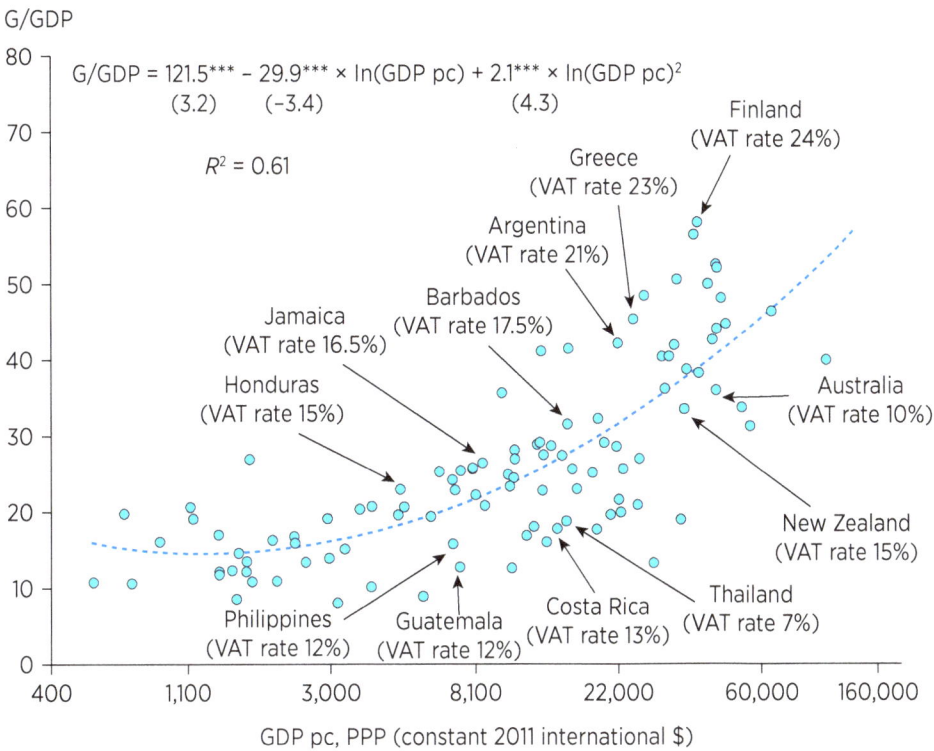

G/GDP

$$G/GDP = 121.5^{***} - 29.9^{***} \times \ln(GDP\ pc) + 2.1^{***} \times \ln(GDP\ pc)^2$$

(3.2)   (−3.4)   (4.3)

$R^2 = 0.61$

Finland (VAT rate 24%)
Greece (VAT rate 23%)
Argentina (VAT rate 21%)
Barbados (VAT rate 17.5%)
Jamaica (VAT rate 16.5%)
Honduras (VAT rate 15%)
Australia (VAT rate 10%)
New Zealand (VAT rate 15%)
Thailand (VAT rate 7%)
Costa Rica (VAT rate 13%)
Guatemala (VAT rate 12%)
Philippines (VAT rate 12%)

GDP pc, PPP (constant 2011 international $)

Source: Gunter et al. 2021b. Data for G/GDP from World Economic Output (International Monetary Fund); data for GDP pc from Penn World Tables.

Note: Data are from 2015. The total number of countries in the sample is 107. GDP = gross domestic product; GDP pc = per capita GDP; G/GDP = government spending over GDP ratio; PPP = purchasing power parity; VAT = value added tax.

Significance level: *** = 1 percent.

Countries above the line spend more than predicted by their income level; those below the line spend less. Excess spending can be defined as the difference between their actual spending ratio (government spending over GDP ratio [G/GDP]) and the predicted ratio from the line. Figure 3.9 shows that countries with higher excess spending (such as Argentina, Greece, Honduras, and Jamaica) tend to have higher VAT rates than those with lower excess spending (such as Australia, Guatemala, Costa Rica, and New Zealand). This evidence suggests that countries such as Guatemala, which provide fewer public goods than expected for their development level, may be able to achieve a typical level of public goods by raising the VAT rate, with minimal impact on economic activity.

Figure 3.9 Relationship between excess spending and the VAT rate

VAT rate

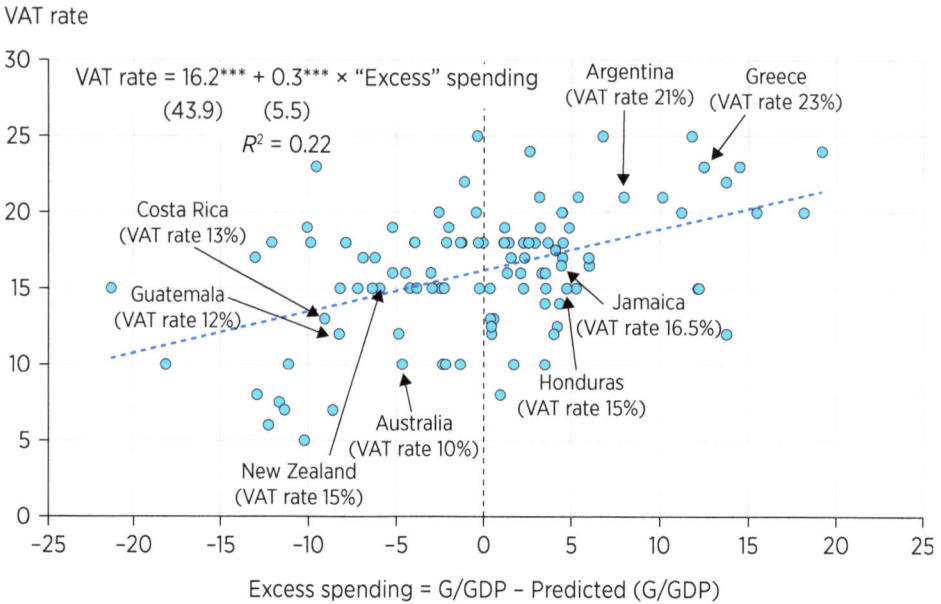

Excess spending = G/GDP – Predicted (G/GDP)

Source: Gunter et al. 2021b. Data for G/GDP from World Economic Output (International Monetary Fund); data for GDP pc from Penn World Tables.

Note: Data are from 2015. The total number of countries in the sample is 107. GDP = gross domestic product; GDP pc = per capita GDP; G/GDP = government spending over GDP ratio; VAT = value added tax.

Significance level: *** = 1 percent.

Revenue Mobilization in Commodity-Dependent Countries

A significant fiscal challenge confronts most commodity-rich countries, especially those that are heavily reliant on commodity revenues. As expected, Figure 3.10 reveals a clear link between an economy's dependence on commodities (measured as the share of commodity GDP in total GDP) and its reliance on commodity revenue (measured as the share of commodity revenue in total government revenue).

Defining excess commodity revenue dependency as the difference between actual commodity revenue and the predicted level represented by the fitted line in figure 3.10 reveals a pattern. Figure 3.11 shows that countries with a positive excess tend to have lower VAT rates (such as Malaysia, Nigeria, and Yemen) or none at all (such as Bahrain, Brunei Darussalam, and Iraq). Conversely, countries with a negative excess (such as Chile, Papua New Guinea, Trinidad and Tobago, and the Republic of Congo) typically have higher VAT rates.

Figure 3.10   Relationship between commodity GDP (as a percentage of GDP) and commodity revenues (as a percentage of total revenues)

Commodity revenues (as % of total revenues)

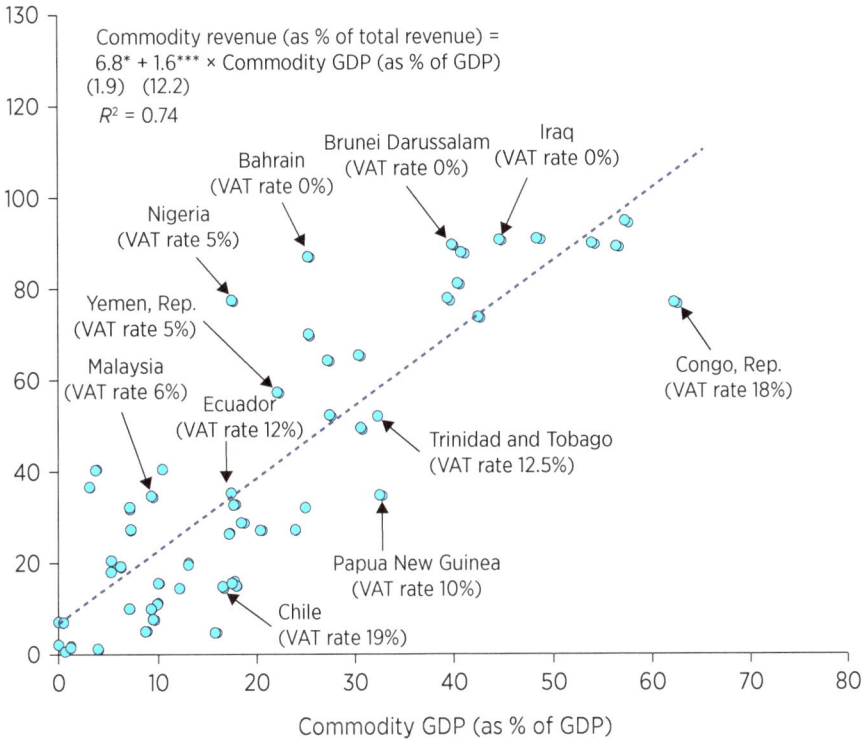

Commodity revenue (as % of total revenue) =
6.8* + 1.6*** × Commodity GDP (as % of GDP)
(1.9)   (12.2)
$R^2 = 0.74$

Bahrain
(VAT rate 0%)
Brunei Darussalam
(VAT rate 0%)
Iraq
(VAT rate 0%)
Nigeria
(VAT rate 5%)
Yemen, Rep.
(VAT rate 5%)
Congo, Rep.
(VAT rate 18%)
Malaysia
(VAT rate 6%)
Ecuador
(VAT rate 12%)
Trinidad and Tobago
(VAT rate 12.5%)
Papua New Guinea
(VAT rate 10%)
Chile
(VAT rate 19%)

Commodity GDP (as % of GDP)

Source: Gunter et al. 2021b. Data for commodity revenues (as percentage of total revenues) and commodity GDP (as percentage of GDP) based on Gunter et al.'s computations, using International Monetary Fund and Inter-American Development Bank data.

Note: Data are from 2010–13. Total number of countries in the sample is 55. GDP = gross domestic product; VAT = value added tax.

Significance level: * = 10 percent, *** = 1 percent.

This evidence suggests that countries such as Nigeria, with high excess commodity revenue dependency and low VAT rates, could quickly mobilize revenues from non-commodity-related activities by increasing their VAT rates. This approach could offer a more stable and sustainable source of government income, reducing reliance on volatile commodity prices.

Figure 3.11 Relationship between excess commodity revenue dependency and the VAT rate

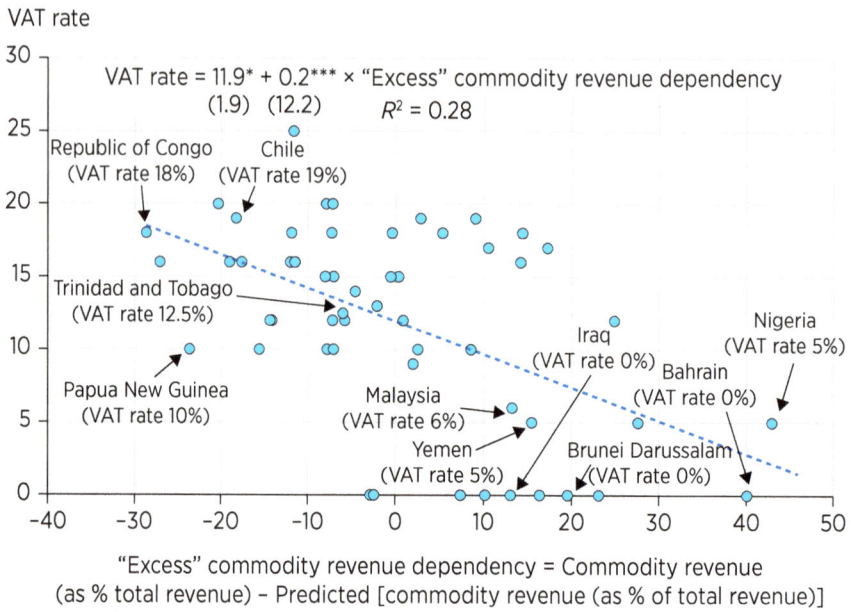

VAT rate

VAT rate = 11.9* + 0.2*** × "Excess" commodity revenue dependency
(1.9) (12.2) $R^2 = 0.28$

Republic of Congo   Chile
(VAT rate 18%)   (VAT rate 19%)

Trinidad and Tobago
(VAT rate 12.5%)

Papua New Guinea
(VAT rate 10%)

Iraq
(VAT rate 0%)   Bahrain

Nigeria
(VAT rate 5%)

Malaysia
(VAT rate 6%)

Yemen
(VAT rate 5%)

Brunei Darussalam
(VAT rate 0%)

"Excess" commodity revenue dependency = Commodity revenue
(as % total revenue) – Predicted [commodity revenue (as % of total revenue)]

Source: Gunter et al. 2021b; data for commodity revenues (as percentage of total revenues) and commodity GDP (as percentage of GDP) based on Gunter et al.'s computations, using International Monetary Fund and Inter-American Development Bank data.

Note: Data are from 2010–13. Total number of countries in the sample is 55. GDP = gross domestic product; VAT = value added tax.

Significance level: * = 10 percent, *** = 1 percent.

Implications for the Laffer Curve

The Laffer curve, developed by Arthur Laffer, proposes a nonlinear relationship between tax rates and tax revenue. Economic behavior also affects the size of the tax base. Laffer argued that when tax rates are below a certain threshold, economic activity faces minimal distortion. Therefore, a higher tax rate applied to this larger economic base can generate more revenue. However, above a certain threshold—leading to significant discouragement of economic activity—further tax hikes can actually lead to lower revenue. This counterintuitive outcome reflects the large response of economic agents to high initial levels of distortion. As shown in figure 3.12, this nonlinear relationship seems to hold true for VAT. The dotted line shows the corresponding increase in revenue as a percentage of GDP for different initial values of the VAT rate.

Figure 3.12 Relationship between initial VAT rate and change in revenues as a percentage of GDP in response to an increase in the VAT rate as of November 2017

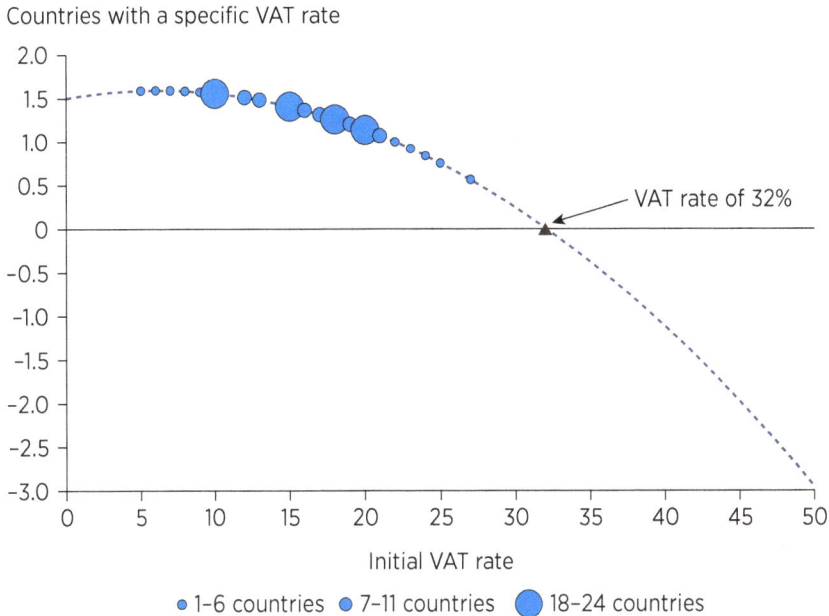

Countries with a specific VAT rate

VAT rate of 32%

Initial VAT rate

● 1–6 countries ● 7–11 countries ⬤ 18–24 countries

Source: Gunter et al. 2021b.

Note: The dotted line indicates the change in revenues (as a percentage of GDP) in response to an increase in the VAT rate, taking into account the nonlinear findings and assuming (without loss of generality) that revenues are given by the VAT rate times GDP. The total number of countries with a VAT rate is 172. The median (and average) VAT rate as of November 2017 was 16 percent, the minimum VAT rate (for countries having such a tax) was 5 percent, and the maximum VAT rate was 27 percent (for only one country). GDP = gross domestic product; VAT = value added tax.

At very low VAT rates (around 1.5 percentage points of GDP in revenue gains), the tax base barely shrinks. However, revenue gains become smaller with higher initial VAT rates. When the initial VAT level is 32 percent or higher, increasing the VAT rate may lead to lower revenue. The size of the dots in figure 3.12 indicates the number of countries with a specific VAT rate. The most common VAT rate (around 16 percent) falls well short of the 32 percent threshold. No country currently exceeds a 27 percent VAT rate. This suggests that, in practice, most countries are likely below the point at which VAT increases become counterproductive for revenue collection purposes.

However, around half of all countries have a VAT rate that exceeds the potential threshold of 16 percent. Notably, it is at or above this 16 percent level that the negative effects on economic activity and tax base reduction start accumulating as the VAT rate increases further. From a distortionary tax perspective, this suggests that a VAT rate reduction toward 16 percent could be economically beneficial for countries currently above this level. Figure 3.13 shows current standard VAT rates around the world and in each LAC country. On average, the LAC region has comparable standard VAT rates to those in Sub-Saharan Africa and South Asia, lower than those observed in Europe and Central Asia, and higher than those in East Asia and the Middle East and North Africa (refer to figure 3.13, panel a). Interestingly, there is large heterogeneity within the LAC region, with lower rates in most Central American and Caribbean countries and larger rates in South America, especially in the Southern Cone (refer to figure 3.13, panel b).

Figure 3.13 Standard VAT rates around the world

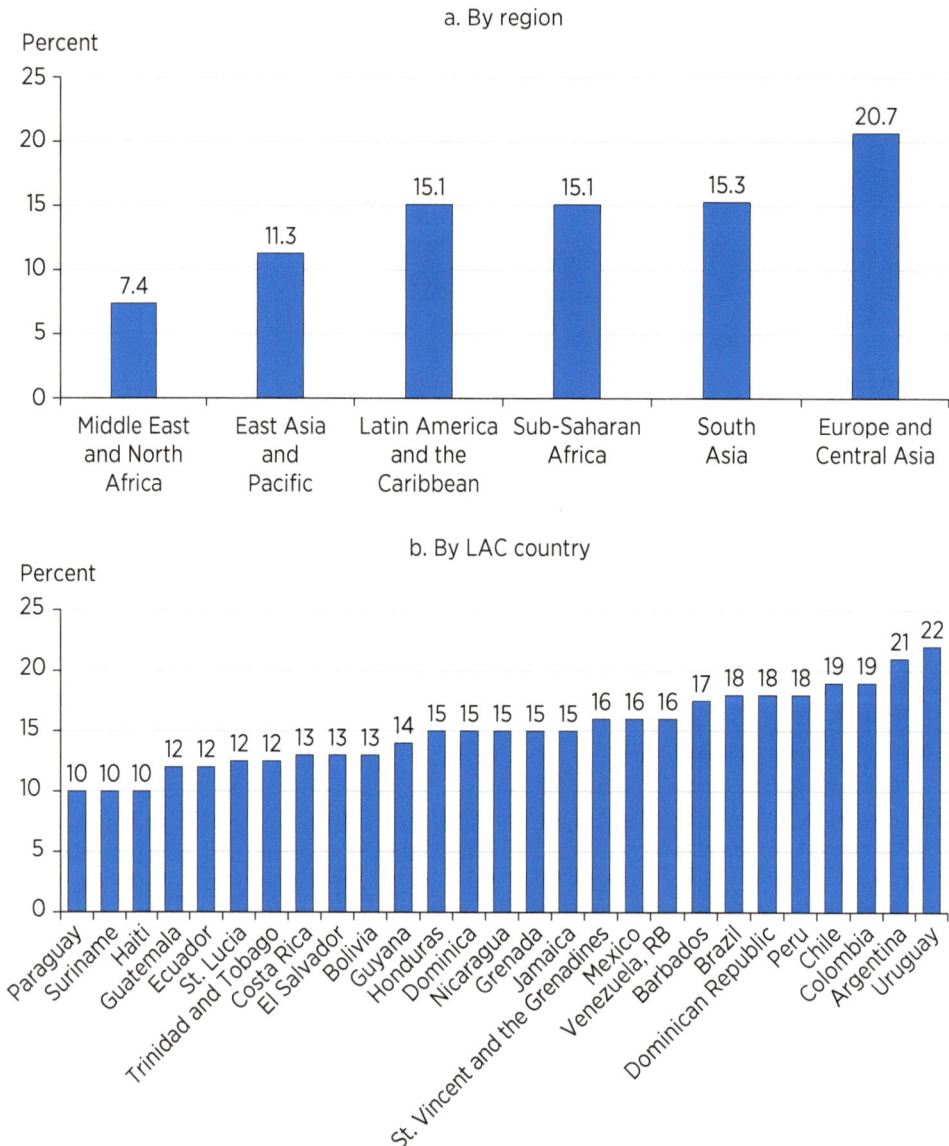

a. By region

b. By LAC country

Source: Vegh and Vuletin 2015 (global tax rate dataset available at www.guillermovuletin.com).
Note: LAC = Latin America and the Caribbean; VAT = value added tax.

No country currently has tax levels so high that further increases would negatively affect revenue collection. Nonetheless, approximately half of the world, including most European nations and many countries in LAC, is in a precarious position. In these regions, escalating tax burdens could potentially disrupt economic activity, posing a risk to progress by introducing distortions. European countries, along with numerous Latin American nations, are particularly experiencing these challenges. Conversely, the economies of Central America and the Caribbean would experience only minor impacts because of their existing tax levels. However, given their economic circumstances, any changes in tax policy should be meticulously planned to prevent adverse effects on economic growth.

Political Economy of VAT Reform: Targeted Transfers and Policy Strategies

VAT reform, particularly the shift toward a less distortionary structure coupled with targeted cash transfers, may face political and implementation risks. The most salient risk stems from the widespread perception of the VAT as inherently regressive. This perception, even if challenged by evidence of a less regressive impact when accounting for consumption patterns and informal markets, can be readily exploited by political actors seeking to mobilize opposition. Policy makers face a delicate balancing act. Reduced VAT rates on essentials, although often inefficient, are politically popular because of their visible impact on consumer prices. Replacing them with less visible cash transfers introduces distrust about government capacity and commitment to deliver promised benefits. Furthermore, implementing targeted cash transfers demands robust administrative capacity for beneficiary identification, efficient delivery, and rigorous monitoring—capabilities often lacking in contexts with weak institutions. These political and administrative hurdles create a challenging environment for enacting and sustaining comprehensive VAT reform.

Despite these inherent risks, evidence from similar successful reforms offers hope and guidance for feasible implementation. Experiences with transitioning from generalized subsidies to targeted transfers, as seen in Mexico's Programa de Educación, Salud y Alimentación (PROGRESA; refer to box 3.1) and many countries' policies after general price subsidies during the coronavirus disease 2019 pandemic, which were subsequently cut or redirected for more targeted cash, underscores the adaptability and scalability of such interventions (refer to box 3.2). Ultimately, success hinges on proactive management of political challenges through clear communication, phased implementation, and a steadfast commitment to strengthening institutional capacity.

Box 3.1

Mexico's shift from generalized subsidies to targeted transfers

Mexico undertook a significant social policy transformation in the late 1990s, shifting away from long-standing generalized subsidies with the elimination of the Compañía Nacional de Subsistencias Populares (CONASUPO) and embracing targeted interventions through the implementation of the Programa de Educación, Salud y Alimentación (PROGRESA). CONASUPO, established in 1961, was a cornerstone of Mexico's social welfare system, designed to achieve the triple objective of stabilizing food prices, supporting rural farmers by guaranteeing purchase prices, and ensuring access to affordable food for Mexico's impoverished population by distributing these staples at subsidized rates. However, by the 1990s, CONASUPO faced mounting criticism that eroded its legitimacy and effectiveness. The program's economic costs became increasingly unsustainable, particularly during the fiscal crises that plagued Mexico in the 1980s and 1990s. Beyond the fiscal burden, CONASUPO's operational efficiency was questioned, and allegations of mismanagement and resource diversion surfaced (Ordóñez-Barba & Silva-Hernández 2019). Perhaps most damning was the growing evidence of its regressive impact. Research demonstrated that wealthier households, because of their higher overall consumption, disproportionately benefited from the subsidized goods, undermining CONASUPO's poverty alleviation goals (Levy 2006). These factors, combined with a broader shift toward neoliberal reforms under the Salinas and Zedillo presidencies, which emphasized reduced state intervention in markets and a preference for targeted social policies, and the compelling evidence that direct transfers could more effectively reduce poverty than generalized subsidies (Niño-Zarazúa 2011), ultimately paved the way for the dismantling of CONASUPO by 1999, with its remaining functions transferred to smaller, specialized agencies.

PROGRESA and its impact

To effectively address the social safety net gaps left by CONASUPO's elimination and to modernize its approach to poverty alleviation, the Mexican government introduced PROGRESA in 1997. This program represented a fundamental paradigm shift in Mexico's social policy, moving away from broad-based price interventions to targeted conditional cash transfers focused on investing in human capital development among the poorest families. PROGRESA's innovative design incorporated several key features. First, it used rigorous targeting methodologies, utilizing both geographic and household-level poverty data to identify and select beneficiary families, ensuring that assistance reached those most in need.

box continued next page

Box 3.1

Mexico's shift from generalized subsidies to targeted transfers *(continued)*

Second, it introduced conditionalities, linking cash transfers to beneficiary households' compliance with specific requirements, most notably investments in children's school attendance, regular health checkups, and participation in nutrition workshops. This conditionality aimed to break the intergenerational transmission of poverty by promoting long-term investments in human capital. Third, recognizing the pivotal role of women in household welfare, PROGRESA directed cash transfers primarily to women within the household, seeking to enhance their agency and decision-making power. PROGRESA's outcomes have been extensively studied, with numerous evaluations demonstrating the program's success in achieving significant reductions in poverty and substantial improvements in key social indicators, including increased school enrollment rates (particularly for girls), better child health and nutritional outcomes, and improved household consumption patterns (Levy 2006; Niño-Zarazúa 2011). The program's efficient targeting mechanisms and relatively low administrative costs (approximately 9 percent of its budget) further contributed to its effectiveness, establishing PROGRESA as a global benchmark and a model for poverty alleviation programs worldwide.

Box 3.2

Postpandemic shift to targeted transfers

The global policy response to the coronavirus disease 2019 pandemic provides a compelling, albeit crisis-driven, demonstration of the adaptability and scalability of targeted transfer programs. In the initial phases of the pandemic, many governments, facing the urgent need to cushion the economic shock of lockdowns and widespread economic disruption, implemented or expanded general price subsidies. These measures, often aimed at stabilizing the prices of essential goods such as fuel, food, and utilities, sought to provide broad relief to households and businesses. However, the limitations and inefficiencies of such generalized subsidies, including their poor targeting and potential to disproportionately benefit wealthier households, became increasingly apparent as the crisis unfolded and fiscal pressures mounted. This experience served as a catalyst for a reevaluation of social safety net mechanisms in many countries.

Subsequently, as the immediate crisis phase subsided, a notable trend emerged toward rationalizing these initial interventions. Governments

box continued next page

Postpandemic shift to targeted transfers *(continued)*

began to cut or redirect the generalized price subsidies, opting for more targeted cash transfer programs. This shift was driven by several factors, including the need to consolidate public finances, improve the efficiency of social spending, and ensure that support reached the most vulnerable populations. The pandemic forced rapid innovation in targeting methodologies and delivery mechanisms, with increased reliance on digital platforms and mobile money to distribute assistance quickly and effectively. Although the specific design and implementation of these programs varied across countries, this widespread transition highlights a growing recognition of the advantages of targeted interventions in providing effective social protection, even under challenging circumstances.

Ultimately, successful VAT reform hinges on strategically navigating political obstacles through integrated policy design. This involves (a) effective communication that clearly articulates the rationale for reform and addresses regressivity concerns, (b) phased implementation to manage disruption and build acceptance, and (c) strengthened institutional capacity to ensure efficient administration and targeted social assistance. In the LAC context, the region's growing experience with implementing and managing targeted social programs provides a valuable foundation for this third pillar because it has demonstrated the capacity to effectively deliver assistance to vulnerable populations. Building on this existing expertise and infrastructure can facilitate the successful integration of VAT reform with compensatory social policies, transforming VAT into a more efficient and equitable fiscal instrument.

Conclusion

This chapter reframes the discourse on VAT, particularly in the LAC context, moving beyond the simplistic notion of its inherent regressivity. It challenges the conventional wisdom by highlighting the limitations of income-based analyses, especially in informal economies, and arguing that consumption offers a more stable measure of long-run well-being. By adopting a consumption-based approach and explicitly considering the dynamics of informal markets, the chapter reveals that VAT's impact on income distribution is far more nuanced and often less regressive, or even progressive, than previously thought. This nuanced understanding is critical for evaluating policy tools such as reduced VAT rates on essential goods, designed to address regressivity.

The analysis underscores the limitations of traditional income measures, especially in economies with significant informal sectors, where consumption provides a more stable and accurate reflection of long-term economic well-being. Furthermore, the chapter highlights the crucial role of the informal sector in mitigating the VAT burden on lower-income households, challenging the assumption that these households bear a disproportionate share of the tax. This also implies that the effectiveness of reduced VAT rates in achieving redistribution may be limited in economies with large informal sectors.

Moreover, the chapter's examination of the nonlinear effects of standard VAT rates introduces a critical dimension to the policy debate. The finding that higher VAT rates can lead to diminishing, and even negative, returns in terms of economic growth has profound implications for fiscal policy design. It suggests that the pursuit of revenue maximization through ever-increasing VAT rates may be self-defeating, potentially undermining the very economic base upon which the tax is levied. This highlights the delicate balance policy makers must strike between revenue needs and economic stability when setting VAT rates, especially in the context of using reduced rates that might necessitate higher standard rates.

Ultimately, this chapter calls for a paradigm shift in how VAT is evaluated and implemented. It advocates for a more holistic approach that integrates a sophisticated understanding of household behavior, market structures, and the nonlinear relationship between tax rates and economic outcomes. This shift suggests a potential policy direction: by reevaluating tax expenditures linked to reduced VAT rates (which may disproportionately favor rich individuals) and decreasing reliance on high standard VAT rates, governments could create fiscal space for a more progressive overall fiscal structure while also minimizing economic distortions and promoting economic growth. Such an approach is essential for crafting tax policies that are not only equitable but also conducive to sustainable economic growth and development. It requires careful consideration of both the distributional impacts of VAT and the potential growth consequences of VAT rate policies.

References

Alesina, A., C. Favero, and F. Giavazzi. 2015. "The Output Effect of Fiscal Consolidation Plans." *Journal of International Economics* 96 (Supplement 1): S19–S42.

Bachas, P., L. Gadenne, and A. Jensen. 2020. "Informality, Consumption Taxes, and Redistribution." Policy Research Working Paper 9267, World Bank, Washington, DC.

Cloyne, J. 2013. "Discretionary Tax Changes and the Macroeconomy: New Narrative Evidence from the United Kingdom." *American Economic Review* 103 (4): 1507–28.

Gil, P., F. Martí, R. Morris, J.J. Pérez, and R. Ramos. 2019. "The Output Effects of Tax Changes: Narrative Evidence from Spain." *SERIEs* 10: 1–23.

Gunter, S., D. Riera-Crichton, C.A. Vegh, and G. Vuletin. 2021a. "Non-Linear Effects of Tax Changes on Output: The Role of the Initial Level of Taxation." *Journal of International Economics* 131: 103450.

Gunter, S., D. Riera-Crichton, C.A. Vegh, and G. Vuletin. 2021b. "Policy Implications of Non-Linear Effects of Tax Changes on Output." Working Paper 28646, National Bureau of Economic Research, Cambridge, MA.

Hayo, B., and M. Uhl. 2014. "The Macroeconomic Effects of Legislated Tax Changes in Germany." *Oxford Economic Papers* 66 (2): 397–418.

Jaimovich, N., and S. Rebelo. 2017. "Nonlinear Effects of Taxation on Growth." *Journal of Political Economy* 125 (1): 265–91.

Kleven, H.J., C.T. Kreiner, and E. Saez. 2016. "Why Can Modern Governments Tax So Much? An Agency Model of Firms as Fiscal Intermediaries." *Economica* 83 (330): 219–46.

Lagakos, D. 2016. "Explaining Cross-Country Productivity Differences in Retail Trade." *Journal of Political Economy* 124 (2): 579–620.

Levy, S. 2006. *Progress Against Poverty: Sustaining Mexico's Progresa-Oportunidades Program*. Washington, DC: Brookings Institution Press.

Niño-Zarazúa, M. 2011. "Mexico's Progresa-Oportunidades and the Emergence of Social Assistance in Latin America." Working Paper Series 142, Brooks World Poverty Institute, University of Manchester, Manchester, UK.

Ordóñez-Barba, G., and A. Silva-Hernández. 2019. "Progresa-Oportunidades-Prospera: Transformations, Reaches and Results of a Paradigmatic Program Against Poverty." *Papeles de Población* 25 (99): 77–109.

Pereira, M.C., and L. Wemans. 2015. "Output Effects of a Measure of Tax Shocks Based on Changes in Legislation for Portugal." *Review of Public Economics* 215 (4): 27–62.

Pessino, C., A. Rasteletti, D. Artana, and N. Lustig. 2023. "Distributional Effects of Taxation in Latin America." Working Paper Series IDB-WP-01534, Inter-American Development Bank, Washington, DC.

Poterba, J. M. 1989. "Lifetime Incidence and the Distributional Burden of Excise Taxes." *American Economic Review* 79 (2): 325–30.

Vegh, D., and G. Vuletin. 2015. "How Is Tax Policy Conducted Over the Business Cycle?" *American Economic Journal: Economic Policy* 7 (3): 327–70.

4

Corporate Income Tax: From Chasing Butterflies to Drawing Bees

Introduction

Corporate income tax (CIT) forms a cornerstone of government revenue in emerging markets and developing economies (EMDEs), especially those in Latin America and the Caribbean (LAC). This tax, levied on company profits after allowable expense deductions, presents a significant policy challenge. Policy makers in LAC grapple with the difficulty of effectively taxing "butterflies"—mobile capital that can easily relocate to lower tax jurisdictions—while simultaneously striving to draw "bees"—crucial foreign investment—and stimulate economic growth. This balancing act is further complicated by high levels of tax evasion and avoidance, which undermine potential revenue gains. Thus, policy makers must carefully navigate CIT's role in funding public services while maintaining competitive rates that foster economic development.

Understanding the specific mechanics of CIT is crucial. Unlike the limited deductions available for personal income tax (PIT), companies are allowed to deduct a wide range of production costs, including costs of goods sold, employee salaries, rent, utilities, marketing, and depreciation. Although most countries use a flat CIT rate, some use a progressive structure in which the tax rate increases with profits or revenues, as observed in countries such as Costa Rica, India, the United Kingdom, and others. This chapter delves into how firms in LAC respond to these CIT structures, exploring the implications for tax policy and economic development in the region.

Figure 4.1 shows that corporate tax collection represents a fairly similar share of gross domestic product (GDP) across world regions. Surprisingly, current CIT rates in LAC are about 30 percent higher than in the rest of the world—29.7 percent higher in LAC versus 23.2 percent higher in the rest of the world. This suggests some large behavioral response in corporations in LAC, including possible tax evasion.

Figure 4.1   Size of corporate income tax revenue

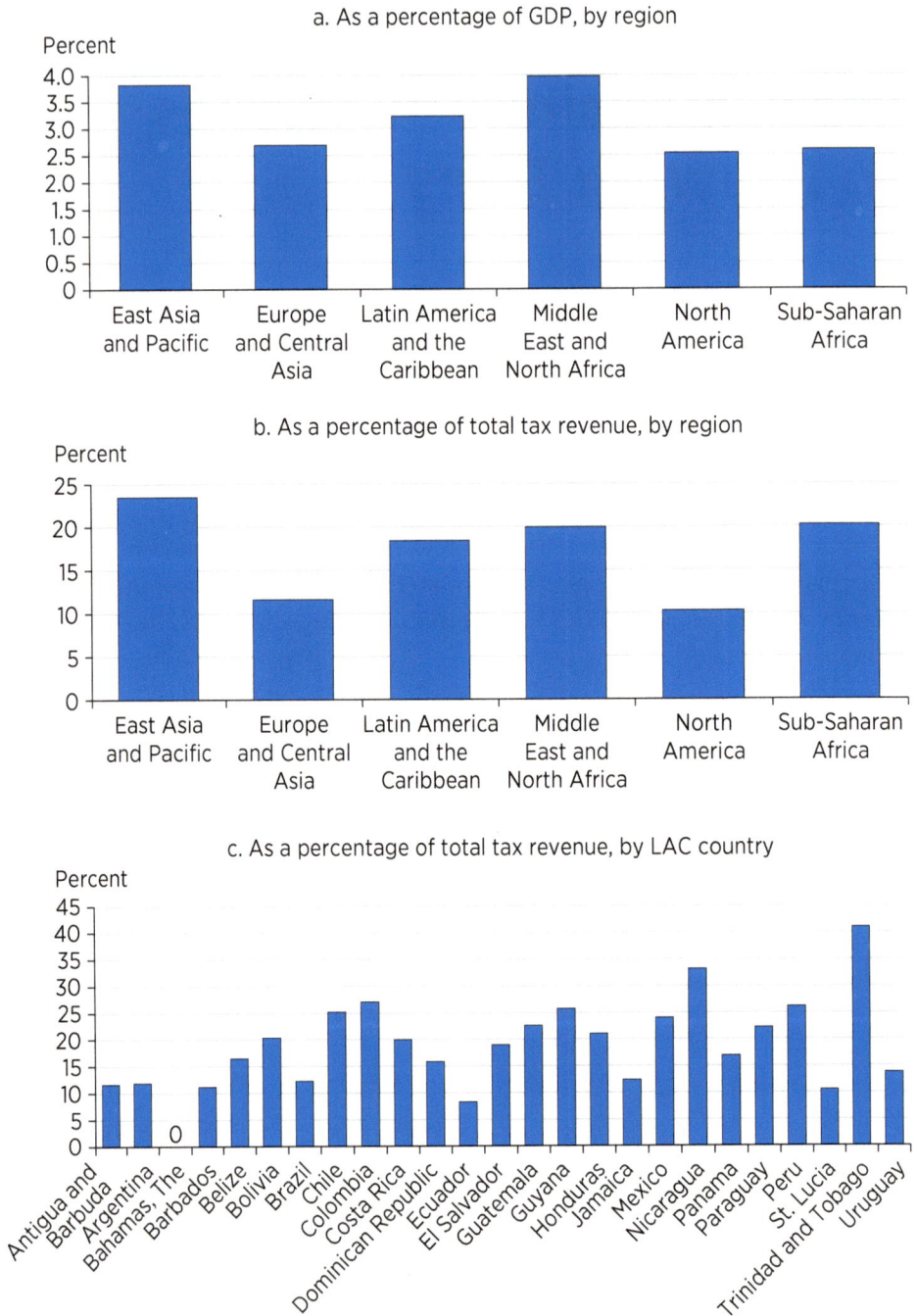

a. As a percentage of GDP, by region

Percent

Region	Percent
East Asia and Pacific	3.8
Europe and Central Asia	2.7
Latin America and the Caribbean	3.3
Middle East and North Africa	4.0
North America	2.6
Sub-Saharan Africa	2.7

b. As a percentage of total tax revenue, by region

Percent

Region	Percent
East Asia and Pacific	23.5
Europe and Central Asia	11.5
Latin America and the Caribbean	18.5
Middle East and North Africa	20
North America	10.5
Sub-Saharan Africa	20.5

c. As a percentage of total tax revenue, by LAC country

Percent

Source: Original calculations for this publication using the Organisation for Economic Co-operation and Development Global Revenue Statistics Database (https://www.oecd .org/en/data/datasets/global-revenue-statistics-database.html) and World Bank data.

Note: Consolidated government statistics. GDP = gross domestic product; LAC = Latin America and the Caribbean.

Corporate tax rates have fallen around the world in the past 40 years. Using the Vegh and Vuletin (2015) tax rate database, figure 4.2 shows a large worldwide fall from more than 40 percent in the 1980s to 24 percent today. A similar picture emerges when focusing on advanced and non-LAC EMDEs. Interestingly, the observed decline in LAC is less dramatic, falling from more than 37 percent in the 1980s to 30 percent today. In other words, CIT rates in LAC seem to show greater resistance to downward changes. In fact, most of the decline occurred during the 1980s and early 1990s, and rates have remained virtually unchanged since then. Whereas the current rate is 27 percent in Chile and 35 percent in Argentina and Colombia, it is 23.7 percent on average in Organisation for Economic Co-operation and Development (OECD) countries, 20.6 percent in Sweden, and 20 percent in Finland. This overtaxed situation aligns with other symptoms of an unfriendly business environment in the LAC region. This unfriendliness is manifested in various forms, including excessive regulation, a poorly skilled workforce, and significant institutional rigidities.

Figure 4.2   Evolution of CIT rate, by region

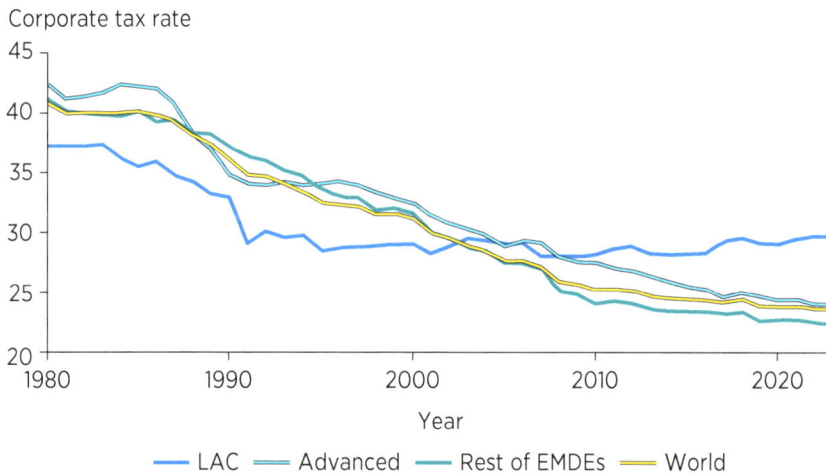

Source: Original calculations for this publication using the Vegh and Vuletin (2015) tax rate dataset.

Note: CIT = corporate income tax; EMDEs = emerging markets and developing economies; LAC = Latin America and the Caribbean.

The Taxman's Knock: Firm Reactions

To evaluate whether increasing corporate tax rates is a realistic policy option to achieve greater progressivity in tax collection, a fundamental understanding of how firms respond to tax hikes is essential for two main reasons. First, it allows us to predict the potential impact on government revenue. If firms significantly reduce profits or investment in response to higher taxes, the overall revenue gain might be lower than anticipated. Second, examining corporate behavior also includes analyzing the incentives created for tax evasion and avoidance when tax rates are increased. By comprehensively examining these multifaceted responses to tax hikes, more informed decisions can be made about the effectiveness of this policy option in achieving a fairer tax system. Similar to the elasticity of taxable income in the PIT literature, profit elasticity with respect to corporate taxation measures the percentage of change in reported corporate profits (that is, the tax base for CIT) in response to a 1 percent increase in the net corporate tax rate.

Evidence from the Global North

Firms' profit elasticity to corporate taxation is typically low in OECD countries. For example, for small firms in the United Kingdom and the United States, Devereux, Liu, and Loretz (2014) and Patel, Seegert, and Smith (2017), respectively, estimate a corporate elasticity of 0.5. This relatively inelastic response suggests that corporate behavior, at least in terms of reported profits, is not dramatically altered by moderate changes in tax rates in these contexts. Several factors contribute to this phenomenon. The findings in Devereux, Liu, and Loretz (2014) highlight the role of foreign direct investment, where tax considerations can influence the location of investment but may not significantly alter the overall profitability of existing firms within a country. Patel, Seegert, and Smith (2017) delve into the impact of investment incentives, such as bonus depreciation, which can have a more pronounced effect on investment decisions than corporate tax rates themselves. In essence, firms may respond to tax changes through investment timing or location rather than drastic profit shifting. The evidence also supports that high levels of enforcement and formality are important factors behind this low elasticity. Strong enforcement mechanisms make it difficult for firms to evade taxes or hide profits. This reduces their ability to manipulate their taxable income and lessen the impact of tax rate changes. Formal tax filing procedures and regulations can limit the flexibility firms have in responding to tax changes.

Evidence from the Global South

Unlike advanced countries, developing economies tend to exhibit higher elasticity of corporate tax revenue. For example, Bachas and Soto (2021) find elasticities of taxable profit in the 3–5 range in Costa Rica, whereas Garriga and Scot (2023) and Lediga, Riedel, and Strohmaier (2019) situate profit elasticities at around 7.4 in Lithuania and at around 1.3 in South Africa, respectively. These higher elasticities indicate that corporate behavior in developing economies is more sensitive to changes in corporate tax rates. It is important to note, as indicated in Waseem (2018), that elasticity estimates often focus on the intensive margin (that is, how existing firms change their behavior). However, in developing economies, the extensive margin (that is, firms' entry and exit) can be particularly important. Tax changes can significantly influence firm creation and survival, further amplifying the overall impact of corporate tax policy. The underlying mechanisms driving these differences, including the roles of tax evasion, avoidance, and labor market effects, are explored in greater detail in the next section.

Factors Contributing to Greater Responsiveness in EMDEs

Factors contributing to greater responsiveness in EMDEs are numerous and multifaceted, often stemming from the unique economic and institutional landscapes of these regions. Understanding these factors is crucial to design effective and equitable tax policies.

Tax Evasion and Avoidance

Within the expanding body of research on EMDEs, tax evasion emerges as a significant concern. In fact, Bachas and Soto (2021) show that strategic tax evasion is observed across firms regardless of profit margin, implying that the incentives to evade are pervasive and not limited to struggling companies. This finding suggests that the decision to evade taxes is more likely driven by the opportunity to reduce tax burden, not necessarily by a company's financial health. In fact, firms in EMDEs use two primary channels to avoid their tax obligations: revenue underreporting and cost overreporting.

Revenue Underreporting

Revenue underreporting can involve companies pocketing cash from unrecorded sales, manipulating their accounting systems to show lower sales figures, fabricating fake sales returns to offset real income, or even funneling sales through fictitious shell companies to create the illusion of a smaller operation. These deceptive maneuvers create a false impression of a company's financial performance, allowing it to dodge taxes but ultimately risking severe penalties and reputational damage if caught.

Cost Overreporting

To reduce their tax burden, companies might resort to deceptive tactics such as inflating invoices from vendors for legitimate purchases, creating entirely fake invoices for fabricated expenses, and even mischaracterizing personal spending as business costs. These manipulations artificially inflate deductible expenses, lowering the company's taxable income and tax bill.

Leveraging a new study by Lobel, Scot, and Zúñiga (2024), box 4.1 explores how corporations adjust their behavior to minimize their tax burden. Focusing on the effects of a minimum corporate tax in Honduras, the analysis provides evidence of these two key strategies.

Box 4.1

Corporations pulling a fast one on the taxman

This box presents key findings of recent insightful research conducted by Lobel, Scot, and Zúñiga (2024). These authors explore the effectiveness of minimum corporate taxes in boosting tax collection in Honduras. Traditionally, corporate income tax is levied on declared profits—what is left after subtracting business expenses from revenue. However, evidence suggests widespread cost overreporting by firms to lower their tax burden.

Minimum taxes are a policy tool designed to ensure that large corporations contribute their fair share. In Honduras, firms exceeding an annual revenue of L 10 million (roughly US$400,000) must pay the higher amount between 25 percent of their declared profits and 1.5 percent of their gross revenue. This mechanism effectively prevents large companies—approximately the top 20 percent by revenue—from escaping taxation by reporting minimal profits. Despite the widespread use and endorsement by the International Monetary Fund of minimum corporate taxes similar to the Honduran experience, their actual impact on tax revenue and corporate behavior remains unclear (Alejos 2017; Best et al. 2015; Mosberger 2016). Lobel, Scot, and Zúñiga (2024) contribute by addressing this gap and providing new evidence for the design of these policies.

Expense-topia: a land in which costs mysteriously multiply

The minimum tax policy was implemented with the goal of establishing a baseline for corporate tax contributions. This policy requires firms exceeding a designated revenue threshold (L 10 million) to pay at least 1.5 percent of their gross revenue in taxes, regardless of their

box continued next page

Box 4.1

Corporations pulling a fast one on the taxman *(continued)*

reported profits. This change aimed to eliminate the possibility of companies lowering their tax burden by inflating costs and minimizing reported profits.

The evidence presented in figure B4.1.1 suggests a significant shift in corporate behavior after the introduction of the minimum tax. In the period before the policy (2011–13), a substantial number of corporations reported profit margins near zero. This pattern changed abruptly in 2014 with the implementation of the minimum tax. Companies began reporting considerably higher profits, as evidenced by the rightward movement of the profit margin distribution. This finding provides strong evidence that corporations were previously using cost overreporting as a tax avoidance strategy.

The analysis quantifies the extent of this prepolicy tax avoidance behavior. The estimate suggests that under the previous profit-based tax system, corporations may have been inflating costs by up to 17 percent of their actual profits to reduce their tax liabilities. This finding aligns with observations from studies conducted with corporations in other countries, such as Pakistan.

Figure B4.1.1   Distribution of firms' profit margins in Honduras

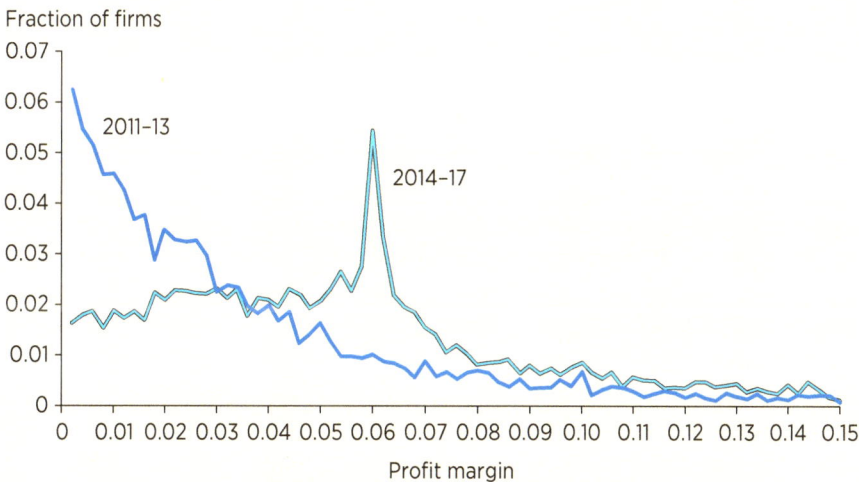

Source: Lobel, Scot, and Zúñiga 2024.
Note: For 2011–13, N = 6,304; for 2014–17, N = 8,612.

box continued next page

Box 4.1

Corporations pulling a fast one on the taxman *(continued)*

Corporate tax filings involve a significant level of complexity, with companies able to claim deductions for more than 100 distinct cost categories. This complexity raises a relevant policy question: are certain cost categories more susceptible to manipulation for tax avoidance purposes? The data analysis reveals a pattern in this regard. There is no observable change in the reporting of easily verifiable cost items, such as labor and financial expenses, after the implementation of the minimum tax. Conversely, a significant response is observed in cost categories that are more challenging to verify, particularly those related to the cost of goods and materials, such as inventories. This finding suggests that government audits could be strategically directed toward these specific cost categories to enhance their effectiveness.

Tax revenues? More like disappearing act revenues

Lobel, Scot, and Zúñiga (2024) examine how companies adjust their reported revenue in response to changes in tax policies. The minimum tax policy exempts firms with revenue below a specific threshold (L 10 million) from its provisions. This exemption creates a sharp point at which a small change in declared revenue can significantly affect tax liability. For instance, a company reporting L 9.99 million in revenue with minimal profits would face negligible taxes (taxed on reported profits). However, declaring revenue of L 10 million triggers a minimum tax liability of L 150,000 (1.5 percent × L 10 million). This scenario creates a strong incentive for firms to strategically position themselves below the exemption threshold.

The data analysis indicates that firms indeed engage in such strategic behavior. There is a noticeable concentration of firms reporting revenue just below the L 10 million threshold during the period when it served as the exemption level (2014–17). This phenomenon, referred to as "bunching," is absent in the prepolicy period (2011–13) and disappears after the exemption level is significantly increased in 2018, as shown in figure B4.1.2.

Established methodologies from the economic literature are used to quantify the changes in declared revenue in response to tax rate adjustments. This analysis aims to determine the elasticity of reported revenue, which reflects the sensitivity of reported revenue to tax

box continued next page

Box 4.1

Corporations pulling a fast one on the taxman *(continued)*

rate changes. The estimated elasticity falls within the range of 0.35–1.00. These estimates are demonstrably higher compared with the findings of similar studies conducted in other contexts, such as Costa Rica. This highlights the potential limitations faced by tax authorities in raising tax revenue under current enforcement structures: increasing tax rates might lead to a significant decrease in the reported tax base.

Figure B4.1.2   Distribution of reported gross revenue in Honduras

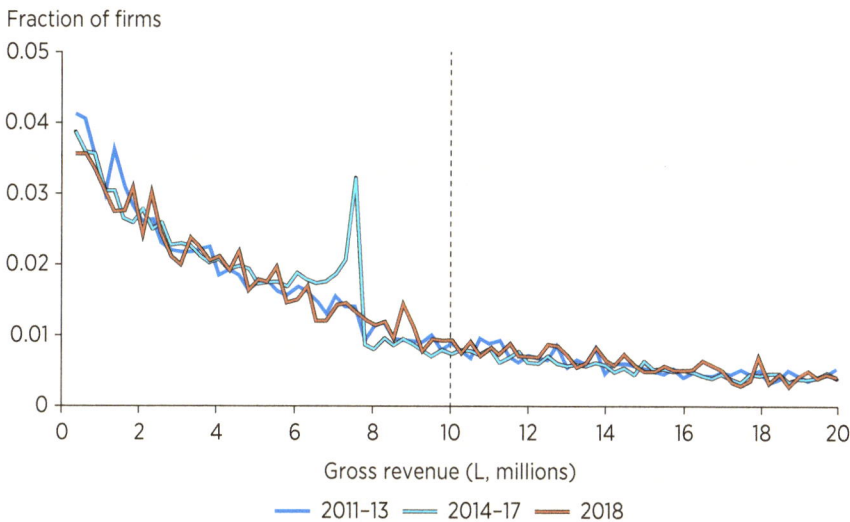

Source: Lobel, Scot, and Zúñiga 2024.

Note: For 2011–13, N = 10,481; for 2014–17, N = 16,043; for 2018, N = 5,046. The vertical dashed line indicates the threshold at which companies incur the minimum tax liability of L 150,000.

Although both overreporting costs and underreporting revenues are methods to manipulate taxable income, evidence suggests that cost overreporting accounts for roughly two-thirds of profit underreporting, with revenue underreporting making up the remaining third (Bachas and Soto 2021; Best et al. 2015; Carrillo, Pomeranz, and Singhal 2017; Garriga and Scot 2023; Lobel, Scot, and Zúñiga 2024; Slemrod et al. 2017). For instance, Carrillo et al. (2023) show that in Ecuador a significant form of tax evasion arises from the operation of "ghost firms"—fictitious entities that issue deceptive receipts, allowing their clients to make illegitimate deduction claims.

Insightful work by Lobel, Scot, and Zúñiga (2024) also shows that, indeed, most of the evasion heterogeneity is determined by the industry, rather than firm characteristics.[1] Figure 4.3 shows the estimated corporate tax evasion in Honduras by industry.

This suggests that certain industries might inherently offer more opportunities for tax evasion than others. Industries with low revenue and cost observability offer more opportunities for tax evasion. Construction, with its cash transactions and complex projects, is a prime example. Companies might underreport revenue or inflate expenses, making it difficult for authorities to track their true financial picture. This is not to imply that all companies within an industry evade taxes. However, an industry's structure can itself create an environment ripe for manipulation. On the one hand, technology companies, with their digital transactions, face less opportunity for traditional evasion but might exploit loopholes related to intellectual property. On the other hand, manufacturing presents a different scenario. Unlike construction with its cash transactions and complex projects, a larger share of a manufacturer's total sales are typically derived from tangible goods. These sales are often documented through

Figure 4.3   Estimated corporate tax evasion in Honduras, by industry

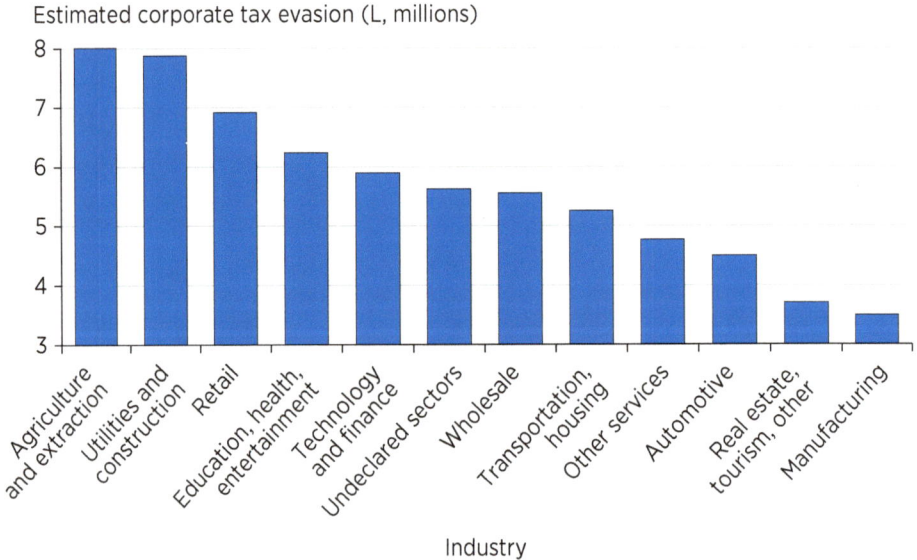

Source: Lobel, Scot, and Zúñiga 2024.

Note: Estimated corporate tax evasion is proxied by the excess mass, defined as the estimated excess number of firms bunching at the L 10 million notch as a ratio of the predicted mass at the notch.

invoices, purchase orders, and production records, creating a more auditable trail. This transparency reduces the opportunities to underreport revenue. Additionally, the cost structure of manufacturing is often more straightforward compared with construction. Although some manipulation of expenses might still be possible, the reliance on raw materials from other firms, labor, and machinery makes it harder to significantly inflate costs without raising red flags. This does not eliminate the possibility of tax evasion in manufacturing entirely, but the industry structure itself inherently offers less room for manipulation compared with some other sectors. In fact, Lobel, Scot, and Zúñiga (2024) show how evasion negatively correlates with the share of revenue informed by third parties (refer to figure 4.4).[2]

In simpler terms, industries in which a larger portion of a company's revenue is documented and reported by independent sources—such as invoices or sales data reported by retailers—experience less tax evasion. This suggests that independent verification makes it more difficult for companies to underreport revenues.

Figure 4.4   Corporate tax evasion and share of revenue reported by third parties in Honduras, by industry

Estimated corporate tax evasion

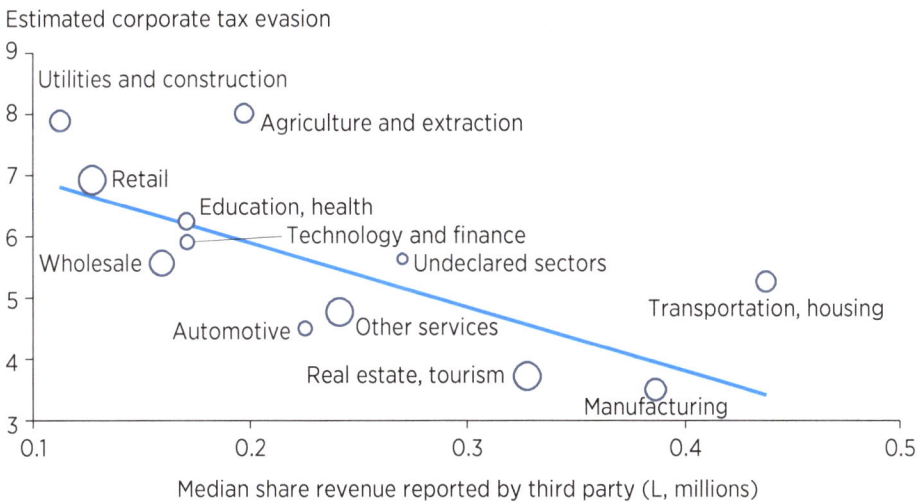

Median share revenue reported by third party (L, millions)

Source: Lobel, Scot, and Zúñiga 2024.

Note: Estimated corporate tax evasion is proxied by the excess mass, defined as the estimated excess number of firms bunching at the L 10 million notch as a ratio of the predicted mass at the notch. Median share of revenue reported by a third party is measured by the median revenue share of self-declared revenue that is independently observed by the tax authority through third-party reporting in each industry.

Partnering for Compliance: The Closer the Better?

High profit elasticities, driven by tax evasion in opaque industries, require policy makers to anticipate these effects while designing policy solutions. This section presents novel evidence on how firms can collaborate with governments to enhance revenue collection in the context of weak enforcement environments, which are prevalent in most EMDEs, including LAC.

Compared with overreporting costs, underreporting revenue is a much riskier proposition for tax evaders. Tax authorities possess a powerful arsenal of auditing techniques—data analysis, third-party verification, and inventory audits—specifically designed to detect inconsistencies in revenue reporting. The sheer volume of sales transactions, documented through receipts, invoices, and digital records, creates a vast and verifiable paper trail that is difficult to manipulate convincingly. Additionally, concealing significant amounts of cash income becomes a logistical nightmare. Banks report large deposits, and unexplained discrepancies between reported sales and cash flow immediately trigger red flags for authorities.

Insightful research by Garriga and Tortarolo (2024) shows that delegating tax collection duties to large firms can bolster tax capacity in weak enforcement settings. Withholding regimes in which third parties collect and remit taxes are ubiquitous. For example, in most countries, employers withhold PIT from employees' monthly paychecks, and this amount is compensated for in their annual tax return. Withholding of business income is particularly common in developing countries in which governments lack the resources and capacity to accurately measure and tax firm activity (Brockmeyer et al. 2019; Slemrod 2008). This collection mechanism relies on financial institutions and large firms to collect taxes owed by other firms in their commercial network. Its use has surged over the past decade, but little is known about its implications.

Garriga and Tortarolo (2024) study the effects of delegating tax collection duties to large firms in the city of Buenos Aires, Argentina, whereby businesses are required to pay a turnover tax on a monthly basis. Historically, a few key players were enrolled as collection agents (CAs) and had to withhold taxes from their commercial partners. These authors analyze an unexpected and major expansion of the withholding scheme in November 2016, in which firms with 2015 annual income above Arg$60 million—roughly US$4 million—were appointed to act as CAs (refer to figure 4.5). As a result, these firms' trade partners—who previously had to pay the tax liability directly to the tax authority—started to pay the tax in advance whenever they made a transaction with CAs. In short, the newly appointed CAs now had to charge an additional amount when selling goods to clients or subtract part of the invoice when purchasing goods from suppliers. This implied an increase in the share of taxpayers' tax liability collected indirectly at source by CAs in lieu of direct payments to the tax authority.

The reform was successful in raising more tax revenue. Figure 4.6 compares the evolution of tax revenue in the city of Buenos Aires with that in the province of Buenos Aires—the two largest jurisdictions in the country in terms of economic activity. Before the reform, the city of Buenos Aires, relative to the province, was on a downward tax revenue trend, which reverted right after November 2016, when the first reform kicked in. By 2019, roughly two years after the reform, the city's tax revenue was 20 percent higher than that of the province in the baseline period.

Figure 4.5   Number of firms acting as collection agents in the city of Buenos Aires, Argentina

Number of active CAs

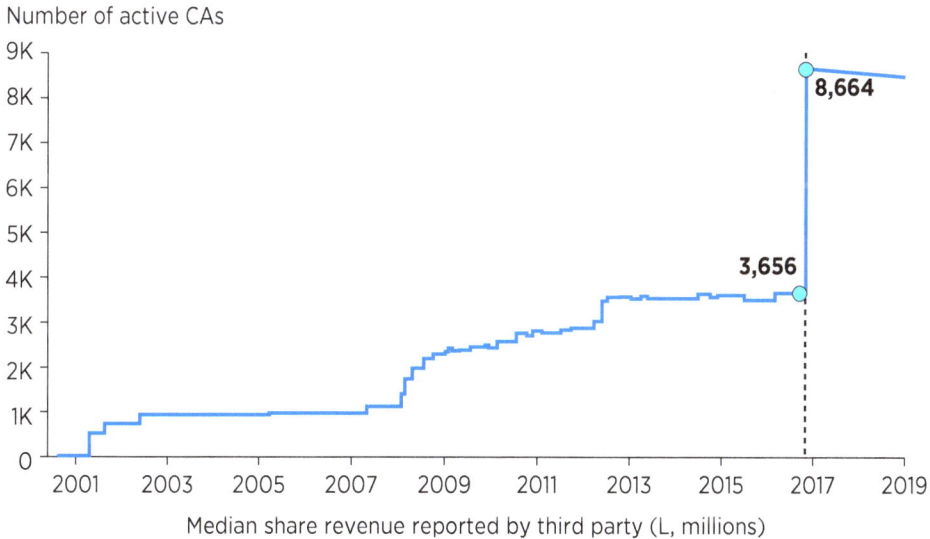

Median share revenue reported by third party (L, millions)

Source: Garriga and Tortarolo 2024.

Note: This figure shows the number of firms that are part of the CA register at any point in time. The vertical line corresponds to November 2016, when the expansion of the withholding scheme went into effect. The number of CAs in October 2016 is shown to the left of the vertical line, and the number in November 2016 is shown to the right. CA = collection agent.

Figure 4.6   Percentage difference in turnover tax revenue between the city of Buenos Aires and the province of Buenos Aires relative to October 2016

Tax revenue CABA versus PBA (% difference)

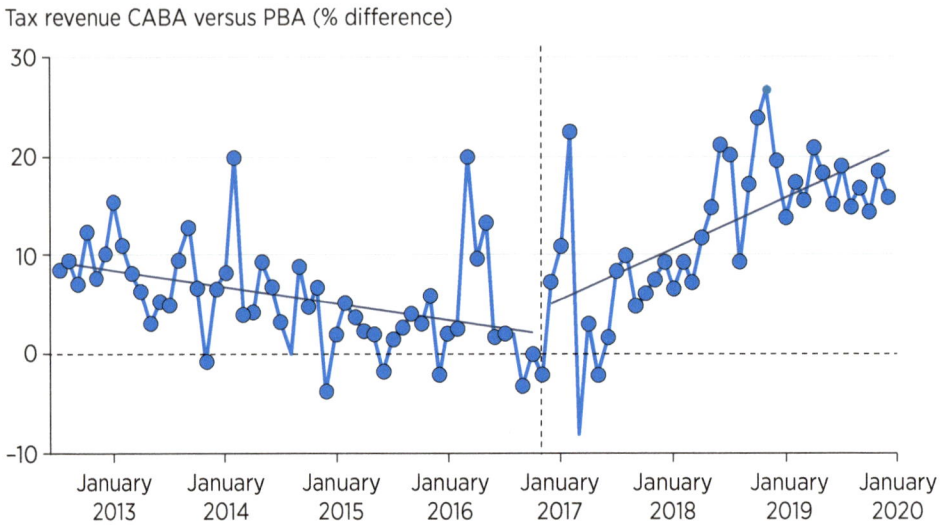

Source: Garriga and Tortarolo (2024).

Note: The figure documents the expansion of the withholding scheme in the city of Buenos Aires by plotting the evolution of aggregate outcomes over time. In particular, the figure shows the percentage difference in turnover tax revenue between CABA and PBA relative to October 2016, which was the month before the reform. The dashed vertical line corresponds to November 2016, when the expansion of the withholding scheme went into effect. CABA = city of Buenos Aires; PBA = province of Buenos Aires.

The Garriga and Tortarolo (2024) study combines the features of this unique policy reform with rich firm-to-firm administrative data to estimate the direct effect of expanding the withholding scheme on CAs—that is, the firms who are put to the task of collecting taxes—and the indirect effect on their trade partners, who now face an increase in the amount of taxes being withheld at source. The main insights and findings from this article are discussed in the following sections.

Does Appointing Firms to Collect Taxes on Behalf of the Government Hurt Firm Performance?

There are several reasons to think that being appointed as a CA might have a negative impact on firms. First, withholding is an administrative burden because it requires CAs to keep track of transactions with trade partners and to file information tax returns. Second, appointment leads to closer scrutiny from the tax administration because CAs must now work side by side with government officials.

The Garriga and Tortarolo (2024) study uses a regression discontinuity design that exploits the Arg$60 million cutoff rule used for enrollment of firms into the program to test whether firms on either side of the threshold fared differently. The authors do not find evidence suggesting an impact on CA business activity. Firms on either side of the cutoff fared similarly in the years after the reform, in both the extensive and the intensive margins (refer to figure 4.7). This result might be due to appointed firms being among the largest—and presumably most formal—in the economy, with highly streamlined tax filing practices, such that collecting taxes from partners and remitting them to the government does not imply an increased burden or a change in enforcement perceptions.

How Does Appointing Firms as Tax Collectors Affect Their Trade Partners?

Garriga and Tortarolo (2024) then move on to the analysis of indirect effects. Their goal was to understand what happens when a firm that was previously paying most of its taxes via self-reported declarations faces an increase in the amount of taxes withheld at source by a third party. They leverage the design of the 2016 reform and use the built-in variation in exposure to CAs to provide a causal effect of withholding on compliance. For firms not directly targeted by the reform— that is, regular taxpayers—the changes that took place in November 2016 had no immediate consequences. However, some taxpayers saw a larger increase in the number of CAs withholding from them as a by-product of their commercial linkages. The study implements a difference-in-differences design relying on this differential exposure to newly appointed CAs: it compares two groups of taxpayers that are very similar, except one group experienced a change in the way taxes are collected—from direct payment to withholding—and the other group did not.

Taxpayers exposed to new CAs exhibit an increase in the share of taxes withheld at source and an increase in their reported sales. Figure 4.8 plots the dynamic difference-in-differences specifications that summarize these findings. Panel a shows the first stage of the analysis: the share of taxes withheld by CAs evolves similarly for both groups in the prereform period, and right at the time of the reform there is a sharp increase for treated firms. This confirms that high exposure to new CAs leads to a larger bite in terms of withheld funds. Panel b shows the behavioral response of firms: there is an immediate increase in reported sales right at the time of the reform. Overall, the estimates suggest that treated firms increased their tax base by about 5.5 percentage points relative to the control group. This effect increases over time, reaching about 9 percentage points by the end of 2019. A similar-size effect is found for tax revenue.

Figure 4.7   Performance of newly appointed CAs and noneligible firms based on the 2015 threshold

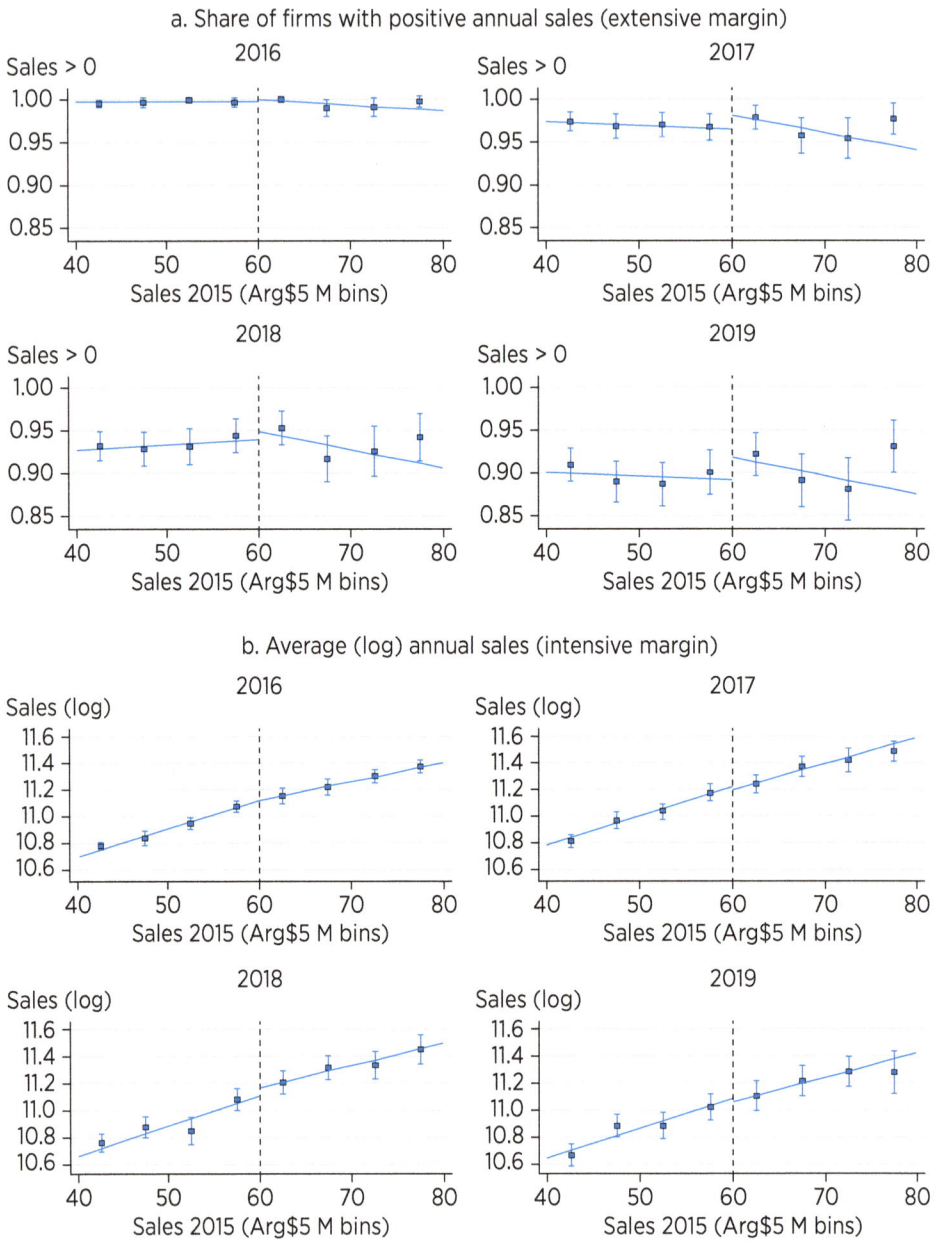

a. Share of firms with positive annual sales (extensive margin)

b. Average (log) annual sales (intensive margin)

Source: Garriga and Tortarolo 2024.

Note: The figure shows estimates from a regression discontinuity specification. The running variable is annual gross sales income in 2015. The vertical line indicates the cutoff variable of Arg$60 million. The dots represent the estimates for the outcome variables using eight equally spaced bins, the spikes represent 95 percent confidence intervals, and the horizontal lines are the linear fit at each side of the cutoff. The 2016 quadrant of each panel shows outcomes excluding November and December, thus reflecting prereform outcomes. CAs = collection agents.

Figure 4.8 Self-reported sales and tax liability of firms linked to newly appointed CAs

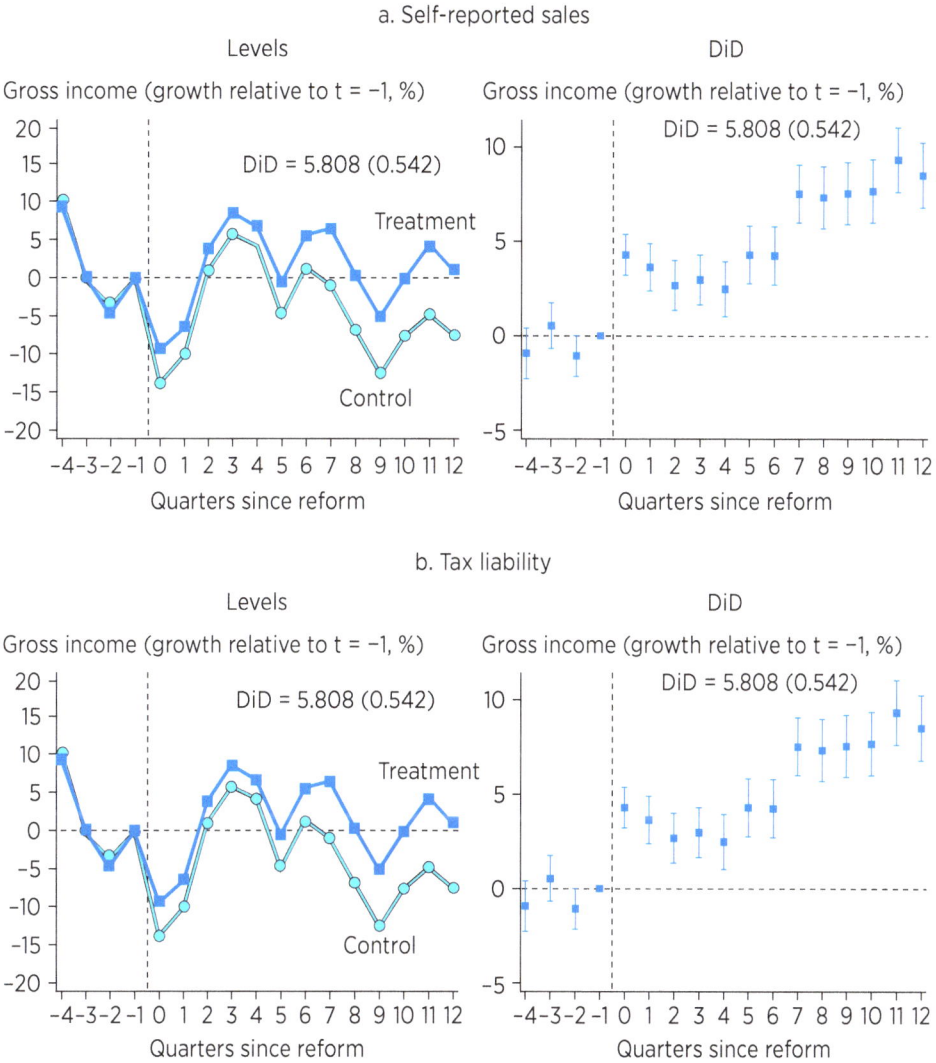

a. Self-reported sales

b. Tax liability

Source: Garriga and Tortarolo 2024.

Note: The figure compares the response on self-reported sales and tax liability for firms connected to newly appointed CAs (treatment group) and firms that are not connected to newly appointed CAs (control group). The spikes indicate 95 percent confidence intervals. CAs = collection agents; DiD = difference-in-differences; t = quarter.

Is the effect compatible with a real increase in sales or, rather, an increase in reported sales? Because the data do not provide information on the volume of sales, it is impossible to provide a definitive answer. Nevertheless, the evidence can be interpreted as suggestive of prereform sales underreporting: the sharp increase in reported sales in the first quarter after the reform, after nearly identical trends before the reform, is consistent with firms correcting their tax filings to match the withheld amounts collected and remitted by CAs. In addition, it would be hard to conceptually rationalize a real increase in sales because of higher withholding.

Main Takeaways

Garriga and Tortarolo's (2024) results suggest that withholding by large firms can be an effective tax collection tool. On the one hand, appointing firms to collect taxes did not seem to directly hurt their activity. On the other hand, substituting direct payments for withholding at the source increases the reported sales of firms linked to CAs, which, in turn, increases total tax revenue. These results are in line with recent research suggesting that reforms to tax administrations can have a considerable impact when it comes to raising revenue and building tax capacity. A plausible interpretation is that, in weak enforcement settings, withholding taxes in advance somehow forces firms to report their sales more truthfully.

Taken together, these findings bolster the argument in recent research by Basri et al. (2021) that administrative reforms can be highly effective in raising revenue and building tax capacity. Moreover, these novel findings could have important implications for the way in which countries determine how to collect taxes. As countries develop and improve their information technology systems, substituting direct means of payment with indirect withholding schemes that rely on firms seems to be a promising path.

However, as promising as these results might be, more research is required to better understand the broader implications of relying on firms to collect taxes. One clear limitation of this tax collection device is the fact that not all firms will be good candidates to perform as CAs. The question that remains open is this: what are the limits to appointing firms as CAs? For sufficiently small firms, the burden associated with this task may outweigh the benefits accrued to the tax administration.

Finally, the consequences of overwithholding—in which the sum of withheld amounts is greater than the tax liability, leading to the taxpayer accumulating a credit in their favor—emerge as an intriguing, yet unexplored topic in this study. Because reclaiming these credits is often a cumbersome process, taxpayers might face liquidity constraints, potentially impairing their activities. This complex interplay between overwithholding and firms' finances is the Achilles heel of tax withholding systems and constitutes a critical avenue for future research.

Behavioral Responses Beyond Tax Evasion and Avoidance

Although tax evasion and avoidance are undoubtedly critical concerns in EMDEs, it is equally as important to acknowledge that corporate tax policies can trigger a wider array of firm responses with significant macroeconomic consequences. As evidenced by Cerda and Larrain (2008) and Waseem (2018), corporate taxation can influence labor demand, capital investment, and firm entry and exit decisions. These real responses can have substantial implications for employment, economic growth, and the overall structure of the economy. Therefore, although efforts to combat evasion and avoidance are essential, policy makers in EMDEs must also consider these broader behavioral responses when designing and evaluating corporate tax policies.

Changes in the Labor Markets and Capital Investment

Although concerns about tax evasion and avoidance are central to corporate tax policy discussions, it is important to recognize that CIT can influence firm behavior and macroeconomic outcomes through various channels. As highlighted by Cerda and Larrain (2008), corporate taxes can have significant impacts on labor demand in developing countries because firms may adjust employment levels in response to tax changes. This labor market response can contribute to the observed higher elasticity of corporate tax revenue, demonstrating that CIT has real implications for the economy.

Cerda and Larrain (2008) delve into the intricate relationship between corporate taxation and factor demand, particularly how tax policies can influence a firm's decisions regarding labor and capital. Their research reveals an asymmetry in how firms of different sizes respond to corporate tax changes. Specifically, they find that the impact on labor demand is more pronounced in large corporations, whereas the demand for capital is more responsive to corporate tax changes in small firms.

This nuanced relationship is illustrated in figures 4.9 and 4.10. Figure 4.9 depicts the long-run effects of corporate taxation on labor demand. As the figure shows, the long-run labor demand is more responsive to corporate tax changes for larger firms. A possible explanation is that large firms, which tend to have more complex organizational structures and greater access to credit, may find it easier to substitute labor for capital when faced with higher corporate taxes. This substitution effect leads to a decrease in labor demand.

Conversely, figure 4.10 illustrates the long-run effects of corporate taxation on capital demand. The figure shows that smaller firms exhibit a greater sensitivity in their capital demand to changes in the corporate tax rate. This finding could be attributed to the fact that smaller firms often face tighter credit constraints. When corporate taxes increase, their access to external financing may be further limited, making it more difficult for them to invest in new capital.

Figure 4.9   Effect of corporate tax on labor demand

Effect of corporate tax on labor demand (regression coefficient)

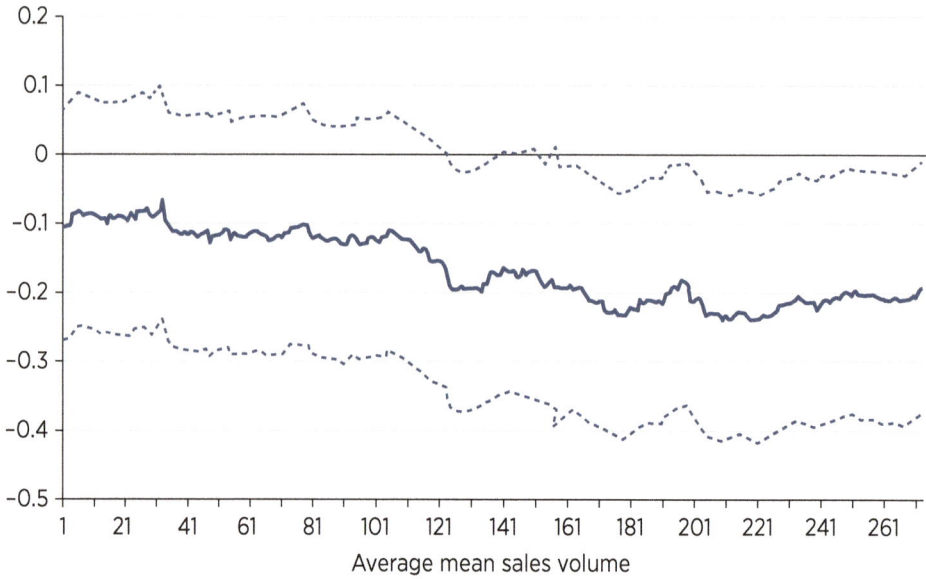

Source: Cerda and Larrain 2008. Used with permission. Further permission required for reuse.

Note: The solid line corresponds to the study's estimated effect in the case of labor demand. The dashed lines correspond to 90% confidence intervals.

Figure 4.10   Effect of corporate tax on the capital demand

Effect of corporate tax on capital demand

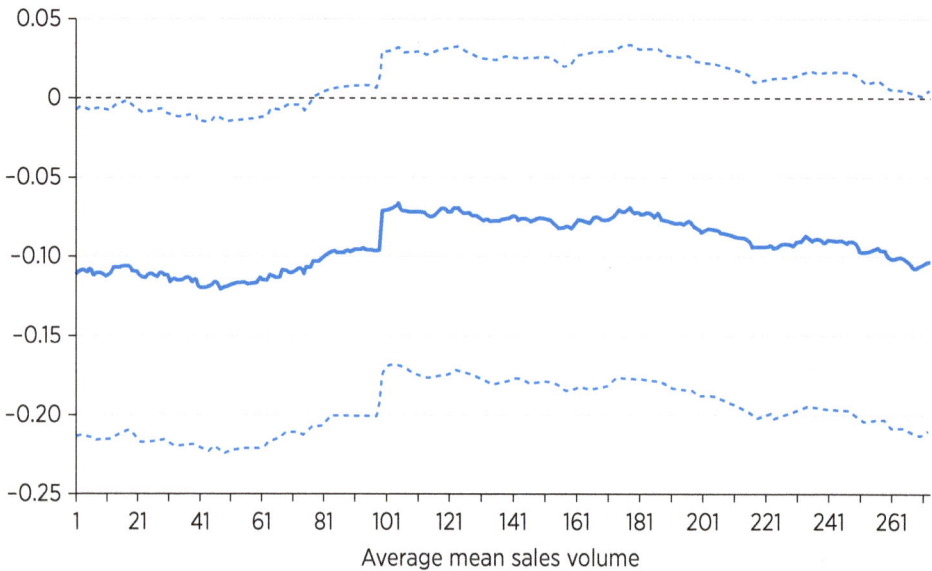

Source: Cerda and Larrain 2008. Used with permission. Further permission required for reuse.

Note: The solid line corresponds to the study's estimated effect in the case of capital demand. The dashed lines correspond to 90% confidence intervals.

Cerda and Larrain's (2008) findings underscore that the effects of corporate taxation extend beyond issues of tax evasion and avoidance. By influencing firms' decisions on labor and capital demand, CIT can have significant implications for employment levels, wage growth, investment, and, ultimately, economic growth. These real-world consequences highlight the importance of considering the broader economic impact of corporate tax policies, particularly in the context of developing economies.

Changes Beyond the Intensive Margin: the Extensive Margin and Firm Dynamics

Traditional analyses of corporate tax effects often concentrate on the intensive margin, which examines how existing firms adjust their behavior in response to tax changes. This includes changes in reported profits, investment levels, and other operational decisions. However, this focus overlooks a crucial dimension of firm behavior, particularly in developing economies: the extensive margin. The extensive margin encompasses changes in the number of firms, specifically firm creation (entry) and firm closure (exit), and its importance is underscored by Waseem (2018).

Waseem (2018) demonstrates that tax policies can have profound effects on the extensive margin. When tax burdens increase, some firms may find it unsustainable to continue operating in the formal sector, leading to closure or a shift into informality. Simultaneously, the attractiveness of starting a new business in the formal sector may decrease, hindering firm creation. These changes in firm entry and exit can have significant consequences for the overall economy.

The distinction between intensive and extensive margins is critical because they capture different aspects of how firms respond to taxation. The intensive margin refers to how existing firms adjust their operations (for example, reducing investment, cutting costs); the extensive margin refers to how the number of firms in the economy changes (for example, through new firms entering or existing firms exiting).

Waseem's (2018) study on a tax reform in Pakistan, which increased taxes on partnerships, provides a compelling illustration of the extensive margin's importance. The reform resulted in a significant 41 percent decrease in the number of formal partnerships immediately after its implementation, followed by further declines of 27 percent and 15 percent in the subsequent two years. This decline had a substantial impact on overall tax revenue and economic activity, effects that would have been missed by an analysis focused solely on the intensive margin.

To illustrate the impact of the tax reform on the number of firms, refer to figures 4.11 and 4.12. Figure 4.11 shows the taxable income distribution, where one can observe the changes in the number of firms pre- and postreform. Figure 4.12 shows the extensive margin response by industry. These figures provide a visual representation of the significant change in the number of firms after the tax increase.

Figure 4.11   Taxable income distribution for corporations

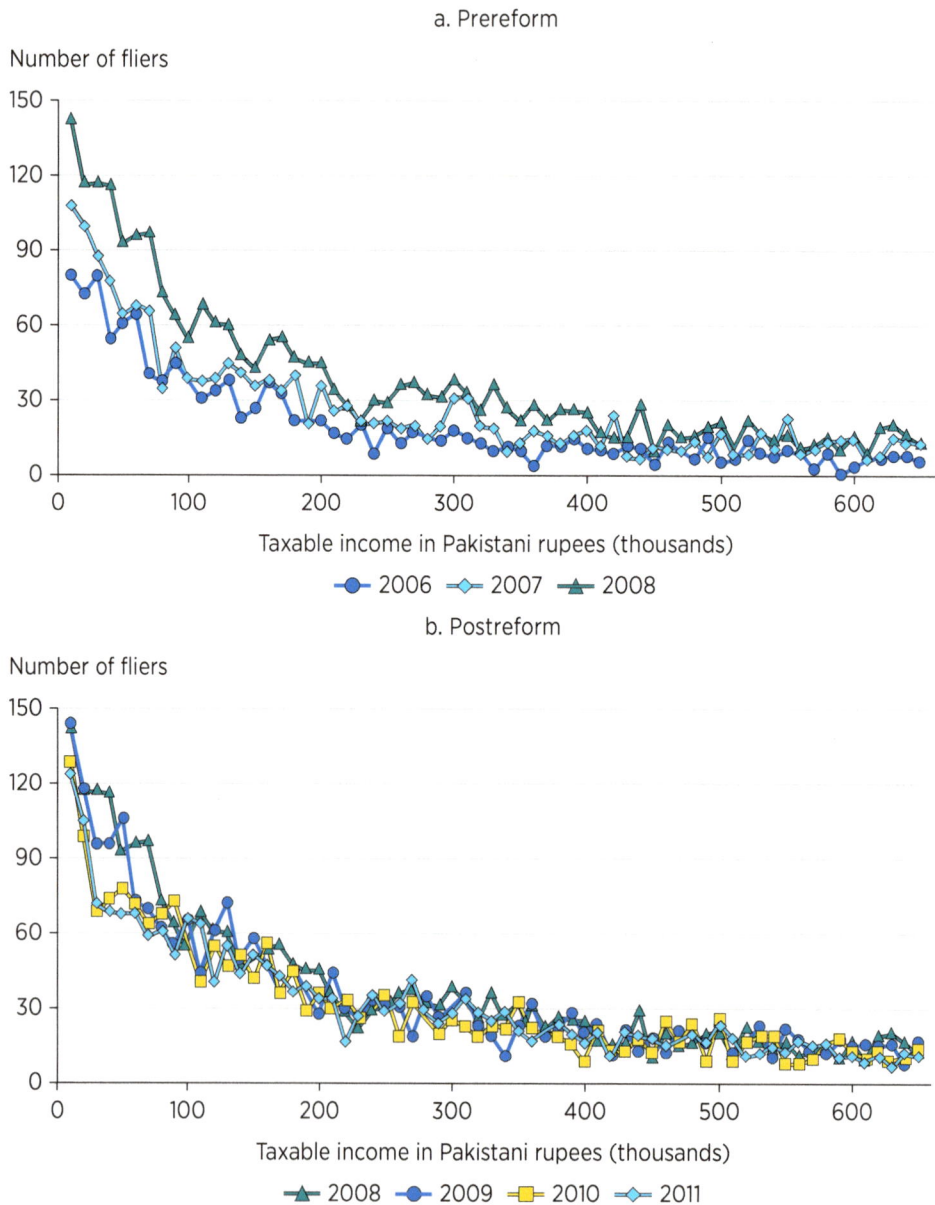

a. Prereform

b. Postreform

Note: The figure compares the pre- and postreform taxable income distributions across the three types of firms.

Figure 4.12   Extensive margin response by industry

Number of partnerships in the industry

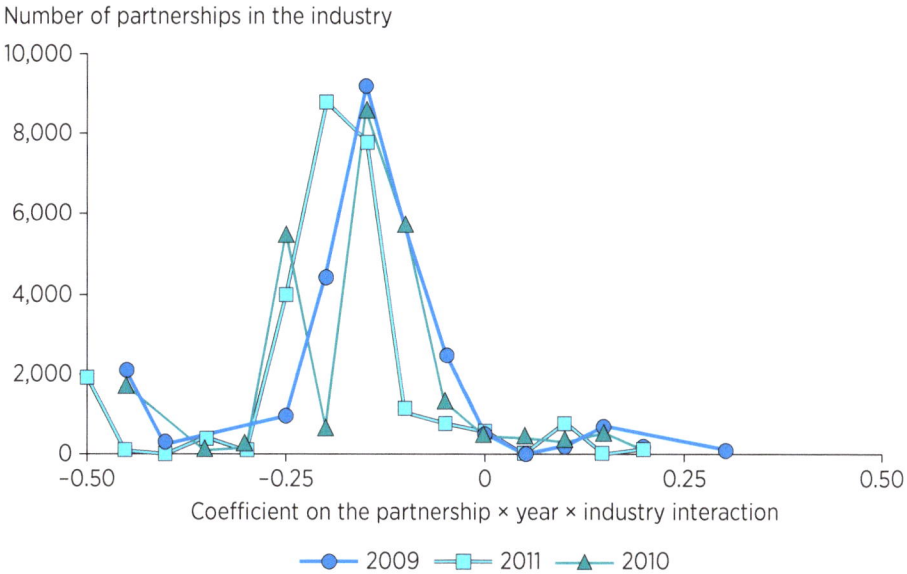

Coefficient on the partnership × year × industry interaction

—●— 2009   —■— 2011   —▲— 2010

Source: Wassem 2018. Used with permission. Further permission required for reuse.

Note: The figure explores heterogeneity in the extensive response across industries.

Waseem's (2018) findings highlight that in developing economies, the extensive margin response to corporate taxation can be substantial and should not be ignored. Policies aimed at increasing corporate tax revenue may have unintended consequences for firm creation and survival, potentially offsetting the intended benefits. A comprehensive understanding of both the intensive and the extensive margins is crucial for designing effective and efficient tax policies.

Conclusion

The analysis in this chapter has highlighted the complexities of CIT policy, particularly in the context of LAC economies. Although CIT is a crucial source of government revenue, its effectiveness is often undermined by challenges such as tax evasion, avoidance, and the sensitivity of firm behavior to tax rates. As this chapter has shown, increasing the CIT rate does not always translate to increased revenue, and it can have unintended negative consequences.

Instead of ineffectively chasing easily evasive butterflies with high CIT rates that hinder growth, policy makers should strategically reduce these rates to improve competitiveness with other EMDEs. This rate reduction should be combined with increased reliance on less distortionary and more easily collected taxes.

Within the CIT framework, bolstering enforcement and fostering innovative public-private partnerships, such as leveraging firms for tax collection (Garriga and Tortarolo 2024), are essential. This comprehensive approach seeks to cultivate a business-friendly environment, stimulate economic growth, and ultimately attract productive bees that generate jobs and flourish in a prosperous and dynamic LAC economy.

This chapter has, moreover, emphasized that the impact of CIT extends beyond the issues of evasion and avoidance. As the evidence from developing economies demonstrates, CIT can significantly affect firms' labor demand, capital investment, and decisions to enter or exit markets. These real-world effects have implications for employment levels, wage growth, investment, and the overall structure of the economy. Therefore, reforms should be designed with a holistic view, considering the potential impacts on the wider economy.

In sum, reforming CIT in LAC requires a multifaceted approach, moving beyond a sole focus on evasion and avoidance to create a tax structure that promotes economic growth and competitiveness. By lowering CIT rates, improving enforcement, and considering the broader economic consequences of CIT policies, LAC countries can create a more favorable environment for businesses and, ultimately, attract those productive bees that generate jobs and drive sustainable development.

Notes

1. In general, this literature finds that firm attributes such as scale, production, and years of reporting do not seem to be crucial determinants of evasion.
2. A growing literature shows that a lack of third-party information and low fiscal capacity lead to widespread tax evasion (Brockmeyer and Hernandez 2016; Khan, Khwaja, and Olken 2016; Naritomi 2019; Pomeranz 2015).

References

Alejos, L. 2017. "Firms' (Mis)Reporting Under a Minimum Tax." *Proceedings. Annual Conference on Taxation and Minutes of the Annual Meeting of the National Tax Association* 110: 1–44.

Bachas, P., and M. Soto. 2021. "Corporate Taxation under Weak Enforcement." *American Economic Journal: Economic Policy* 13 (4): 33–71.

Basri, M. C., M. Felix, R. Hanna, and B. A. Olken. 2021. "Tax Administration vs. Tax Rates: Evidence from Corporate Taxation in Indonesia." *American Economic Review* 111 (12): 3827–71.

Best, M. C., A. Brockmeyer, H. J. Kleven, J. Spinnewijn, and M. Waseem. 2015. "Production versus Revenue Efficiency with Limited Tax Capacity: Theory and Evidence from Pakistan." *Journal of Political Economy* 123 (6): 1311–55.

Brockmeyer, A., and M. Hernandez. 2016. "Taxation, Information, and Withholding: Evidence from Costa Rica." Policy Research Working Paper 7600, World Bank, Washington, DC.

Brockmeyer, A., S. Smith, M. Hernandez, and S. Kettle. 2019. "Casting a Wider Tax Net: Experimental Evidence from Costa Rica." *American Economic Journal: Economic Policy* 11 (3): 55–87.

Carrillo, P., D. Donaldson, D. Pomeranz, and M. Singhal. 2023. "Ghosting the Tax Authority: Fake Firms and Tax Fraud in Ecuador." *American Economic Review: Insights* 5 (4): 427–44.

Carrillo, P., D. Pomeranz, and M. Singhal. 2017. "Dodging the Taxman: Firm Misreporting and Limits to Tax Enforcement." *American Economic Journal: Applied Economics* 9 (2): 144–64.

Cerda, R. A., and M. Larrain. 2008. "Corporate Taxes and Labor Demand: Evidence from Developing Countries." Discussion Paper 3640, Institute of Labor Economics, Bonn, Germany.

Devereux, M., L. Liu, and S. Loretz. 2014. "The Elasticity of Corporate Taxable Income: New Evidence from UK Tax Records." *American Economic Journal: Economic Policy* 6 (2): 19–53.

Garriga, P., and T. Scot. 2023. "Corporate Responses to Size-Based Tax Rates in Lithuania." Policy Research Working Paper 10500, World Bank, Washington, DC. http://documents.worldbank.org/curated/en/099313106262317603.

Garriga, P., and D. Tortarolo. 2024. "Firms as Tax Collectors." *Journal of Public Economics* 233: 105092.

Khan, A. Q., A. I. Khwaja, and B. A. Olken. 2016. "Tax Farming Redux: Experimental Evidence on Performance Pay for Tax Collectors." *Quarterly Journal of Economics* 131 (1): 219–71.

Lediga, C., N. Riedel, and K. Strohmaier. 2019. "The Elasticity of Corporate Taxable Income: Evidence from South Africa." *Economics Letters* 175: 43–6.

Lobel, F., T. Scot, and P. Zúñiga. 2024. "Corporate Taxation and Evasion Responses: Evidence from a Minimum Tax in Honduras." *American Economic Journal: Economic Policy* 16 (1): 482–517.

Mosberger, P. 2016. "Accounting versus Real Production Responses among Firms to Tax Incentives: Bunching Evidence from Hungary." MNB Working Paper 2016/3, Magyar Nemzeti Bank, Budapest, Hungary.

Naritomi, J. 2019. "Consumers as Tax Auditors." *American Economic Review* 109 (9): 3031–72.

Patel, E., N. Seegert, and M. Smith. 2017. "At a Loss: The Real and Reporting Elasticity of Corporate Taxable Income." SSRN Working Paper. https://doi.org/10.2139/ssrn.2608166.

Pomeranz, D. 2015. "No Taxation without Information: Deterrence and Self-Enforcement in the Value Added Tax." *American Economic Review* 105 (8): 2539–69.

Slemrod, J. 2008. "Does It Matter Who Writes the Check to the Government? The Economics of Tax Remittance." *National Tax Journal* 61 (2): 251–75.

Slemrod, J., B. Collins, J. L. Hoopes, D. Reck, and M. Sebastiani. 2017. "Does Credit-Card Information Reporting Improve Small-Business Tax Compliance?" *Journal of Public Economics* 149 (C): 1–19.

Vegh, C. A., and G. Vuletin. 2015. "How Is Tax Policy Conducted Over the Business Cycle?" *American Economic Journal: Economic Policy* 7 (3): 327–70.

Waseem, M. 2018. "Taxes, Informality and Income Shifting: Evidence from a Recent Pakistani Tax Reform." *Journal of Public Economics* 157: 41–77.

5

Personal Income Tax Beyond Top Rates

Introduction

One of the most widely used methods to tax high earners is the personal income tax (PIT). Although its administration can involve complexities, its core principle is simple. It divides taxable individual income into brackets, and each bracket gets taxed at a designated rate that progressively increases for higher income brackets. This structure allows for a progressive system in which high earners pay a greater proportion of their individual income in taxes than low earners. Latin America and the Caribbean (LAC) collect, on average, the least from PIT—approximately 2 percent of GDP or 10 percent of total tax revenue (refer to figure 5.1, panels a and b). At the other extreme, the United States and Canada (bundled in the North America region) collect about half their tax revenue from PIT. Figure 5.1, panel c shows that the low relevance of PIT for revenue purposes is quite widespread in most LAC countries. Their low reliance on PIT suggests a potential to increase tax collection from this source. A key question is how to achieve this, and a crucial step is to thoroughly understand the PIT tax structure and anticipate taxpayers' potential behavioral responses.

This chapter relies heavily on recent research work by Riera-Crichton, Venturi, and Vuletin (forthcoming), which fills an existing gap in the literature by estimating the aggregate income and labor effects of PIT for LAC. Most of the work in this area so far has been conducted for the United States because of the availability of average marginal PIT rates (AMPITR) series relying on administrative data on tax returns and individual reported income. AMPITR represent the average tax rate paid on an additional dollar of income for individuals or households in specific income brackets. Riera-Crichton, Venturi, and Vuletin's (forthcoming) work includes the creation of novel long-time series of AMPITR for Argentina, Brazil, Colombia, Ecuador, Paraguay, and Peru. These series are based on official tax codes and individual income reported in household surveys. Additionally, they estimate the so-called elasticity of taxable income (ETI), or the responsiveness of taxable income to changes in the marginal tax rate, indicating how much taxable income is expected to change when the tax rate on the last dollar earned is altered. This metric provides valuable insights into taxpayer behavior in response to changes in tax policy, and it relies on narrative-based identification work that follows Romer and Romer's (2010) seminal methodology.

Figure 5.1   Size of personal income tax revenue

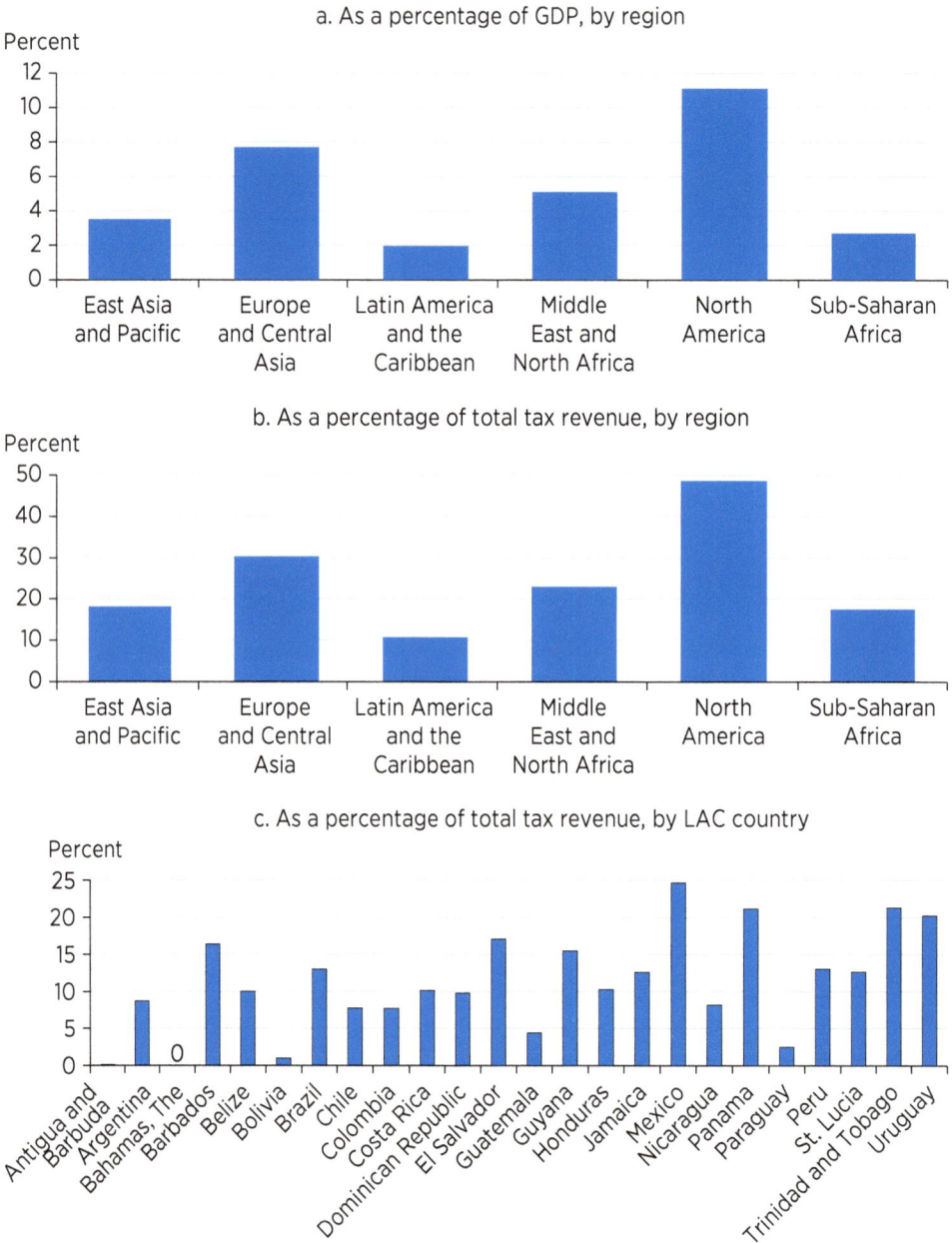

a. As a percentage of GDP, by region

b. As a percentage of total tax revenue, by region

c. As a percentage of total tax revenue, by LAC country

Source: Original calculations for this publication using Organisation for Economic Co-operation and Development Global Revenue Statistics Database (https://www.oecd .org/en/data/datasets/global-revenue-statistics-database.html) and World Bank data.

Note: Consolidated government statistics. GDP = gross domestic product; LAC = Latin America and the Caribbean.

Low Average Marginal PIT Rates: Narrow Tax Base and Marked Progressivity

LAC countries typically exhibit low levels of AMPITR compared with their more advanced counterparts, such as the United States. Although the AMPITR for the entire income distribution reaches 24.1 percent in the United States (table 5.1)—indicating that, on average, the tax rate paid on an additional dollar of income for individuals is almost a quarter of that dollar—this figure is significantly lower in LAC. Paraguay, which only introduced the tax in 2012 (a relatively recent development), exhibits the lowest AMPITR at 1.1 percent, whereas Brazil has the highest AMPITR, at 9.3 percent.[1]

These low levels of AMPITR in the selected LAC sample do not necessarily reflect a tax structure with particularly low marginal rates. As shown in Table 5.1, this phenomenon occurs because a large share of taxpayers face a zero marginal tax rate, concentrating the tax burden on high earners. To illustrate this empirical fact, rows 2–10 in table 5.1 report descriptive statistics for different quantiles of the tax units' income distribution showing who actually pays this tax. A zero reflects that no tax unit is reached in that income group.[2]

Rows 2–6, which split the income distribution of each country into quintiles, show that the individual income tax is concentrated at the top 20 percent of the income distribution in all LAC countries except Argentina—even though the AMPITR paid by the four lowest quintiles is significantly lower than the AMPITR paid by the top 20 percent—and, to a lesser extent, Peru. This is very different from the United States, where even the first quintile is reached by this tax in a quantitatively relevant manner.

Moreover, when looking at rows 7 and 8 in table 5.1, which divide the tax units' income distribution between the top 10 percent and bottom 90 percent, it is clear that mainly the top 10 percent of the income distribution of these countries pay, by and large, the individual income tax. The bottom 90 percent pay a much significantly lower AMPITR than the top 10 percent. Although the ratio of the top 10 percent to the bottom 90 percent is about 1.6 in the United States, it is 193 in Peru, 77 in Brazil, 38 in Ecuador, and 11 in Argentina, and it is not defined (because the mean AMPITR of the bottom 90 percent is zero) in Colombia and Paraguay.

Table 5.1   Basic AMPITR statistics using a pooled regional-year sample for each country

Sample	Mean	SD	CV	Min	Max	Mean	SD	CV	Min	Max
			Argentina					Brazil		
1. All sample	5.4	5.2	1.0	0	27.7	9.3	2.4	0.3	2.0	19.8
2. Lowest 20%	0.02	0.1	3.2	0	0.7	0	0	0	0	0
3. Second 20%	0.03	0.1	2.5	0	1.0	0	0	0	0	0
4. Third 20%	0.11	0.4	3.3	0	2.5	0	0	0	0	0
5. Fourth 20%	1.2	3.2	2.7	0	15.7	0	0	0	0	0
6. Top 20%	11.1	8.8	0.8	0	32.6	16.4	2.3	0.1	3.8	23.8
7. Bottom 90%	1.4	2.7	1.9	0	17.4	0.3	0.3	0.9	0	1.3
8. Top 10%	15.1	10.4	0.7	0	34.9	21.7	2.0	0.1	7.8	25.7
9. Top 1%	23.7	11.1	0.5	0	35.0	27.3	0.8	0	25.0	29.8
10. Top 10%–2%	12.7	10.8	0.8	0	34.8	19.6	2.2	0.1	7.8	24.4
			Colombia					Ecuador		
	Mean	SD	CV	Min	Max	Mean	SD	CV	Min	Max
1. All sample	5.0	1.9	0.4	1.7	12.1	4.7	2.5	0.5	0.7	16.2
2. Lowest 20%	0	0	0	0	0	0	0	0	0	0
3. Second 20%	0	0	0	0	0	0	0	0	0	0
4. Third 20%	0	0	0	0	0	0	0	0	0	0
5. Fourth 20%	0	0	0	0	0	0	0	0	0	0
6. Top 20%	10.3	2.4	0.2	5.0	17.7	8.9	3.9	0.4	1.6	26.0
7. Bottom 90%	0	0	0	0	0	0.3	0.5	1.7	0	3.6
8. Top 10%	14.94	2.5	0.2	9.4	22.1	12.1	4.5	0.4	2.6	29.7
9. Top 1%	30.4	0.8	0	28.0	32.5	21.3	5.7	0.3	8.6	34.0
10. Top 10%–2%	10.0	1.6	0.2	5.6	14.9	8.2	3.6	0.4	0	15.0

table continued next page

Table 5.1   Basic AMPITR statistics using a pooled regional-year sample for each country *(continued)*

Sample	Paraguay					Peru				
	Mean	SD	CV	Min	Max	Mean	SD	CV	Min	Max
1. All sample	1.1	1.0	0.9	0.1	4.7	3.7	1.8	0.5	0	10.4
2. Lowest 20%	0	0	0	0	0	0	0	0	0	0
3. Second 20%	0	0	0	0	0	0.002	0.01	4.9	0	0.1
4. Third 20%	0	0	0	0	0	0.003	0.02	5.1	0	0.2
5. Fourth 20%	0	0	0	0	0	0.005	0.02	3.9	0	0.2
6. Top 20%	1.8	1.4	0.8	0.3	6.2	7.5	2.6	0.3	0	13.4
7. Bottom 90%	0	0	0	0	0	0.06	0.1	2.4	0	1.0
8. Top 10%	2.3	1.5	0.6	0.4	6.9	11.2	3.3	0.3	0	18.6
9. Top 1%	6.0	1.8	0.3	2.5	9.1	17.0	2.6	0.2	4.7	26.0
10. Top 10%–2%	0	0	0	0	0	9.5	3.5	0.4	0	15.0

	United States				
	Mean	SD	CV	Min	Max
1. All sample	24.1	2.4	0.1	19.5	37.8
2. Lowest 20%	6.8	1.4	0.2	2.0	10.7
3. Second 20%	14.7	0.9	0.1	12.9	18.7
4. Third 20%	19.3	1.7	0.1	16.6	27.0
5. Fourth 20%	24.0	2.6	0.1	19.5	37.0
6. Top 20%	31.6	4.1	0.1	26.6	50.3
7. Bottom 90%	21.2	2.0	0.1	17.5	29.8
8. Top 10%	33.6	5.0	0.1	27.9	53.2
9. Top 1%	38.5	6.3	0.2	28.0	63.4
10. Top 10%–2%	32.4	4.9	0.2	27.2	48.3

Source: Original table for this publication.

Note: AMPITR = average marginal personal income tax rate; CV = coefficient of variation; Max = maximum; Min = minimum; SD = standard deviation.

Last, we further split the top 10 percent (row 8) between the top 1 percent (row 9) and the top 10–2 percent (row 10). Interestingly, when focusing on the top 1 percent, the AMPITR in most Latin American countries (except for Paraguay) is now much closer to that of the United States. Whereas the AMPITR in the United States for the top 1 percent is 38.5 percent, it is 30.4 percent in Colombia, 27.3 percent in Brazil, 23.7 percent in Argentina, 21.3 percent in Ecuador, and 17 percent in Peru. In fact, for example, although the highest marginal individual income tax rate in the United States reached 39.6 percent in 2017, this value ranged between 27.5 percent and 35.0 percent in Argentina, Brazil, and Ecuador.[3] Therefore, the relatively low AMPITR in Latin American countries primarily stems from tax concentration among high-income earners rather than significantly lower top marginal tax rates. In other words, the PIT in Latin American countries exhibits a high degree of progressivity, surpassing that observed in the United States.

When analyzing the LAC sample, the geographically disaggregated nature of household survey datasets allows the construction of both national and subnational AMPITR series—the latter for 139 regions or statelike areas. Subnational estimates show a larger variation in AMPITR within each LAC country vis-à-vis the United States, which mainly reflects a substantially larger heterogeneity in the income distribution across regions.

Map 5.1 sheds some light on this topic by displaying the share of each country's top 10 percent tax units in each region. Notice that although such a share in the United States ranges between 4.5 percent in West Virginia and 21.5 percent in Alaska—and 16.7 percent in the second-highest state, Maryland—these discrepancies tend to be much larger in LAC countries. For example, in Argentina, this share ranges between 4 percent in Santiago del Estero and 40.6 percent in Tierra del Fuego. Even the second, third, and fourth regions with the highest shares are above 20 percent (Santa Cruz with 27.4 percent, the city of Buenos Aires with 27.1 percent, and Chubut with 21.5 percent). In Brazil, this share ranges between 3.9 percent in Maranhão and 26.7 percent in the Federal District.

Map 5.1 Share of top 10 percent tax units per region in each country

a. Argentina

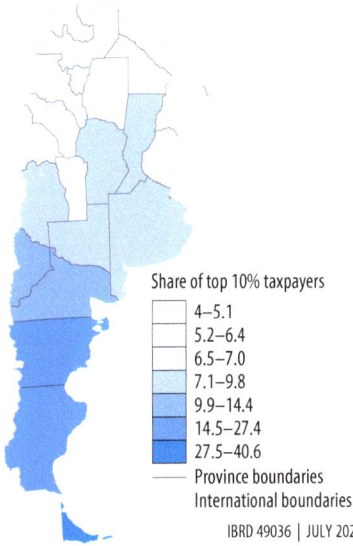

Share of top 10% taxpayers

- 4–5.1
- 5.2–6.4
- 6.5–7.0
- 7.1–9.8
- 9.9–14.4
- 14.5–27.4
- 27.5–40.6
- —— Province boundaries
- —— International boundaries

IBRD 49036 | JULY 2025

b. Brazil

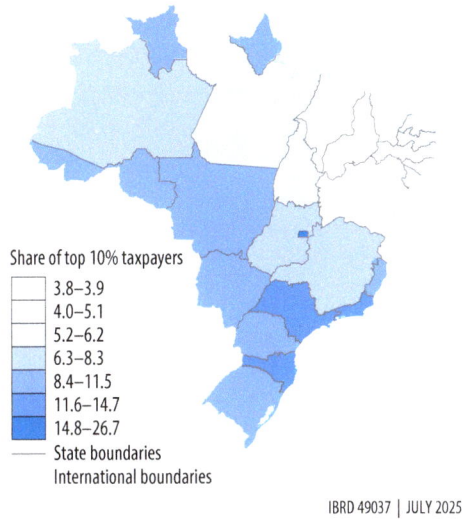

Share of top 10% taxpayers

- 3.8–3.9
- 4.0–5.1
- 5.2–6.2
- 6.3–8.3
- 8.4–11.5
- 11.6–14.7
- 14.8–26.7
- —— State boundaries
- —— International boundaries

IBRD 49037 | JULY 2025

c. Colombia

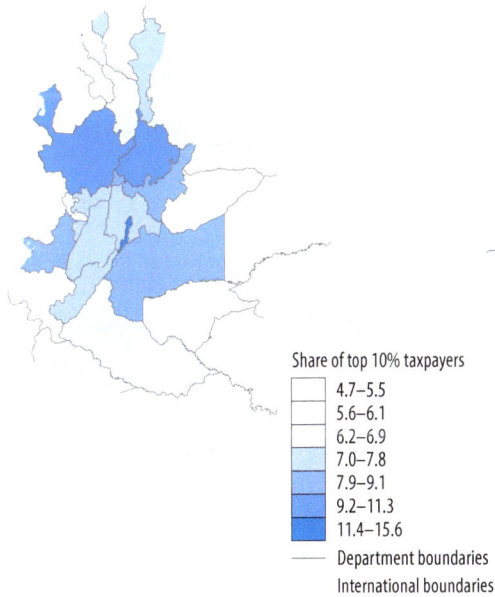

Share of top 10% taxpayers

- 4.7–5.5
- 5.6–6.1
- 6.2–6.9
- 7.0–7.8
- 7.9–9.1
- 9.2–11.3
- 11.4–15.6
- —— Department boundaries
- —— International boundaries

IBRD 49038 | JULY 2025

d. Ecuador

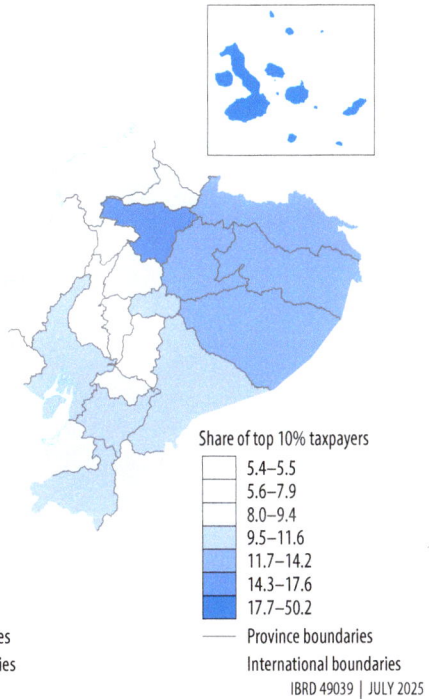

Share of top 10% taxpayers

- 5.4–5.5
- 5.6–7.9
- 8.0–9.4
- 9.5–11.6
- 11.7–14.2
- 14.3–17.6
- 17.7–50.2
- —— Province boundaries
- —— International boundaries

IBRD 49039 | JULY 2025

map continued next page

Map 5.1   Share of top 10 percent tax units per region in each country *(continued)*

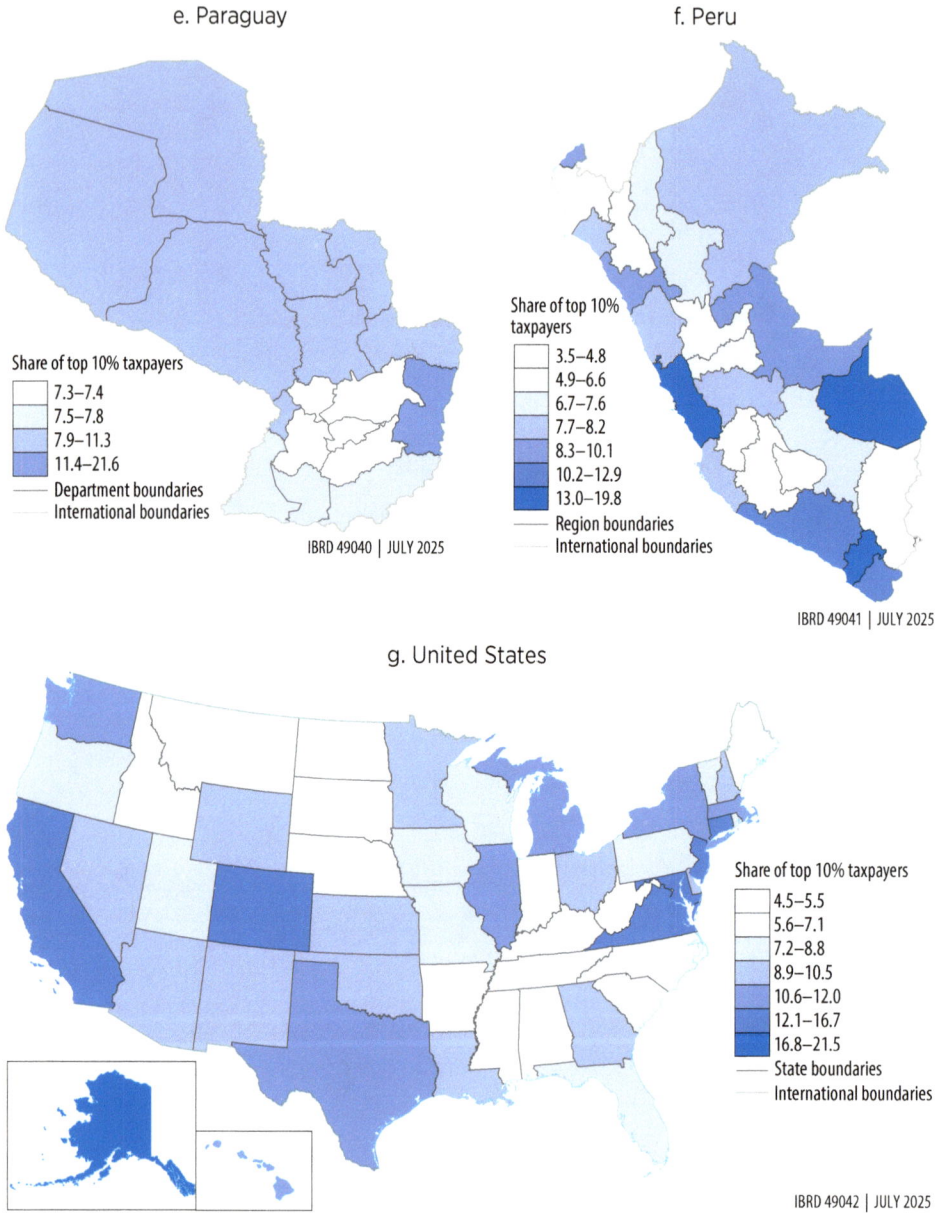

e. Paraguay

Share of top 10% taxpayers
- 7.3–7.4
- 7.5–7.8
- 7.9–11.3
- 11.4–21.6
— Department boundaries
— International boundaries

IBRD 49040 | JULY 2025

f. Peru

Share of top 10% taxpayers
- 3.5–4.8
- 4.9–6.6
- 6.7–7.6
- 7.7–8.2
- 8.3–10.1
- 10.2–12.9
- 13.0–19.8
— Region boundaries
— International boundaries

IBRD 49041 | JULY 2025

g. United States

Share of top 10% taxpayers
- 4.5–5.5
- 5.6–7.1
- 7.2–8.8
- 8.9–10.5
- 10.6–12.0
- 12.1–16.7
- 16.8–21.5
— State boundaries
— International boundaries

IBRD 49042 | JULY 2025

Source: Original map for this publication.

Note: Because household surveys in Argentina are representative solely of urban areas, and, in some cases, there is more than one urban area belonging to the same province, the value assigned to each province in the map is a population-weighted average of the share of the top 10 percent taxpayers in the urban areas belonging to each province. It is worth noting that the share of urban-to-total population in Argentinean provinces ranges between 74 percent (in Misiones) and 100 percent (in the city of Buenos Aires). The regions in Colombia with no value are not included in the country's household survey. It is worth noting that these excluded regions represent only 3 percent of Colombia's total population.

Aggregate Income Responses to PIT Changes

Accurate tax policy design hinges on comprehending how individuals react to tax changes, a concept quantified by the ETI. Ignoring behavioral responses, as is common in static tax analyses, can lead to significantly flawed policy outcomes. In regions such as LAC, where ETI estimates are substantial, particularly among top earners, revenue projections based on static assumptions can dramatically underestimate the effect on the labor market and overestimate the impact of tax changes. For instance, a seemingly straightforward increase in the AMPITR can produce significantly different revenue outcomes when behavioral responses are considered. Crucially, knowing these responses also allows policy makers to tailor tax policy reforms to more effectively achieve their intended goals. This discrepancy underscores the critical need to incorporate behavioral adjustments into revenue estimations, ensuring that policy decisions are grounded in realistic assessments of how taxpayers will modify their behavior in response to tax reforms. Failure to do so can result in unintended revenue shortfalls and distorted economic outcomes.

Higher ETI Estimates, Particularly Among Top Earners

Short-term ETI estimates for the United States range between 0.02 in Saez (2004) to 1.2 in Mertens and Montiel-Olea (2018). As these estimates suggest, a 0.02 ETI indicates minimal change in income due to tax rate adjustments, whereas a 1.2 ETI suggests a more-than-proportional response.

In novel work, Riera-Crichton, Venturi, and Vuletin (forthcoming) find that short-term ETI estimates in LAC are around 0.5, pointing to a modest (and statistically not significant) average effect somewhere in the middle of current ETI estimates for the United States. Figure 5.2 shows the response of the cumulative pretax income to an exogenous and unanticipated net-of-tax AMPITR shock one year after the shock.

Top income earners (the top 5 percent) in LAC are more responsive to changes in tax rates than the bottom 95 percent of the population, who exhibit virtually inelastic behavior. These findings align with estimates from the United States, such as those in Saez (2004) and Gruber and Saez (2002), who show that top earners exhibit greater ability to respond to tax shocks.

Figure 5.2   Cumulative ETI one year after the shock

Elasticity of taxable income (ETI)

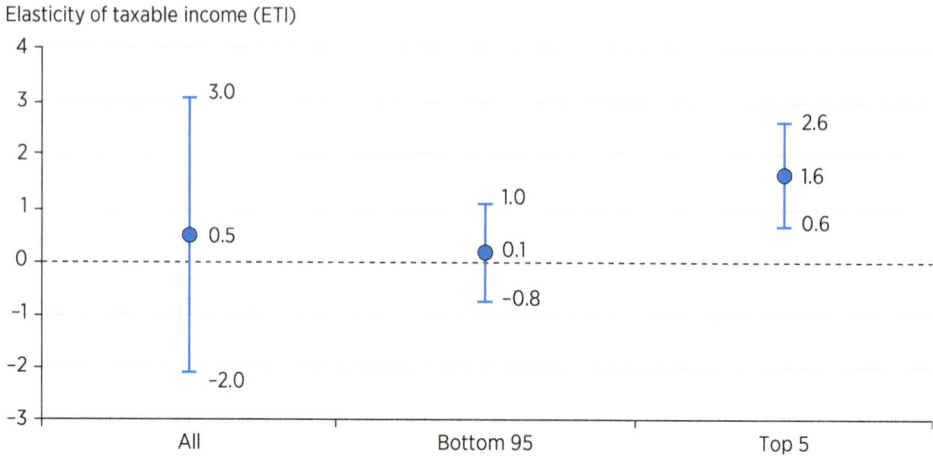

Source: Original figure for this publication.

Note: Dots represent the country-level response of pretax income to an exogenous and unanticipated net-of-tax average marginal personal income tax rate shock solely driven by legislated tax changes one year after the tax shock. The spikes represent the 95% confidence intervals. ETI = elasticity of taxable income.

Factors Contributing to Greater Responsiveness of Top Earners

Although disentangling all the interconnected effects is challenging, three key forces seem to strongly drive the greater income responsiveness of top earners in LAC: a larger labor behavioral response, larger presence of tax evasion, and higher income inequality with more income concentrated at the top.

Larger Labor Behavioral Response

Individuals, especially top earners, exhibit larger labor market responses, on both the extensive and the intensive margins. As predicted by simple labor market models, both labor force participation rates and working hours decrease in response to tax hikes, and vice versa. These heterogeneous labor responses also reflect higher educational attainment and greater entrepreneurship at the top of the income distribution. Individuals with higher levels of education often possess greater flexibility in their labor market choices, such as the ability to adjust their working hours, switch jobs, or even pursue self-employment (Autor, Katz, and Kearney 2008; Cullen and Gruber 2000). For example, although on average only about 25 percent of the LAC labor force have completed tertiary education, this increases to 60 percent when focusing on the last decile. Entrepreneurs, by their very nature, have more control over their income and can potentially adjust their business activities, investment decisions, or even the timing of income recognition in response to tax changes (Blanchard and Katz 1999; Hamilton 2000).

Higher Evasion at the Top

Larger ETI estimates might also be due to a greater tendency for high-income earners to evade taxes when rates increase. Informality is a prevalent feature of labor markets in developing countries with important consequences for economic development and government tax collection. Traditional views define an informal employee as one who is not registered with social security and is therefore not likely to engage with the tax authority. These employees could be working in fully informal firms, such as street vendors or small-scale repair shops, or as off-the-book workers in a registered firm.

However, by focusing on a dichotomous definition of an informal worker, standard research overlooks the informal connections between registered firms and registered workers. This omission aligns with the prevalent notion that income sources reported by third parties are less susceptible to evasion, because collusion between the involved parties is challenging to sustain. Using online surveys of formal workers, Feinmann, Hsu Rocha, and Lauletta (2022) have challenged this idea, showing that informal ties between formal workers and firms are prevalent in the Brazilian labor market, where formal workers receive part of their wages under the table. They define the practice of payments under the table (PUT) as when formal workers in registered firms receive part of their wages off the books. The measurement of this practice is challenging because, by definition, it does not show up in administrative data and, different from traditional informality, it is not present in the vast majority of standard household and labor force surveys. To circumvent this issue, Feinmann, Hsu Rocha, and Lauletta (2022) use a novel survey design to elicit truthful responses from respondents.

In an upcoming study, Feinmann et al. (forthcoming) use the same survey design to extend the analysis of Feinmann, Hsu Rocha, and Lauletta (2022), which focused on Brazil, to other countries in the LAC region. In addition to Brazil, this new study includes Argentina, Chile, Colombia, and Mexico. This allows them to document the prevalence of PUT at a regional scale and to understand what drives differences across countries.

The results indicate that 16 percent of formal workers in the region receive some part of their compensation under the table. Among those who receive PUT, on average 24 percent of their labor earnings are paid off the books. Conditional to receiving PUT, workers in the upper part of the income distribution in LAC receive a larger fraction of their income outside of regular channels (refer to figure 5.3).

Figure 5.3   Percentage of total payroll as PUT

Total payroll as PUT (%)

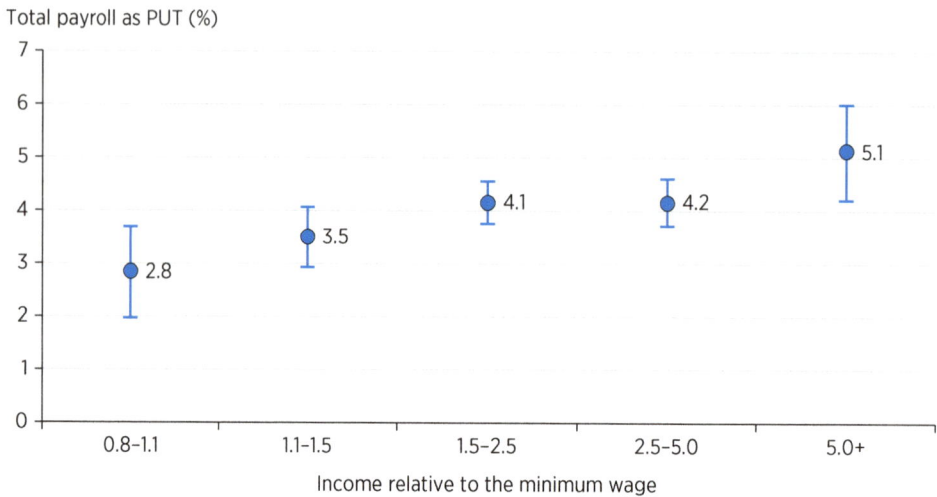

Income relative to the minimum wage

Source: Feinmann et al. (forthcoming).

Note: Dots represent the average percentage of total payroll as PUT. The spikes represent the 95% confidence intervals. PUT = payment under the table.

Higher Income Inequality

Although the top 5 percent of income earners in the United States account for 20 percent of total income, this figure is about 30 percent in LAC. This greater concentration of income at the top, combined with the larger responsiveness of this group to tax changes, mechanically leads to a larger overall impact of tax hikes to this group on total income. In other words, the higher ETI in LAC reflects not only the larger behavioral response of top earners but also the larger relevance of this group in terms of their participation in total income. This interplay between high income concentration and the responsiveness of top earners has significant implications for the design and effectiveness of tax policies in LAC. The following discussion provides quantitative insights into how PIT changes affect estimated fiscal revenues after correcting for behavioral responses.

Policy Implications for Revenue Collection

A critical limitation of many traditional tax reform analyses is the common assumption of no behavioral response to tax changes. This static approach, often used in microsimulation exercises, assumes that income levels remain constant regardless of tax policy adjustments. Although such simplifications can be useful for initial estimations, they can lead to significantly misleading conclusions, particularly in contexts in which behavioral responses are substantial.

When behavioral responses are not considered (that is, income levels stay the same, as is common in microsimulation exercises), tax increases lead to higher revenue and vice versa. However, for the LAC sample, for which behavioral responsiveness is high, the change in revenue is much weaker when these behavioral changes are factored in. Figure 5.4 illustrates these key findings.

When assuming no behavioral response (that is, no adjustments in income), tax hikes naturally drive revenue increases, and tax cuts drive reductions. In particular, a 1-percentage-point hike in the AMPITR leads to a revenue increase of 0.38 percentage points of the previous year's pretax income when no behavioral response is assumed. Moreover, the null hypothesis that such a revenue response equals zero can be rejected. However, and in light of the large behavioral responsiveness found in the LAC sample, the change in revenues is much weaker when properly allowing for behavioral responses in incomes affecting the estimated revenue collection. In particular, when accounting for behavioral adjustments, a 1-percentage-point hike in the AMPITR increases the estimated individual income tax revenue collection by 0.20 percentage points of pretax income, almost half that obtained when not allowing for a behavioral response. Notably, the null hypothesis that such a revenue response equals zero cannot be rejected.

Figure 5.4   Country-level impact response of individual income tax revenues to exogenous unanticipated changes in AMPITR

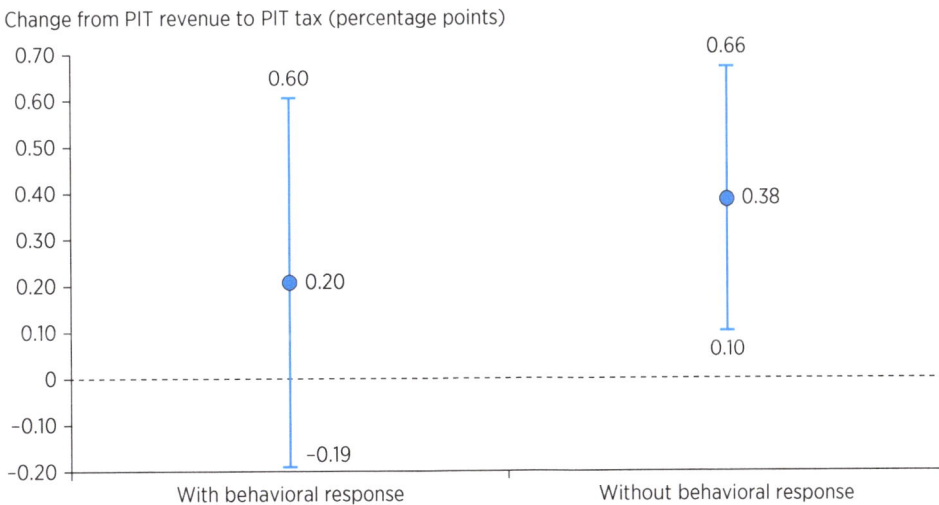

Change from PIT revenue to PIT tax (percentage points)

Source: Original figure for this publication.

Note: Dots represent the estimated country-level impact response of individual income tax revenues to exogenous unanticipated changes in AMPITR. The spikes represent the 95% confidence intervals. AMPITR = average marginal personal income tax rate; PIT = personal income tax.

As demonstrated by the findings for the LAC sample, for which behavioral responsiveness is high, neglecting these responses can drastically overestimate the revenue impact of tax changes. This stark difference underscores the crucial importance of incorporating behavioral responses into tax policy analysis to ensure accurate revenue projections and effective policy design. Relying on static analysis in the face of significant behavioral responses can lead to flawed policy decisions with unintended consequences for government revenues and economic activity.

Expanding the Base: A Familiar Tax Evolution

The combination of a very narrow PIT tax base in LAC, which taxes top income earners in a way that resembles that of more advanced economies, with ETI estimates showing high behavioral responsiveness (including labor and entrepreneurial responses), particularly among the top 5 percent of earners, and virtually low ETI in lower high-income groups, suggests that rather than focusing on further increasing already high top rates, LAC countries should focus on moderately expanding the tax base. Obviously, this expansion cannot reach vulnerable or poor populations, many of whom are already in the informal sector. This recommendation to broaden the tax base in LAC finds strong support in the historical experience of the United States. The evolution of the United States' PIT demonstrates a clear shift from a narrow-based, high-rate system to a broader-based one.

A Historical Perspective from the United States

The proposed approach of broadening the base is not novel; the history of the PIT in the United States exemplifies this. The federal income tax in the United States has a long and complex history. Its origins can be traced back to the Civil War (1861–65), when Congress enacted a temporary income tax in 1861 to finance the war effort. This initial tax was short-lived and expired in 1872. The modern income tax system in the United States was established with the ratification of the 16th Amendment to the Constitution in 1913, which granted Congress the power to levy an income tax without apportionment among the states.

Early US PIT Characteristics

Before the mid-20th century, the US income tax system exhibited striking similarities to the current tax systems observed in many Latin American countries in terms of structure and reach. It had the following features:

- *Extremely high top marginal tax rates.* These rates often exceeded 80 percent, reaching levels considered confiscatory by today's standards (refer to figure 5.5, panel a).

- *A very narrow tax base.* The income tax primarily targeted a small segment of the population, typically the wealthiest individuals, with only a small fraction of the adult population subject to the tax. This limited base, despite the high top rates, resulted in a relatively low average marginal income tax rate for the overall population (refer to figure 5.5, panel b).

- *A low average marginal income tax rate.* Despite the presence of extremely high top marginal rates, the narrow tax base resulted in a relatively low average marginal income tax rate for the overall population (refer to figure 5.5, panel c).

Broadening the PIT During World War II

The advent of World War II necessitated a significant expansion of the federal government's revenue sources. To fund the war effort, the US government undertook a major overhaul of the income tax system. Key changes included the following:

- *Reduced top marginal rates.* Although still substantial, the highest marginal tax rates were gradually reduced from their prewar levels (refer to figure 5.5, panel a).

- *Significant base broadening.* The tax base was dramatically expanded to include a much larger share of the population, eventually reaching approximately half of all adults by the end of the war. This expansion brought millions of middle-class Americans into the income tax system (refer to figure 5.5, panel b).

- *Increased average marginal tax rate.* These changes, particularly the significant expansion of the tax base, led to a substantial increase in the average marginal income tax rate, which rose to approximately 20–25 percent for the overall population (refer to figure 5.5, panel c).

The historical experience in the United States demonstrates how significant tax base expansion can dramatically increase the overall revenue yield of the income tax system, even with potentially lower top marginal rates.

Figure 5.5   History of PIT in the United States, pre-World War II and after

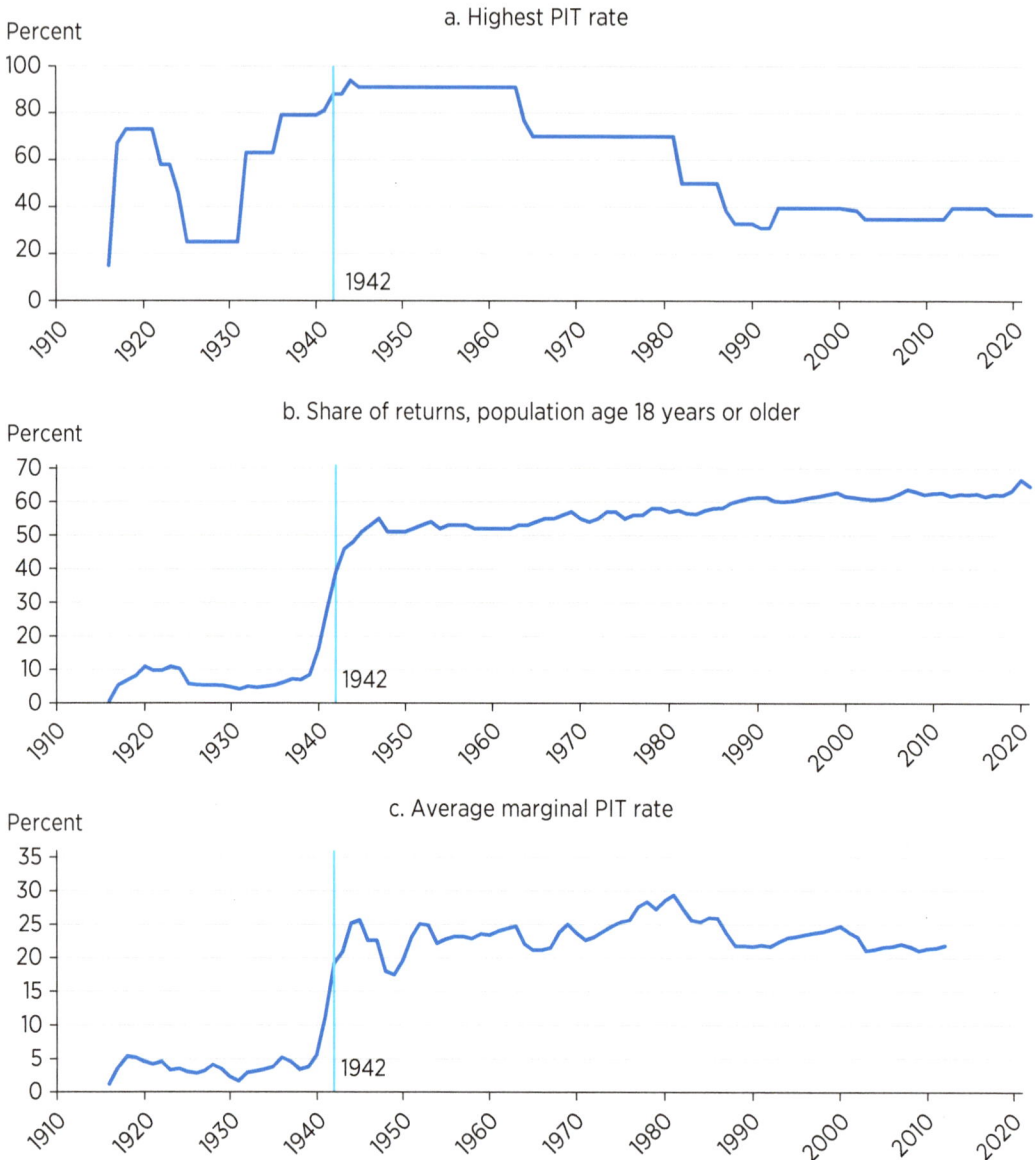

a. Highest PIT rate

Percent

1942

b. Share of returns, population age 18 years or older

Percent

1942

c. Average marginal PIT rate

Percent

1942

Source: Barro and Sahasakul 1983; Saez 2004.

Note: The vertical line represents the US entry into World War II. PIT = personal income tax.

Conclusion

This analysis reveals a critical tension in LAC PIT policy. Although top earners are taxed at rates resembling those in advanced economies, the narrow tax base and high ETI among this group limit revenue. Simply raising already high top rates is likely to be counterproductive, triggering behavioral responses and diminishing revenue. Instead, a moderate broadening of the tax base is a more effective strategy and is supported by the US historical experience.

Before the mid-20th century, the United States faced a similar challenge: high top rates applied to a small segment of the population, resulting in low average tax rates. World War II forced a shift toward a broader base, significantly increasing revenue. In a sense, LAC faces a similar crossroads. Although taxing the wealthy is politically appealing, focusing solely on high top rates within a narrow base is inefficient. By learning from US history, LAC can unlock greater revenue and achieve a more sustainable tax system by moderately expanding the base, excluding vulnerable and informal populations. This offers a more promising path to enhancing fiscal capacity.

Notes

1. Individual income tax in Argentina, Brazil, Colombia, Ecuador, and Peru dates back to 1932, 1922, 1927, 1926, and 1934, respectively.
2. People in the province of Tierra del Fuego in Argentina have not paid individual income tax since 1974 (Law 19,640); hence, the value in the "Min" column is always "0" for this country.
3. In Paraguay, the highest marginal individual income tax rate is 10 percent.

References

Autor, D., L. F. Katz, and M. S. Kearney. 2008. "The Polarization of the U.S. Labor Market: Implications for Workers, Families, and Policy." *Annual Review of Economics* 4 (1): 187–221.

Barro, R. J., and C. Sahasakul. 1983. "Measuring the Average Marginal Tax Rate from the Individual Income Tax." *Journal of Business* 56 (4): 419–52.

Blanchard, O. J., and H. C. Katz. 1999. "The Future of the U.S. Labor Market: An Agenda." Working Paper 7380, National Bureau of Economics, Cambridge, MA.

Cullen, J. B., and J. Gruber. 2000. "Does Unemployment Insurance Increase Job Matching? Evidence from Seasonal Layoffs." *Econometrica* 68 (3): 705–31.

Feinmann, J., A. P. Franco, P. Garriga, N. Gonzalez-Prieto, R. Hsu Rocha, and M. Lauletta. Forthcoming. "Payments Under the Table in Latin America." Washington, DC: World Bank.

Feinmann, J., R. Hsu Rocha, and M. Lauletta. 2022. "Payments Under the Table: Employer-Employee Collusion in Brazil." *SSRN*. https://doi.org/10.2139/ssrn.4270665.

Gruber, J., and E. Saez. 2002. "The Elasticity of Taxable Income: Evidence and Implications." *Journal of Public Economics* 84 (1): 1–32.

Hamilton, B. H. 2000. "Does Entrepreneurship Pay? An Empirical Analysis of Self-Employment in the United States." *Journal of Political Economy* 108 (1): 60–81.

Mertens, K., and J. L. Montiel-Olea. 2018. "Marginal Tax Rates and Income: New Time Series Evidence." *Quarterly Journal of Economics* 133 (4): 1803–84.

Riera-Crichton, D., L. Venturi, and G. Vuletin. Forthcoming. "The Income and Labor Effects of Individual Income Tax Changes in Latin America: Evidence from a New Measure of Tax Shocks." Working Paper, World Bank, Washington, DC.

Romer, C. D., and D. H. Romer. 2010. "The Macroeconomic Effects of Tax Changes: Estimates Based on a New Measure of Fiscal Shocks." *American Economic Review* 100 (3): 763–801.

Saez, E. 2004. "Reported Incomes and Marginal Tax Rates, 1960–2000: Evidence and Policy Implications." *Tax Policy and the Economy* 18: 117–72.

6

Wealth Tax: Toward a Practical Wealth Tax in Latin America and the Caribbean

Introduction

This chapter asserts that the effectiveness of wealth taxes (WTs) hinges on a clear recognition of the assets being taxed. In Latin America and the Caribbean (LAC), where property constitutes the largest share of wealth, a strategic focus on property taxation is essential. The inherent challenges of taxing financial assets—their easy concealment and transfer—stand in stark contrast to the relative simplicity of taxing property. To maximize revenue potential and minimize economic distortions, LAC countries should prioritize policies that leverage the unique characteristics of property within their wealth structures.

To understand this distinction, it is important to first define what constitutes a WT. At its core, a WT is based on the concept of net worth, which represents the total value of an individual's assets minus their liabilities. Much like the personal income tax, the WT often follows a progressive structure, meaning the tax rate increases as net worth rises. By taxing very wealthy individuals at a higher rate, WTs have the chance to be even more progressive than the personal income tax (Saez and Zucman 2016).

WTs have been enacted or considered in various countries at various times. Several European nations implemented WTs in the aftermath of World War II to generate resources to rebuild their economies; more recently, the coronavirus disease 2019 pandemic spurred discussions and, in some cases, temporary WTs to offset stimulus costs. Interest in WTs is spreading in LAC. President Lula da Silva of Brazil has pushed for a minimum global WT, as has President Emmanuel Macron of France. The EU Tax Observatory, which advises the G-20 Brazilian presidency, has proposed imposing a minimum 2 percent levy on the world's 3,000 richest billionaires, which in Brazil's case is estimated to raise an additional US$2.1 billion (Leali 2024). President Gustavo Petro of Colombia has proposed an annual WT on savings and property above US$460,000. WTs were first introduced in Colombia in 1935, repealed in 1992, and then introduced again in 2002 to finance Seguridad Democratica—the Uribe administration's security effort against drug trafficking and guerrilla and paramilitary groups—with revenues earmarked for defense and security expenditures (Londoño-Vélez and Ávila-Mahecha 2021). Chile has repeatedly considered implementing a WT but has yet to enact one. Although proposals have been introduced in recent years, including a significant attempt in 2023, the measure has faced opposition and remains under debate. In December 2020, Bolivia implemented a WT targeting individuals with assets exceeding US$4 million (Bolivian Law Number 1357). The tax features progressive rates ranging from 1.4 percent to 2.4 percent. In its first year, the tax affected 204 taxpayers and generated approximately $35 million in revenue, accounting for merely 0.38 percent of the country's total tax income for that year. Argentina's WT was first introduced in 1972 and allowed for debt deductions. This net wealth taxation was discontinued in 1989 but reintroduced in 1991 as a global tax on gross wealth, without debt deductions. The Uruguayan WT applies to individuals; it is based on their assets in the country and is progressive, ranging from 0.1 percent to 0.4 percent for residents and from 0.7 percent to 1.5 percent for nonresidents.

Which Wealth to Tax?

WTs have been criticized for requiring intensive administrative capacity, for discouraging investment, and for sometimes leading to wealth flight and low collection, but these criticisms depend greatly on precisely what type of wealth is targeted (Enache 2024; OECD 2018). For instance, even in advanced economies, taxing liquid assets can be challenging, especially in countries with weak enforcement, because these assets are easy to move across borders and hide offshore. Strengthening global enforcement efforts to track them, and to address concerns related to crime and money laundering, will continue to be a priority, although the levels of international coordination needed will likely remain elusive over the medium term.

Property taxation, however, has fewer negative behavioral consequences and more manageable administrative burdens. By nature, property is a relatively fixed and easily identifiable asset, and hence less susceptible to flight, and real estate is the main type of wealth in LAC. Despite relatively standard marginal taxation rates, low valuations have led to real estate being underused as a revenue source. The availability of modern platforms to obtain more accurate market value data and identify the locations of wealthy neighborhoods offers potential to remedy this going forward. Moreover, this tax could be a valuable tool for empowering subnational governments and reducing their excessive reliance on transfers from higher levels of government.

More important, property taxes are less likely to hinder growth. Property holdings generally contribute less to economic dynamism in terms of fostering innovation, creating positive synergies with other strategic productive sectors, or nurturing human capital. Thus, taxing property can potentially create jobs and accelerate growth. By contrast, excessively high marginal rates in corporate and personal income taxes and other distortive taxes, such as gross receipts and financial transaction taxes, penalize investors and entrepreneurs, who may be adding innovation and jobs to the economy. The double taxation implied because wealth is often the accumulation of savings from already taxed income can deter investment and innovation or encourage productive entrepreneurs to relocate to jurisdictions with lower tax rates. Lowering taxes for high-return and skilled individuals could reallocate capital; in turn, the higher yields could potentially motivate greater savings (Guvenen et al. 2023). Numerous European countries have repealed or refocused WTs over the past decade.

As a final caveat, the chapter also suggests that although proposals for taxing billionaires in LAC should be taken seriously and can probably reach their stated goals for raising funds for the green transition, they are not a silver bullet for generating fiscal space more generally. Even without considering potential mobility responses, the potential revenue gains are modest because of the region's relatively smaller number of billionaires and their lesser wealth compared with billionaires in more advanced economies and emerging markets. However unpopular, to reach both revenue and equity goals, all tax systems will need to increase the base of those taxed.

A Tale of Two Models: Wealth Taxation in Advanced Economies

Essential to the analysis of WTs is the concept of net worth, which is the total value of an individual's assets minus their liabilities. Assets encompass a broad spectrum of possessions, including readily tradable financial ones such as stocks and bonds as well as tangible assets such as real estate, artwork, and even luxury vehicles. Liabilities, however, represent financial obligations, such as mortgages, student loans, and credit card debt (Rudnick and Gordon 1996). In principle, the idea is to levy taxes on the net position, and, even more than the personal income tax, WTs often follow a progressive structure, meaning the tax rate increases as net worth rises.[1]

This said, the advanced world has taken very different approaches to implementing WTs. In North America, neither the United States nor Canada has a federal general WT. However, property taxes on real estate (property taxes, hereinafter) are a cornerstone of local revenue, primarily funding schools, public safety, and infrastructure. This heavy reliance on property taxes can impose significant burdens on homeowners, especially in areas with high property values. Furthermore, some states impose estate taxes, a form of WT levied on the transfer of assets at death, contributing to the overall tax burden on high-net-worth individuals in these jurisdictions. Although estate taxes can in principle be a source of revenue, they can also be difficult to enforce and may incentivize wealthy individuals to engage in tax avoidance strategies, such as gifting assets during their lifetime, establishing trusts, or holding assets in foreign jurisdictions.

In contrast, many European countries have adopted a broader approach to taxing wealth. Germany's WT is levied on net assets exceeding a specific threshold, including real estate, financial assets, and business holdings. Switzerland, known for its tax-friendly environment, imposes a relatively low WT but applies it to a broad range of assets. Countries such as the United Kingdom, France, and Germany impose substantial taxes on wealth transfers at death. The United Kingdom's inheritance tax, for example, applies to estates exceeding a certain value, with progressive rates based on the size of the inheritance. France and Germany also have progressive inheritance tax systems, with higher rates for larger inheritances. Recently, European countries have reduced the scope of those who are wealth taxed. France now focuses on a real estate WT targeting high-value properties. Other countries have also joined a recent trend of repealing WTs, including Austria (1994); Denmark and Germany (1997); the Netherlands (2001); Finland, Iceland, and Luxembourg (2006); and Sweden (2007). In 2021, the Netherlands Supreme Court ruled that the country's WT violated European law primarily because of issues of property rights and nondiscrimination.[2] In fact, as of 2024, only three Western European countries still levy the broader net WTs: Norway, Spain, and Switzerland.

These divergent paths of wealth taxation in North America and Europe are deeply intertwined with the historical and political evolution of each. The United States, founded on principles of individual property rights and limited government, developed a system heavily reliant on property taxes for local revenue (Bailyn 1967). This emphasis on local property taxes reflects the nation's agrarian roots (where land is often the most valuable asset) and a political culture averse to strong central authority. In contrast, European nations experienced earlier industrialization and the subsequent concentration of wealth. These factors, coupled with Europe's more centralized authority, led to discussions about larger welfare states (Esping-Andersen 1990) and the implementation of direct WTs as a means to address inequality (Piketty 2014).

WT Revenues

The contribution to total government revenue from WTs on both net wealth and property varies greatly by region and, within them, by country (refer to figure 6.1). As discussed, North America and Europe are the regions with the most significant wealth taxation, with North America relying more heavily on property taxes compared with Europe (refer to figure 6.1, panels a, b, d, and e). Although the United States and Canada lack a federal-level WT like some European nations, property taxes constitute a substantial revenue source for subnational governments in both countries. These taxes can be considerable, especially in areas with high property values. Consequently, it is inaccurate to claim that the United States and Canada do not tax wealth. In fact, overall revenue in these North American nations often far exceeds that of their European counterparts (refer to figure 6.1, panels a, b, and e).

WT collection in the LAC region is very low, representing only about 0.5 percent of gross domestic product (GDP; refer to figure 6.1, panel a) or 2.7 percent of total revenue collection (refer to figure 6.1, panel b). Sub-Saharan Africa is the only region with lower WT collection. There is, however, high variation among LAC countries: WT collection exceeds or centers around 5 percent of total tax revenues in Uruguay, Barbados, the Bahamas, Chile (refer to figure 6.1, panel c), and Colombia. Variation is also high in other emerging markets and developing economies (EMDEs; refer to figure 6.1, panel e).

Figure 6.1   Size of wealth tax revenue by region and country

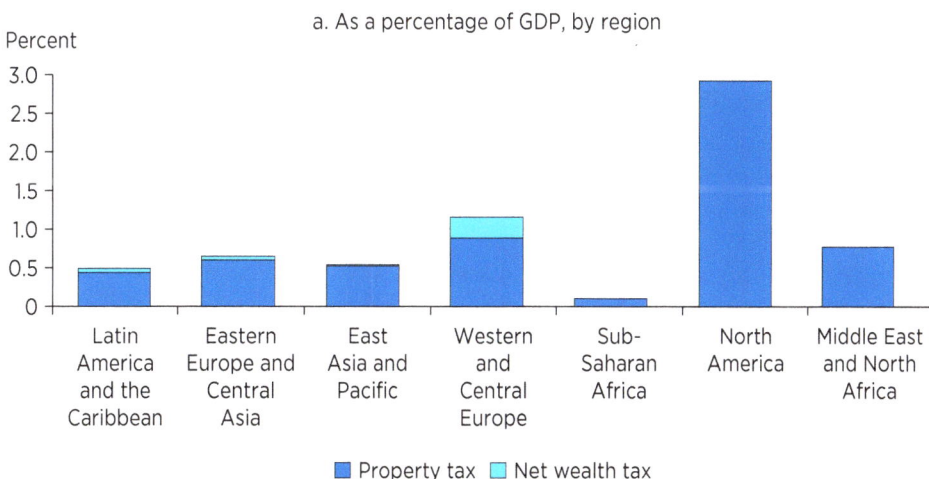

a. As a percentage of GDP, by region

figure continued next page

Figure 6.1   Size of wealth tax revenue by region and country *(continued)*

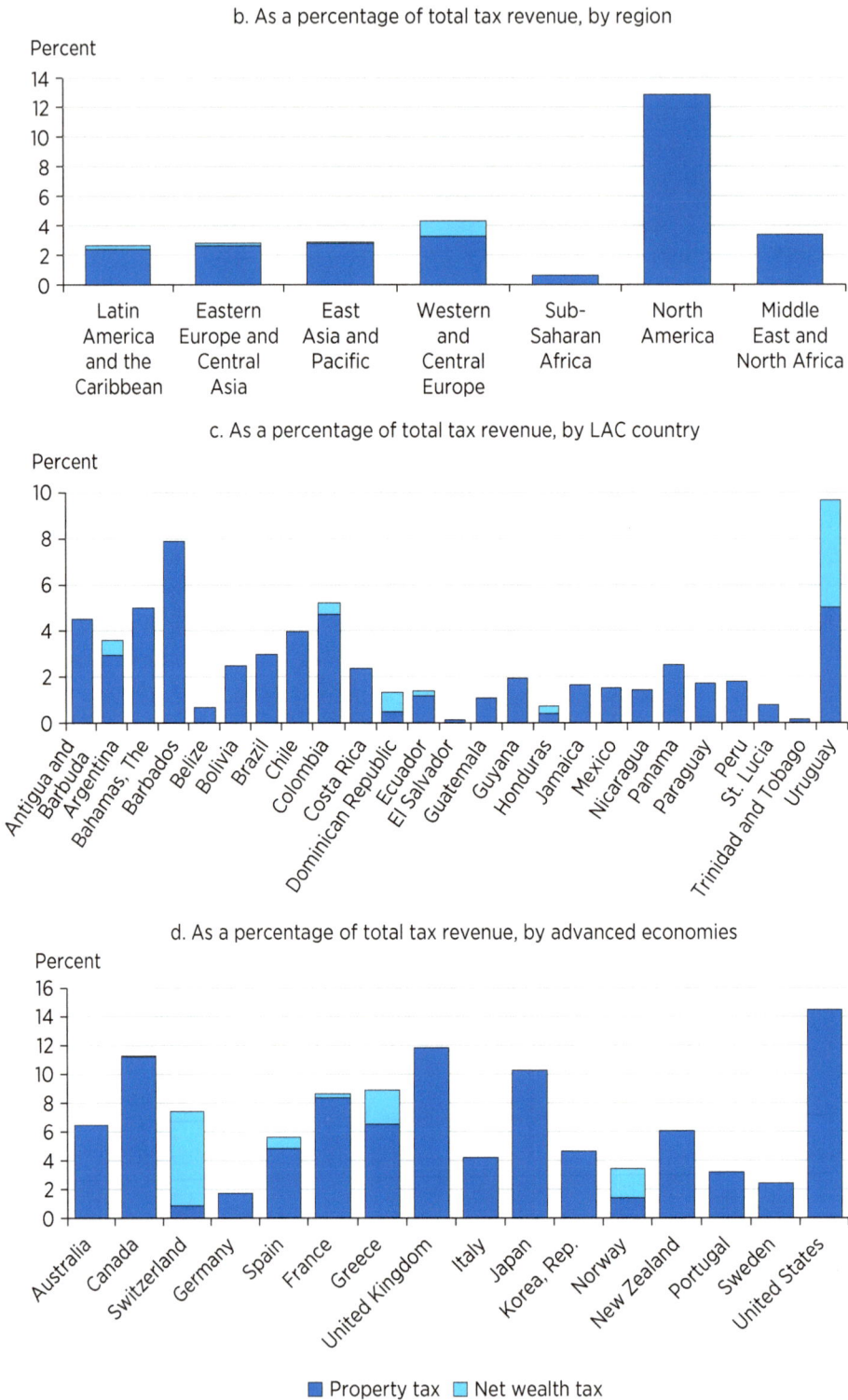

b. As a percentage of total tax revenue, by region

c. As a percentage of total tax revenue, by LAC country

d. As a percentage of total tax revenue, by advanced economies

■ Property tax   ■ Net wealth tax

figure continued next page

Figure 6.1 Size of wealth tax revenue by region and country *(continued)*

e. As a percentage of total tax revenue,
by emerging markets and developing economies

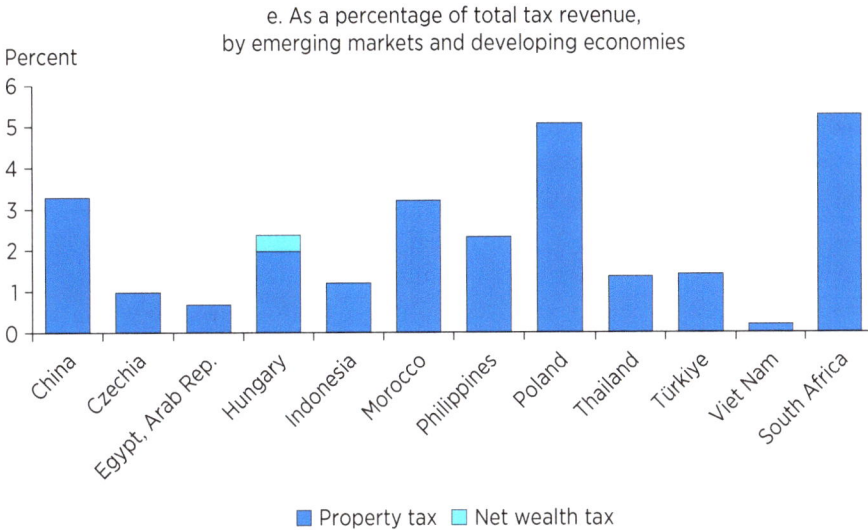

■ Property tax □ Net wealth tax

Source: Original calculations for this publication using Organisation for Economic Co-operation and Development Global Revenue Statistics Database (https://www .oecd.org/en/data/datasets/global-revenue-statistics-database.html) and World Bank data.

Note: Social security revenues are excluded from total tax revenues. The figure uses consolidated government statistics. GDP = gross domestic product; LAC = Latin America and the Caribbean.

Another dimension on which LAC countries differ in their taxation regards the main property that is subject to taxation from a revenue collection point of view. Many countries in the region, such as Barbados and Chile, primarily tax land values. Others, such as Argentina, Colombia, and Peru, primarily tax building values. Brazil and Mexico, like other countries, incorporate land value into their property tax calculations in addition to building value. Several, such as Costa Rica and Uruguay, have made efforts to shift the tax burden more toward land values, recognizing the potential for fairer and more efficient taxation.

Tax rates, exemptions, deductions, and administrative structures also differ widely. For instance, some nations offer generous exemptions for residential property, especially for low-income owners (Chile, Colombia), and others impose higher rates on commercial and luxury properties (Argentina, Brazil).

Administrative systems vary dramatically. Countries such as Costa Rica and Uruguay have centralized property valuation, ensuring consistent assessments. Conversely, many LAC nations, including Mexico and Peru and Central American countries, rely on self-reported values, often leading to underassessment.

Administrative Challenges of WTs: Chasing the Elusive Liquid Asset

Although WTs may seem attractive, their administrative feasibility can be challenging, depending on the type of wealth. This is particularly the case in environments with weak enforcement, such as those prevalent in EMDEs, including those in LAC. The Achilles' heel of policies to tax highly liquid assets (such as stocks, bonds, and cash) is the ease with which wealthy individuals can transfer these assets across borders. Tax havens, offering minimal or no WTs, secrecy, and lax regulations, further exacerbate this issue. The ability to relocate liquid wealth poses a substantial risk of tax evasion and avoidance (Atkinson, Piketty, and Saez 2011). These tax havens, which complicate wealth tracking, also undermine the overall effectiveness of the tax system.

Plugging the Wealth Loophole: Can the World Act Together?

Governments worldwide face challenges in taxing financial assets because of opacity and cross-border mobility. International cooperation is crucial. Advanced economies are leading the way with innovative strategies. This dictates a need for a coordinated international approach. Several strategies are emerging to this end, particularly in advanced economies:

- *Information-sharing agreements.* Governments are increasingly collaborating to exchange data on taxpayers' foreign assets. These agreements enable tax authorities to access information on individuals' holdings in other countries, making it more difficult to conceal offshore wealth. This coordinated effort, led by organizations such as the Organisation for Economic Co-operation and Development (OECD), aims to create a global framework to prevent the exploitation of tax loopholes by wealthy individuals.

- *Closing loopholes in tax havens.* The international community is actively working to curtail the advantages offered by tax havens. These jurisdictions often provide secrecy and minimal regulations, hindering wealth tracking. Initiatives such as the OECD's Base Erosion and Profit Shifting project are establishing minimum tax standards, reducing the appeal of shifting profits and assets to these havens (OECD 2023). Indeed, the fear of being caught and punished appears to be an effective deterrent. For instance, the increased scrutiny from Colombian authorities after the Panama Papers leak significantly discouraged tax evasion (Londoño-Vélez and Ávila-Mahecha 2021). This heightened scrutiny led to a remarkable 15-fold increase in voluntary disclosures of foreign assets by Colombian taxpayers.

- *Disincentivizing asset flight.* Some countries are implementing measures to deter the movement of liquid assets, including levying exit taxes on high-value assets. These taxes are imposed on certain valuable assets, such as stocks, when transferred offshore beyond a specific threshold. This discourages individuals from relocating wealth to avoid taxes (Brondolo 2011). The practice of presumptive taxation assumes a minimum level of income from foreign assets, even without reported income. This incentivizes taxpayers to keep their assets within the country's tax jurisdiction to avoid the presumptive tax burden (Brondolo 2011). By using exit taxes and presumptive taxation, countries can discourage the offshore movement of liquid wealth.

In a world in which tax authorities can seamlessly access a comprehensive overview of a taxpayer's global assets, tax havens are neutralized. Although advances have been made in developing the infrastructure and capacity for such a system, advanced economies still face challenges, and EMDEs, including those in LAC, even more so. Establishing the necessary systems is complex, resource intensive, and fraught with bureaucratic obstacles. Developing technical infrastructure, training personnel, and ensuring robust data security are demanding tasks, compounded by often pervasive corruption. Furthermore, achieving the necessary consensus among all countries can be arduous, and even a very small number of noncompliant countries provide havens for tax evaders and undermine the effort. For these reasons, even advanced economies with robust tax systems are recognizing the difficulties of taxing highly liquid assets. Box 6.1 shows the paradigmatic and recent case of France, which in 2017, under President Emmanuel Macron, replaced the long-standing broad-based WT, the *Impôt de Solidarité sur la Fortune,* with the *Impôt sur la Fortune Immobilière,* a tax specifically targeting real estate holdings.

The great French wealth tax shuffle

Origins and history of the wealth tax

The French wealth tax (WT) has a complex history, marked by periods of implementation and abolition. Introduced in 1981 by the Socialist Party under President François Mitterrand as the *Impôt sur les Grandes Fortunes,* it was aimed at redistributing wealth and reducing inequality. However, the tax was abolished in 1986 by the right-wing government of Jacques Chirac.

box continued next page

Box 6.1

The great French wealth tax shuffle *(continued)*

Reinstated in 1988 as the *Impôt de Solidarité sur la Fortune* (ISF) after Mitterrand's reelection, the tax underwent several modifications over the years. It imposed a levy on individuals with assets exceeding a certain threshold, with the proceeds intended to fund social programs. Despite its reintroduction, the ISF remained a controversial policy, with critics arguing that it discouraged investment, prompted wealthy individuals to leave the country, and generated limited revenue.

The shift to the wealth tax on real estate

In September 2017, the French government, led by President Emmanuel Macron, abolished the ISF and replaced it with the *Impôt sur la Fortune Immobilière* (IFI), a WT specifically targeting real estate holdings. This significant policy change was driven by several factors:

- *Economic concerns.* Critics of the ISF argued that it hindered economic growth by discouraging investment and prompting wealthy individuals to relocate their assets or residences (Cheysson-Kaplan 2024a, 2024b).

- *Equity considerations.* The IFI was seen as fairer because it focused on a tangible asset that is less easily hidden or transferred in comparison with other forms of wealth.

- *Political considerations.* The shift to the IFI aligned with Macron's pro-business agenda and his desire to curb asset flight and attract investment to France.

This policy change seems to have had led to some shifts in the French economy. A recent paper has found that five years after the reform, the IFI appears to have incentivized individuals to at least modestly reallocate their assets away from real estate toward financial assets (Le Guern Herry 2024).

The challenge of achieving global consensus on these initiatives is exacerbated by the fact that not all countries benefit equally from them. Countries that stand to lose the most revenue or investment from increased international cooperation may be less inclined to participate fully, especially if the additional revenue generated globally is not shared. Moreover, as more countries agree to participate in these initiatives, the incentives for some countries to deviate and not agree may increase. These factors pose a significant challenge to the implementation of such policies.

Targeting the Tangible: Real Estate as a Potential Anchor for WTs in LAC

Unlike stocks, bonds, and cash, which can be easily transferred across borders, real estate is an immobile physical asset with a fixed location and hence offers a potentially more promising target for WTs. Moreover, taxing less productive wealth, such as unused land, instead of capital accumulation, shifts incentives toward projects with higher returns. As with income taxes, systems can be designed to ensure progressivity by targeting high-value properties or providing exemptions or credits for low-income homeowners.

Furthermore, property is by far the greatest type of wealth in LAC, as documented by survey-based microdata from the OECD, as well as from local sources for Chile, Colombia, Mexico, and Uruguay (refer to figure 6.2). Thus, property is a logical target for revenue. Relative to financial and other assets (such as cars), owner-occupied and secondary housing are dominant in LAC (86 percent) compared with Eastern Europe (75 percent); Greece, Italy, Portugal, and Spain (73 percent); and other advanced economies (62 percent; refer to figure 6.2, panel a). Within individual countries in LAC, the importance of real estate in total wealth is even higher than the regional average: 90.5 percent in Mexico, 85.7 percent in Colombia, 85.2 percent in Chile, and 83.2 percent in Uruguay. It represents a considerably lower share in some major advanced economies, including Canada (56.4 percent), the United Kingdom (54.6 percent), and the United States (38.6 percent; refer to figure 6.2, panel b).

The case is even stronger for the top 10 percent of income earners in LAC (refer to figure 6.3), where real estate accounts for 81 percent of household wealth, compared with 55 percent in Greece, Italy, Portugal, and Spain, and 47 percent in other advanced economies (refer to figure 6.3, panel a). Although the importance of real estate in total wealth of households is 88.1 percent in Uruguay, 79.3 percent in Colombia, 78.8 percent in Chile, and 76.7 percent in Mexico, it is 46.3 percent in Canada and 24.3 percent in the United States (refer to figure 6.3, panel b).

Figure 6.2 Composition of gross household wealth in LAC, Eastern Europe, GIPS, and the rest of the OECD countries

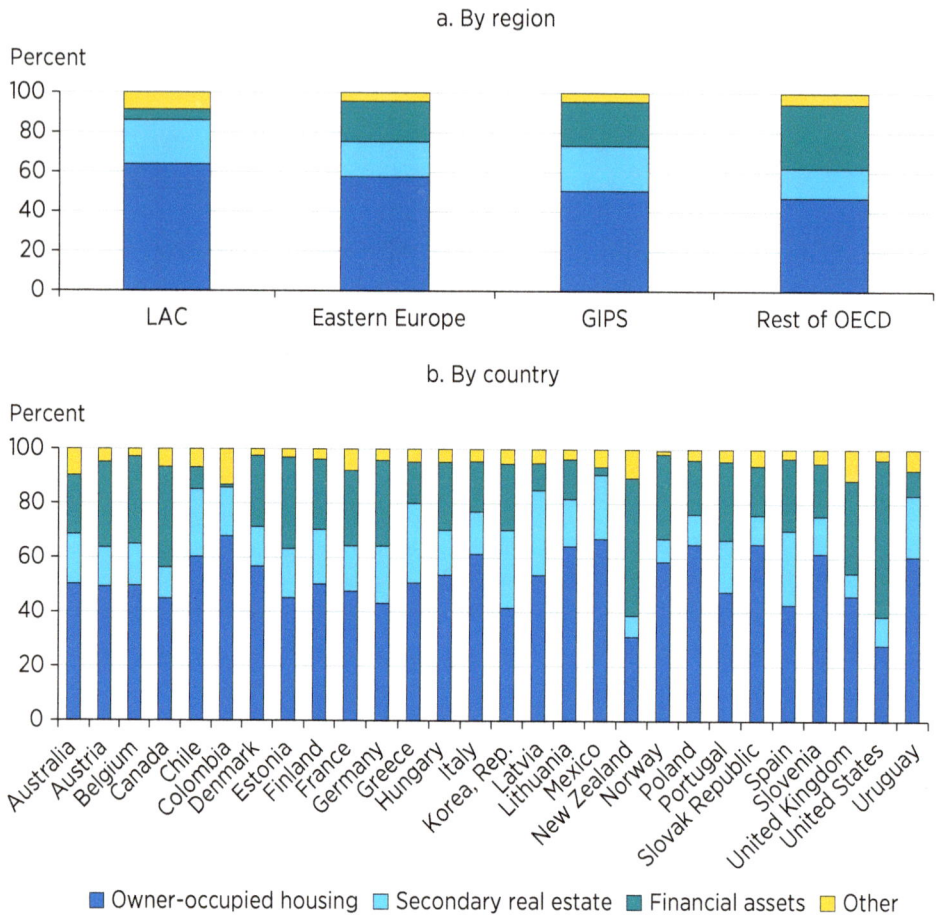

a. By region

b. By country

■ Owner-occupied housing ■ Secondary real estate ■ Financial assets □ Other

Source: Original calculations for this publication using OECD and survey-based microdata for Chile, Colombia, Mexico, and Uruguay. National data sources include the Survey of Financial Security, 2019 (Canada, Statistics Canada); Encuesta Financiera de Hogares, 2017 (Chile, Banco Central de Chile); Encuesta de Carga Financiera y Educación, 2017 (Colombia, Departamento Administrativo Nacional de Estadística); Encuesta Financiera de las Familias, 2017 (Spain, Banco de España); Encuesta Nacional sobre las Finanzas de los Hogares, 2019 (México, Instituto Nacional de Estadística y Geografía); Módulo Financiero de los Hogares Uruguayos, 2017 (Uruguay, Universidad de la República); Wealth and Assets Survey, 2016–18 (United Kingdom, Office for National Statistics); and Survey of Consumer Finances, 2019 (United States, Federal Reserve System).

Note: All countries in the data set belong to the OECD, except for Uruguay (in LAC). The regional groups are composed as follows: LAC (Chile, Colombia, Mexico, Uruguay), Eastern Europe (Estonia, Hungary, Latvia, Lithuania, Poland, Slovak Republic); GIPS (Greece, Italy, Portugal, Spain); rest of OECD (Australia, Austria, Belgium, Canada, Denmark, Finland, France, Germany, Republic of Korea, New Zealand, Norway, Slovenia, United Kingdom, United States). GIPS = Greece, Italy, Portugal, Spain; LAC = Latin American and the Caribbean; OECD = Organisation for Economic Co-operation and Development.

Figure 6.3   Composition of gross household wealth for the top 10 percent of income earners in LAC

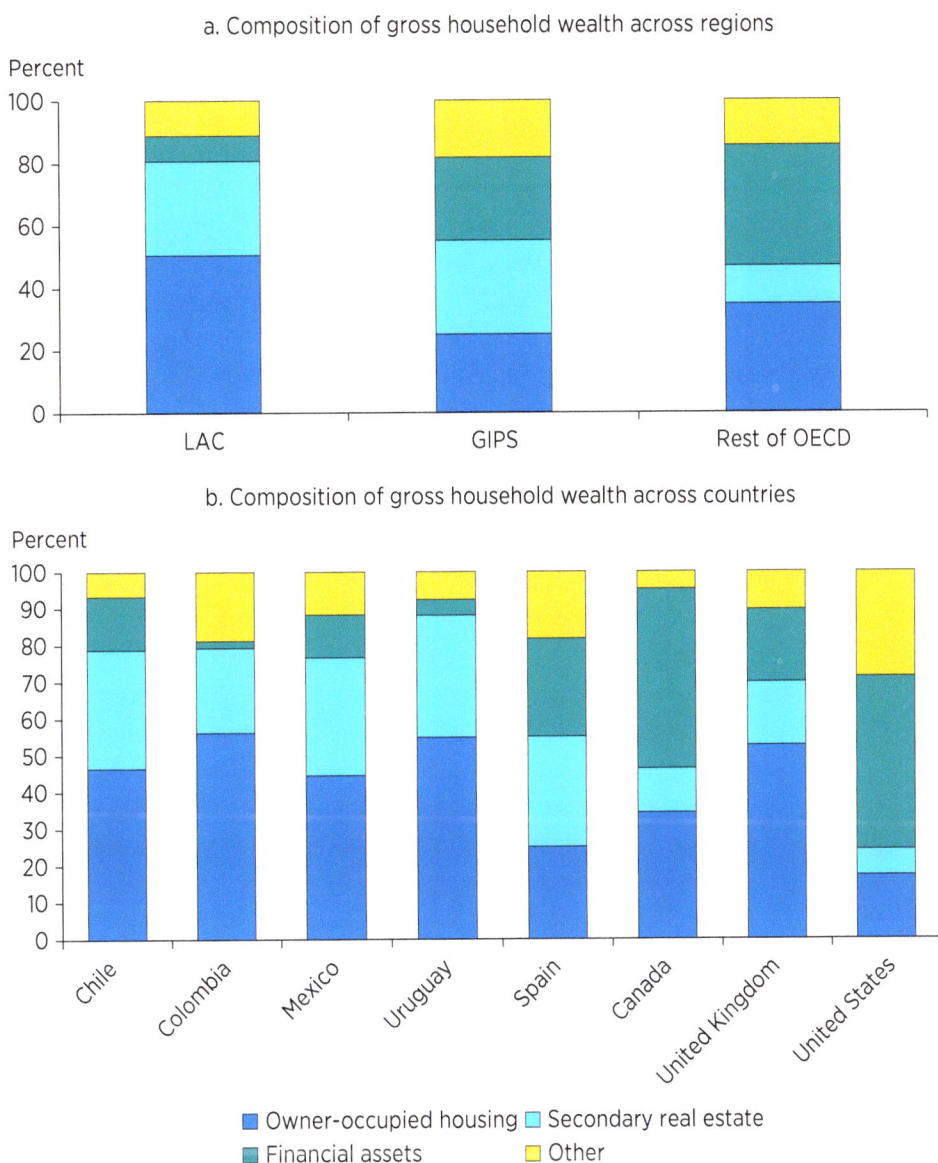

a. Composition of gross household wealth across regions

b. Composition of gross household wealth across countries

Owner-occupied housing ■ Secondary real estate
Financial assets   ■ Other

Source: Original calculations for this publication using OECD and survey-based microdata.

Note: All countries in the dataset belong to the OECD, except for Uruguay (in LAC). The groups are composed as follows. LAC (Colombia, Chile, Mexico, Uruguay); GIPS (Spain); rest of OECD (Canada, United Kingdom, United States). GIPS = Greece, Italy, Portugal, Spain; LAC = Latin America and the Caribbean; OECD = Organisation for Economic Co-operation and Development.

Figure 6.4 sheds further light on wealth distribution across income percentiles in LAC countries compared with the United States. A closer look at the data reveals several significant patterns:

- *The enduring importance of real estate in LAC.* First, real estate remains a significant wealth holding across income levels in LAC, even more than in the United States or other advanced economies (refer to figure 6.4, panels a and b). Although the importance of real estate in total wealth declines between the first and last income percentile by 20.4 percent in Chile (from 93.4 percent to 74.3 percent), by 18.4 percent in Mexico (from 97.4 percent to 79.5 percent), by 9.7 percent in Colombia (from 94.8 percent to 85.5 percent), and by 9.1 percent in Uruguay (from 96.8 percent to 88 percent), it falls considerably more in the United States, by 65.1 percent (from 60.9 percent to 21.2 percent). This finding suggests that real estate taxation could be an effective tool for taxing wealth in LAC countries.

- *The rise of secondary housing.* The rise of secondary housing is a notable trend across all studied countries, with its importance increasing as income rises (refer to figure 6.4, panel c). This suggests a growing emphasis on investment properties or vacation homes among wealthier individuals. Moreover, many of these secondary properties are located in different areas than the primary residence. This geographic separation, as in the case of vacation homes or weekend getaways, could offer additional benefits from a taxation point of view. In some cases, it could simplify taxation because the properties are situated in regions with different tax constituencies than the primary residence. For instance, a highly valued vacation home located in a wealthy neighborhood, owned by a wealthy nonresident and subject to low property taxes, could create opportunities to increase property taxes on such properties, thereby capturing more revenue from wealthy nonresidents. This potential revenue increase could alleviate the tax burden on local homeowners, who would likely be the primary voters on any such tax increase.

- *The lag in financial assets in LAC, even at the top of the income distribution.* The picture of financial assets differs between LAC and, for example, the United States. In LAC, the importance of financial assets such as stocks and bonds increases modestly only for the very top earners (refer to figure 6.4, panel d). For example, the proportion of financial assets in total wealth for the top 5 percent of income earners reaches 14.3 percent in Chile, 11.6 percent in Mexico, 4.8 percent in Uruguay, and 2.3 percent in Colombia. In contrast, in the United States, the presence of financial assets is strong across all income levels, including middle-income households. For example, the share of financial assets in total wealth for median income earners in the United States reaches 32.9 percent, far surpassing that of the top 5 percent of earners in LAC.

Figure 6.4   Composition of gross household wealth in LAC countries, Spain, Canada, and the United States by income percentile

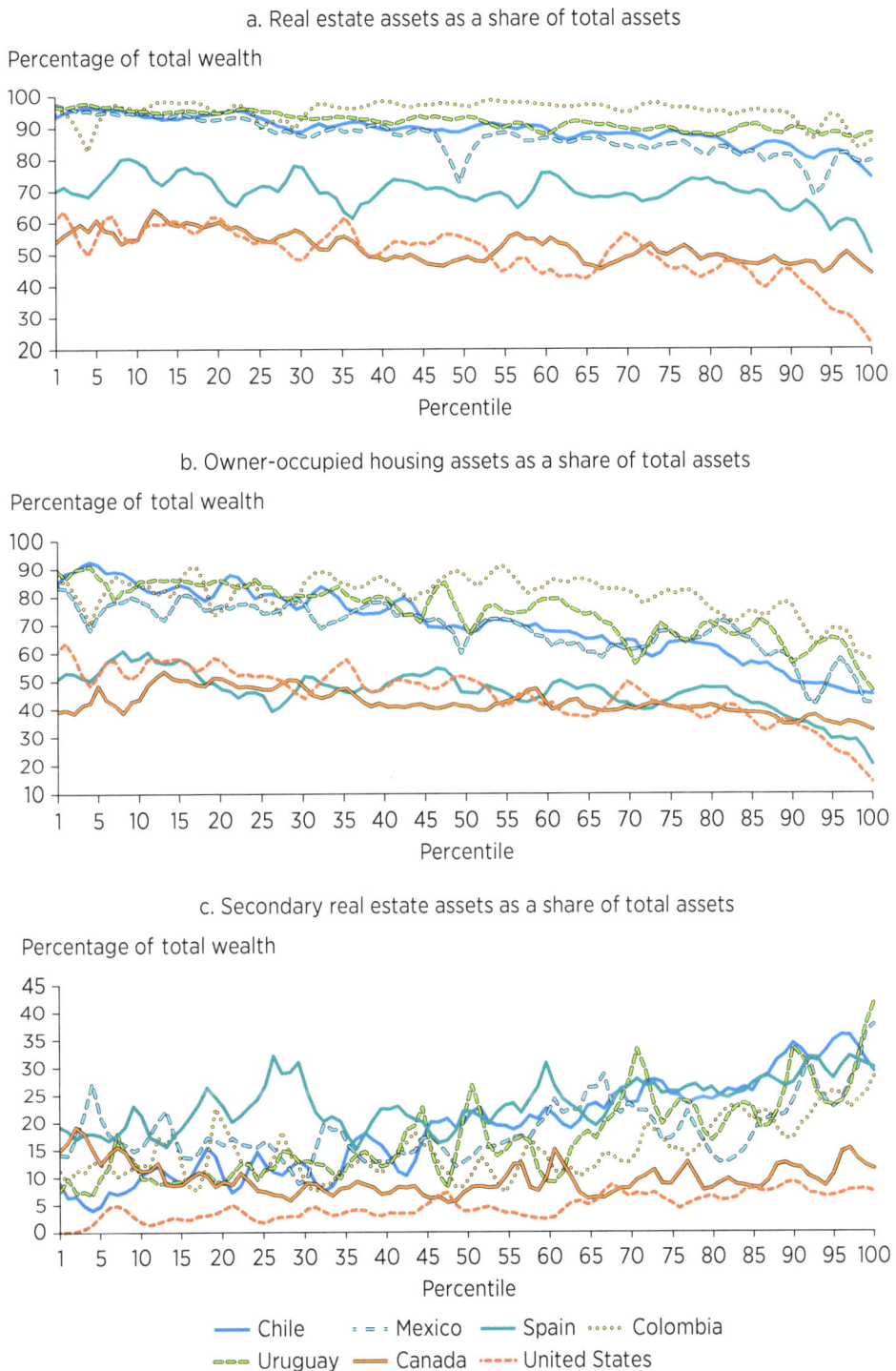

a. Real estate assets as a share of total assets

Percentage of total wealth

b. Owner-occupied housing assets as a share of total assets

Percentage of total wealth

c. Secondary real estate assets as a share of total assets

Percentage of total wealth

Chile   Mexico   Spain   Colombia
Uruguay   Canada   United States

figure continued next page

Figure 6.4   Composition of gross household wealth in LAC countries, Spain, Canada, and the United States by income percentile *(continued)*

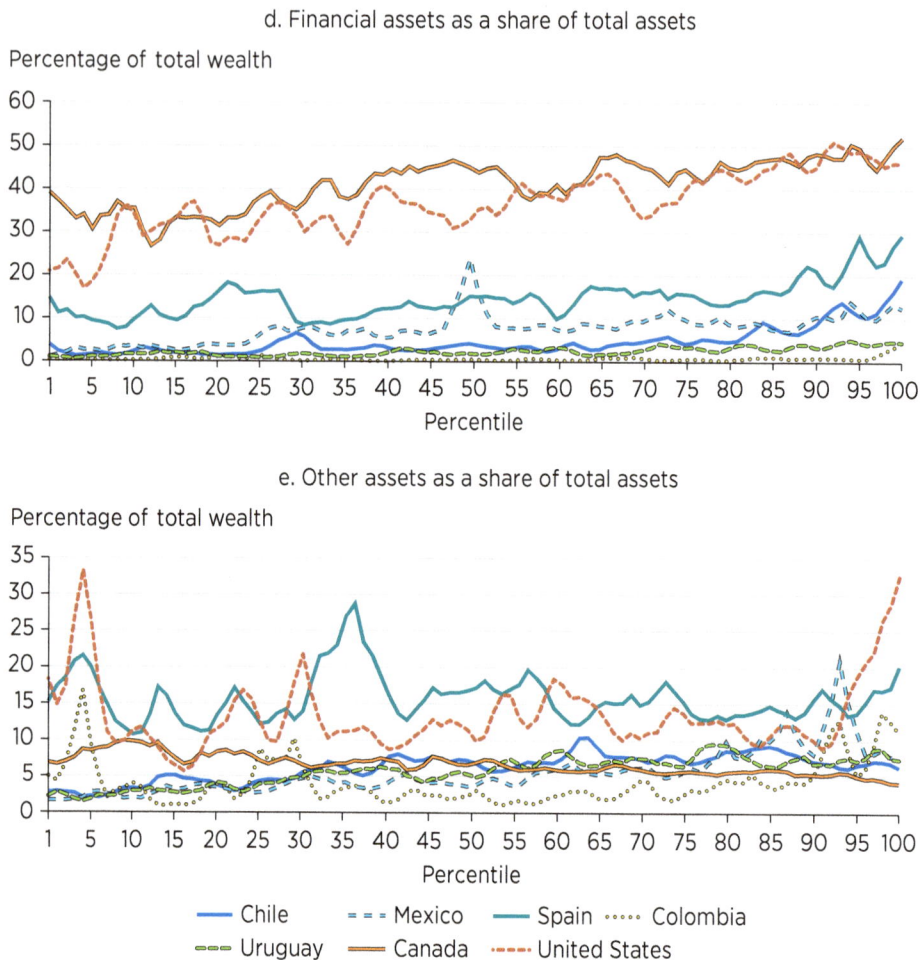

d. Financial assets as a share of total assets

Percentage of total wealth

e. Other assets as a share of total assets

Percentage of total wealth

| — Chile | = = Mexico | — Spain | ····· Colombia |
| === Uruguay | — Canada | -···- United States | |

Source: Original calculations for this publication using survey-based microdata.

Note: The share of each percentile is built from actual data smoothed by a weighted average that combines the evaluated data point and the four closest percentiles. The weights were based on a Gaussian kernel with bandwidth 0.6. LAC = Latin America and the Caribbean.

The cross-country evidence highlights a strong relationship between wealth composition and economic development. For middle-income countries, real estate remains the dominant asset class, accounting for about 80–90 percent of total wealth (refer to figure 6.5, panel a). However, this importance diminishes in countries with higher income per capita. Conversely, the share of financial assets tends to increase with the level of economic development (refer to figure 6.5, panel b). Assets other than real estate and financial assets (such as cars) appear to be negatively related to income levels, yet not as markedly (refer to figure 6.5, panel c). This suggests that as countries develop, their wealth composition shifts from being concentrated in real estate to a more diversified portfolio that includes a greater share of financial assets.

Figure 6.5   Total wealth versus economic development, LAC and OECD countries

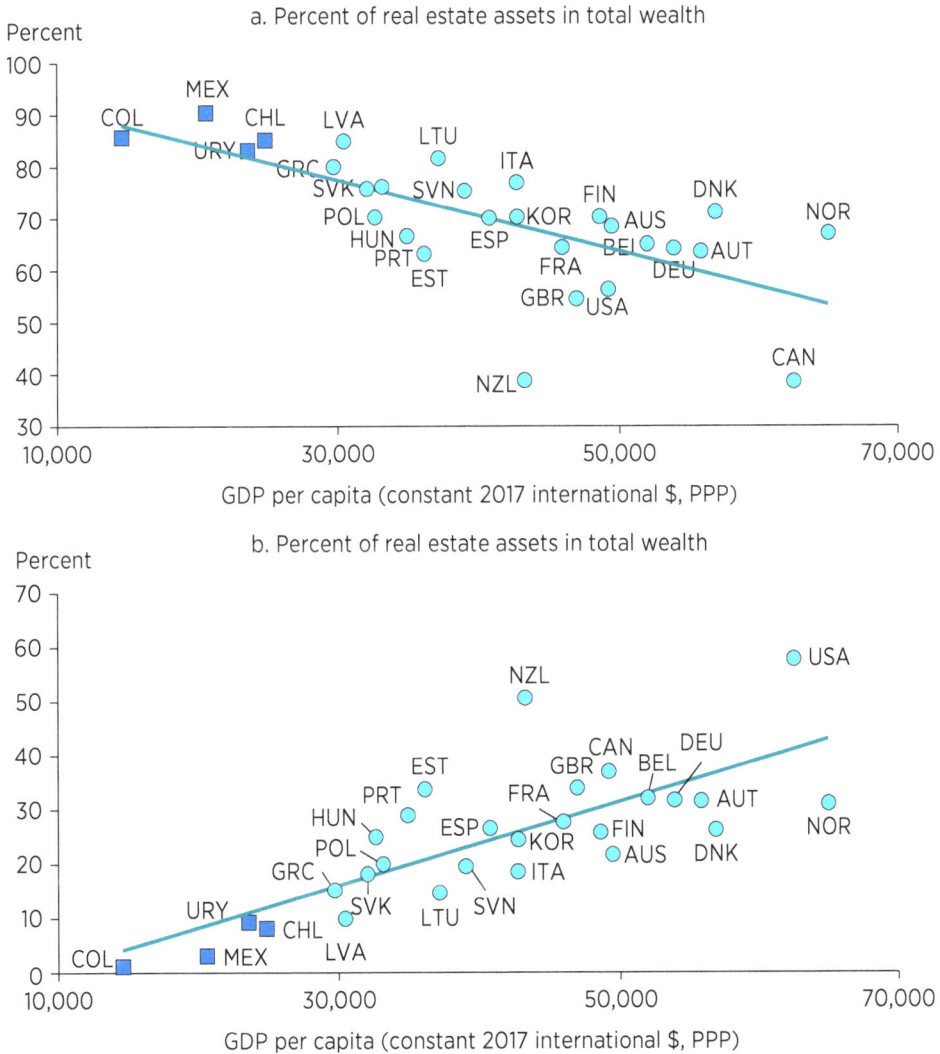

a. Percent of real estate assets in total wealth

b. Percent of real estate assets in total wealth

figure continued next page

Figure 6.5   Total wealth versus economic development, LAC and OECD countries *(continued)*

c. Percent of other assets in total wealth

Percent

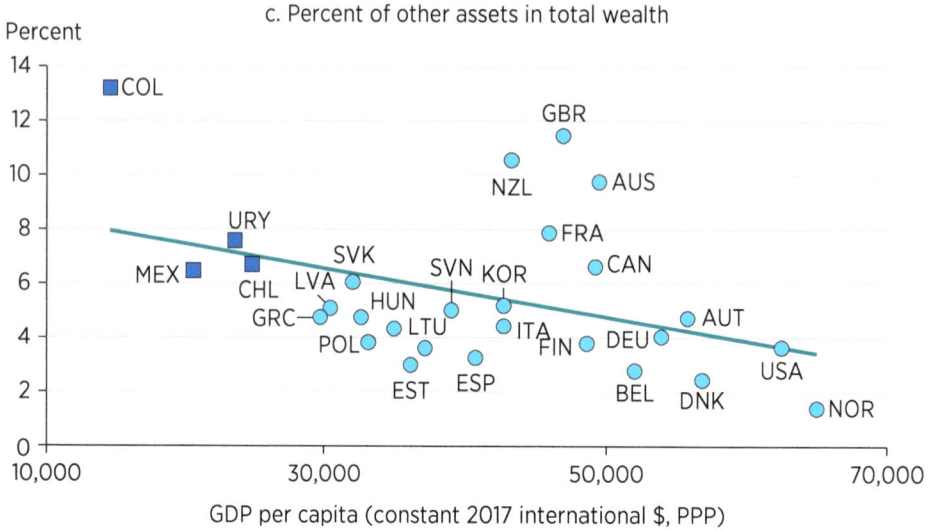

GDP per capita (constant 2017 international $, PPP)

Source: Original calculations for this publication using OECD 2022 and survey-based microdata.

Note: Data labels use International Organization for Standardization country codes. For a list of country codes, go to https://www.iso.org/obp/ui/#search. Countries in Latin America and the Caribbean are shown as squares. GDP = gross domestic product; LAC = Latin America and the Caribbean; OECD = Organisation for Economic Co-operation and Development; PPP = purchasing power parity.

In light of the evidence, it is clear that wealth concentration in real estate is a prominent feature in LAC, persisting even among high-income earners. This suggests a strong reliance on real estate as a wealth-building tool across income levels in the region. However, the dynamics shift as countries develop economically. As development progresses, the significance of real estate in overall wealth composition tends to decline dramatically, particularly for the very top earners. Wealth holdings diversify toward other asset classes, such as financial instruments, as economies mature.

Why Does Real Estate Reign Supreme as a Form of Wealth in LAC?

The prominence of real estate in LAC portfolios arises from several factors:

- *Restricted variety of investment vehicles.* Developing countries, including many in LAC, often have nascent or immature financial markets with limited options for investment. In such an environment, real estate emerges as the primary, and sometimes the only, viable option for those seeking to build wealth or invest their savings. For example, in Colombia and Mexico, where stock and bond markets are relatively underdeveloped, real estate has historically been a dominant asset class (Cavallo and Serebrisky 2016).

- *Tangibility and security.* Real estate offers a unique sense of tangibility and security, as well as serving as an inflation hedge, particularly in countries with a recent past history of economic crises. Investors may view land and buildings as a safer way to store value compared with the perceived risks associated with stock market fluctuations, currency devaluation, or even confiscation. A study by the Inter-American Development Bank found that real estate acts as a hedge against inflation in LAC (Bouillon 2012), especially in countries such as Argentina and Brazil, which have experienced periods of high inflation and economic instability.

- *Low levels of financial literacy.* Societies in advanced economies often have higher levels of financial literacy, leading to more diversified investment approaches. In LAC, limited knowledge about liquid assets can concentrate wealth into real estate (Klapper, Lusardi, and van Oudheusden 2015).

- *Cultural preference for land ownership.* In many countries, there is a strong cultural preference for land ownership, driven by factors such as social status and inheritance. This can influence investment decisions, leading individuals to prioritize real estate ownership even if alternative options might offer higher returns. For example, in countries such as Colombia and Mexico, where social hierarchies have historically been tied to land ownership, acquiring property can be a way to elevate one's social standing.

The Property Tax Paradox in LAC

This unusual concentration of wealth in real estate, combined with the low share of tax collection from this source, constitutes an LAC property tax paradox (refer to figure 6.6, panels a and b). Although 80 percent of wealth, on average, is held as real estate, LAC collects about 2 percent of tax revenues from real estate taxes, and many countries in the region collect almost none (refer to figure 6.6, panel c). The Bahamas, Barbados, Chile, Colombia, and Uruguay lead, collecting about 5 percent of their tax revenues from this source. Conversely, Argentina, Ecuador, Mexico, and Paraguay collect about 2 percent, and Bolivia, Cuba, El Salvador, and Trinidad and Tobago collect almost none.

Figure 6.6 Property tax collection across regions and by LAC country

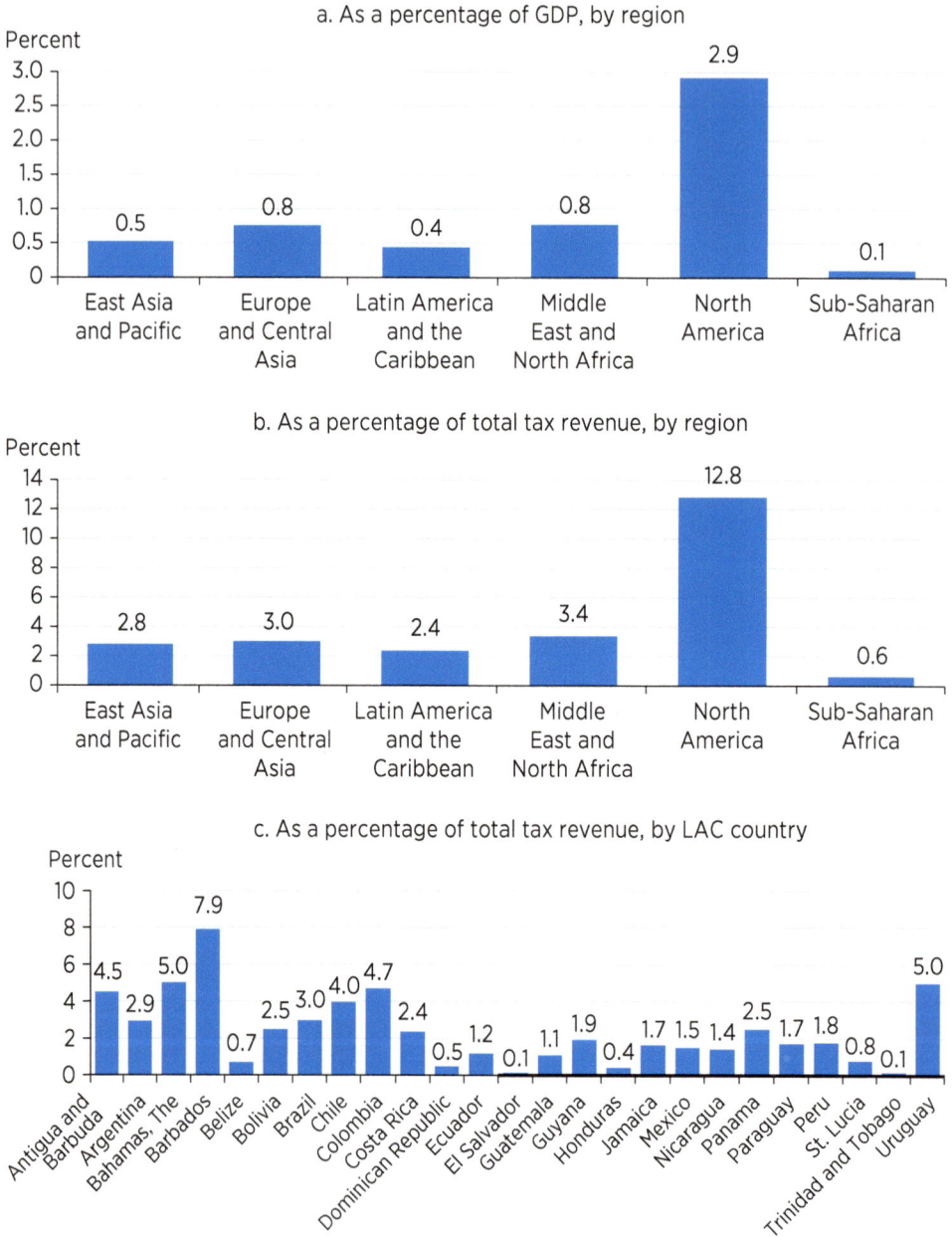

a. As a percentage of GDP, by region

b. As a percentage of total tax revenue, by region

c. As a percentage of total tax revenue, by LAC country

Source: Original calculations for this publication using Organisation for Economic Co-operation and Development Global Revenue Statistics Database (https://www.oecd.org/en/data/datasets/global-revenue-statistics-database.html) and World Bank data.

Note: Social security revenues are excluded from total tax revenues. Consolidated government statistics. GDP-weighted regional averages. GDP = gross domestic product; LAC = Latin America and the Caribbean.

Indeed, LAC's adjusted real estate revenue—the difference between the predicted value as a share of GDP given real estate wealth and actual collections—illustrates the paradox: LAC countries (except for Uruguay) tend to collect too little—about 30 percent less than what would be expected on the basis of the relevance of wealth (refer to figure 6.7, panels a and b). The adjusted revenue tends to increase with the level of development, but LAC is largely below trend (panel c).

Figure 6.7   Estimates of over- and undertaxation in real estate, by region and country

a. Adjusted real estate tax revenue, by region

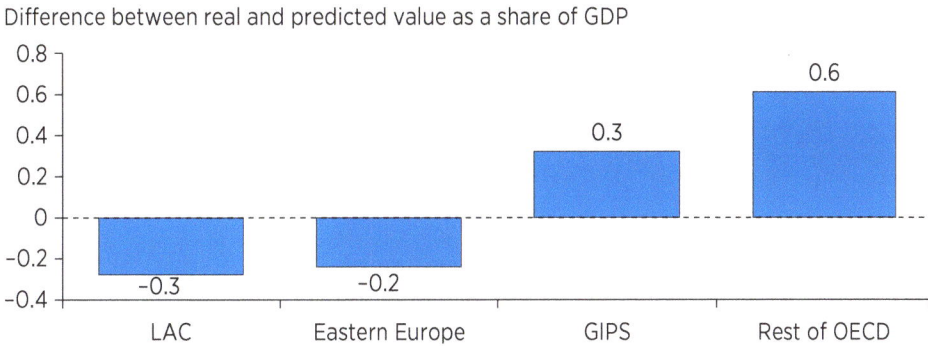

b. Adjusted real estate tax revenue, by country

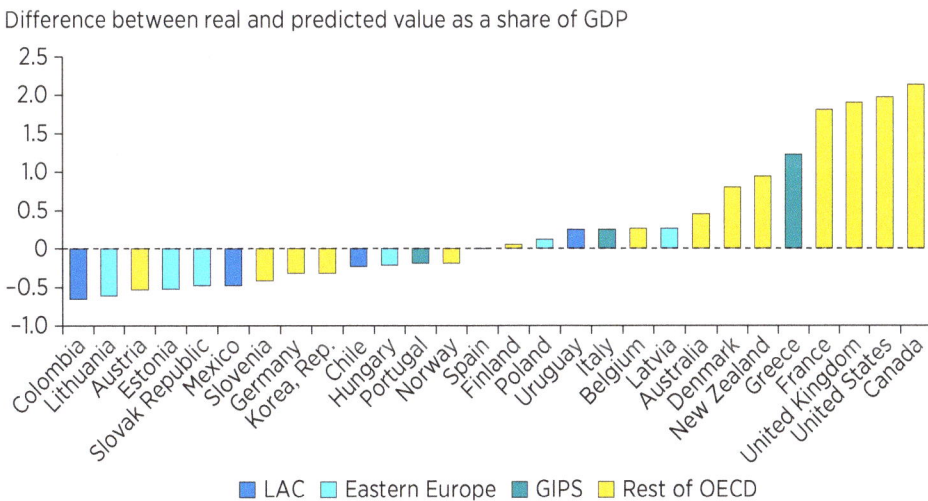

figure continued next page

Figure 6.7   Estimates of over- and undertaxation in real estate, by region and country *(continued)*

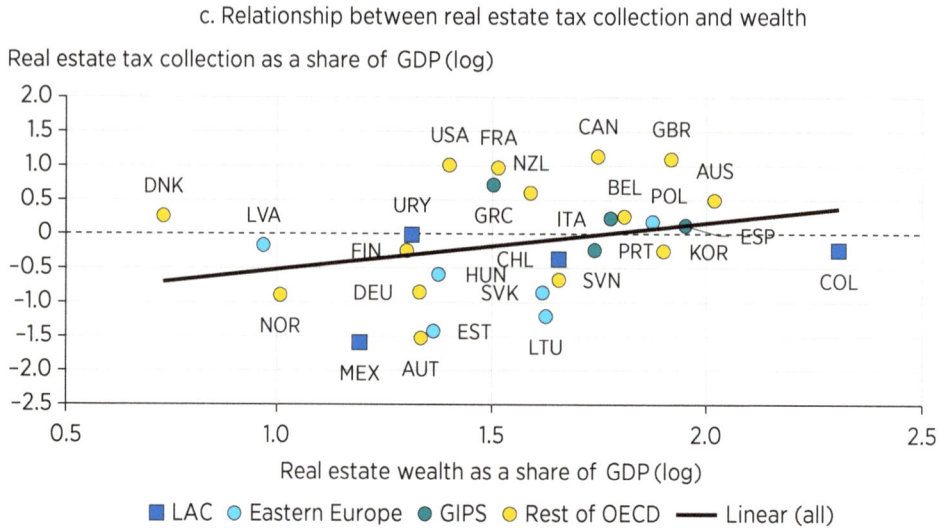

c. Relationship between real estate tax collection and wealth

Real estate tax collection as a share of GDP (log)

Real estate wealth as a share of GDP (log)

■ LAC   ○ Eastern Europe   ● GIPS   ○ Rest of OECD   ── Linear (all)

Source: Original calculations for this publication using OECD 2022 and survey-based microdata.

Note: Adjusted real estate revenue refers to the difference between the predicted value as a share of GDP given real estate wealth and actual collections. Data labels use International Organization for Standardization (ISO) country codes. For a list of country codes, go to https://www.iso.org/obp/ui/#search. Countries in Latin America and the Caribbean are shown as squares. GDP = gross domestic product; GIPS = Greece, Italy, Portugal, Spain; LAC = Latin America and the Caribbean; OECD = Organisation for Economic Co-operation and Development.

A modern analysis, using simulations for 2014, supports the significant potential for growth in property tax revenue collection in LAC (Ahmad, Brosio, and Jiménez 2019). This potential is based on reasonable assumptions about the tax base (value of immovable property) and tax effort (tax rates, exemptions, and administration). Figure 6.8 presents the study's findings in terms of actual revenue collection for 2014 as well as potential revenue collection, expressed in terms of GDP. Although on average the actual property revenue reaches about 0.3 percent of GDP, its potential is estimated to be about 3 percent. Given that the average share of consolidated government expenditure in LAC is about 34 percent of GDP,[3] and about 40 percent of this corresponds to subnational governments, this means additional financing could represent about 8 percent of consolidated expenditure and about 20 percent of subnational expenditure.

Figure 6.8   Actual and potential revenues from property taxes in LAC: Simulations for 2014 as a percentage of GDP

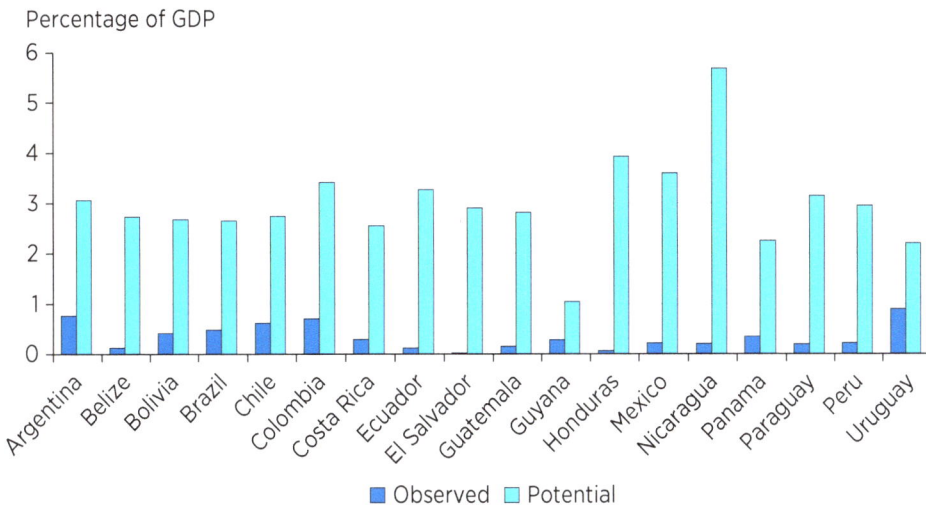

Source: Ahmad, Brosio, and Jiménez 2019.

Note: GDP = gross domestic product; LAC = Latin America and the Caribbean.

If LAC countries were to fully realize this kind of potential, the impact on their ability to finance public services, reduce poverty, and support a pro-growth tax reform agenda could be substantial. Additional revenues could be used to fund education, health care, infrastructure, and other essential services. Furthermore, these increased revenues could help reduce corporate taxes, excessively high personal income marginal rates, and other distortive types of taxation. Such a reduction would promote economic growth by encouraging investment and enhancing productivity.

Anatomy of the Real Estate Tax in LAC: A Patchwork of Systems with a Serious Valuation Problem

The roots of the paradox do not seem to originate in the tax rates themselves. As figure 6.9 shows, in the United States, a country with high real estate taxes, tax rates on residential properties range from 0.32 percent in Hawaii to 2.23 percent in New Jersey, and they average 1.04 percent for all 50 states and the District of Columbia. In LAC, these rates range between 0.20 percent in República Bolivariana de Venezuela to 2.28 percent in Uruguay, averaging 0.91 percent in the entire region (all LAC countries), 1.43 percent in the Southern Cone, and 0.85 percent in Central America and the Caribbean.

Figure 6.9   Average residential property tax rates across LAC countries and the United States

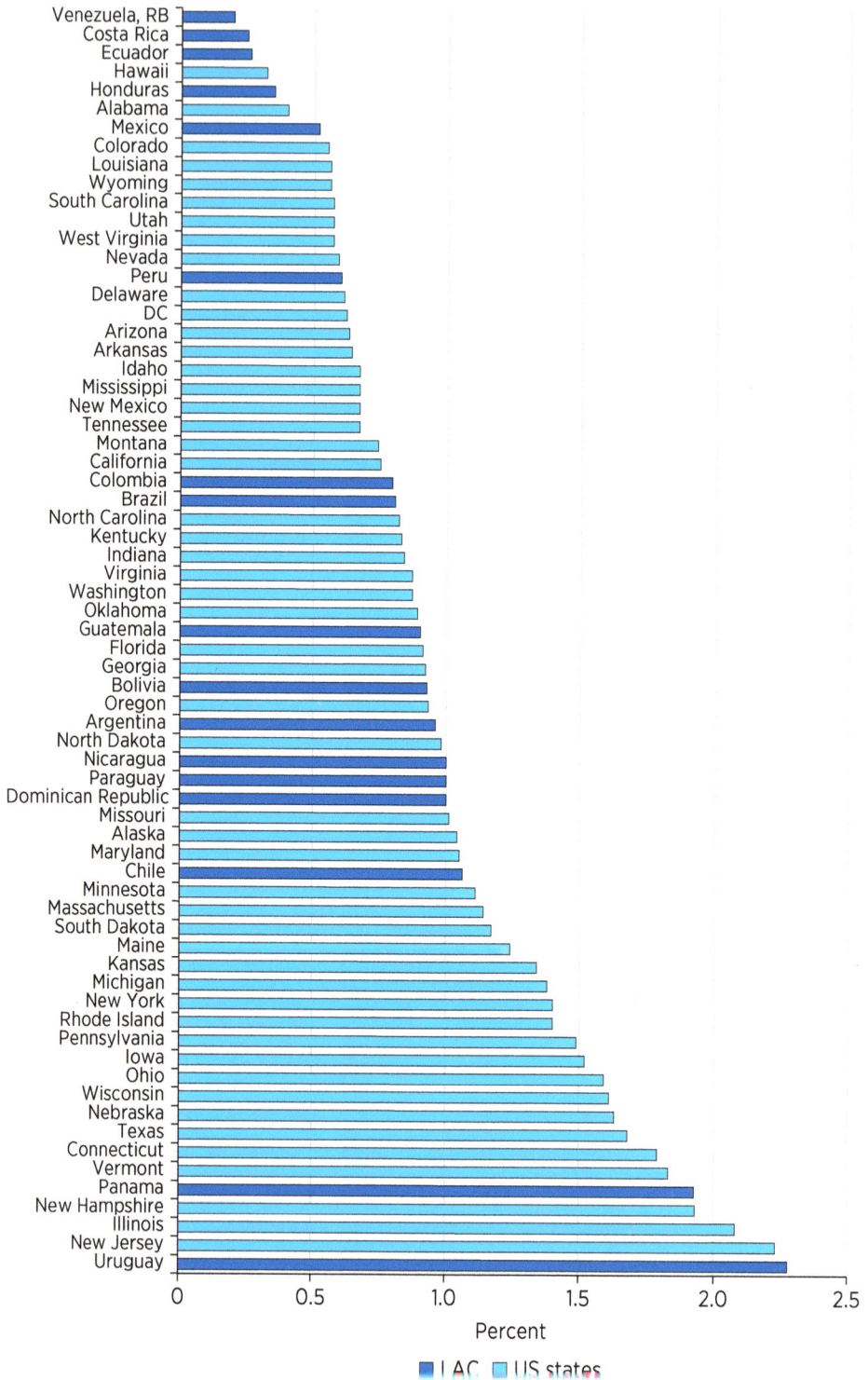

Source: Original calculations for this publication based on Lincoln Institute (https://www
.lincolninst.edu/data/property-tax-in-latin-america/) and Grace and Yale 2024.

Note: DC = District of Columbia; LAC = Latin America and the Caribbean.

The problem lies, rather, in low and poorly calculated property valuation (Bahl and Martinez-Vazquez 2008; Norregaard 2015). Outdated cadastral systems (land ownership records) often struggle to keep pace with rapid urbanization and the emergence of informal settlements. This lack of accurate data makes it difficult to determine the true value of properties, leading to undervaluation and lower tax bills for landowners. Moreover, lower-priced properties are assessed at a higher proportion of their market value than higher-priced ones, increasing the regressivity in practice.

For example, figure 6.10 shows that fiscal valuation in the city of Buenos Aires, Argentina, is, on average, only 18 percent of market value. This means that for a property with a market value of US$100,000, the fiscal valuation used to calculate property taxes might be only about US$18,000.

Similar, although less dramatic, discrepancies exist in other LAC countries. Data from the Lincoln Institute suggest that property valuations in Chile were at 55 percent of market value in 2013, and in Colombia they ranged from 45 percent to 60 percent in different localities in 2011. In contrast, Uruguayan property valuations were closer to 80 percent in Montevideo, potentially explaining the higher adjusted value there. In the United States, fiscal property valuations typically range between 80 percent and 90 percent of market value.

Reliance on Presumptive Taxes

Attempting to more solidly ground property valuations, many LAC countries have turned to presumptive taxes as a tool to generate revenue from the real estate sector. Presumptive taxes are a type of indirect tax levied to estimate property value on the basis of proxies such as size, location, and property type. In the context of real estate taxation, these assumptions might be based on factors such as the following:

- *Property size.* Although property size (that is, square footage) is a common approach for presumptive real estate taxes, it raises concerns. Larger properties are generally assumed to be more valuable, but this can be inaccurate and inequitable. A small, luxurious condo packed with amenities might be worth more than a sprawling, outdated house. Similarly, warehouses with vast square footage used for storage might be taxed heavily despite generating lower rental income compared with a smaller, well-located office space.

- *Location.* Properties in prime locations are presumed to be more valuable than those in less desirable areas. Location is another factor used in presumptive taxes, but it has its own conceptual issues. Defining *prime location* can be subjective. Up-and-coming areas or those with unique

Figure 6.10   Fiscal valuation estimate, as a percentage of market value, in Buenos Aires, by neighborhood, 2018–21

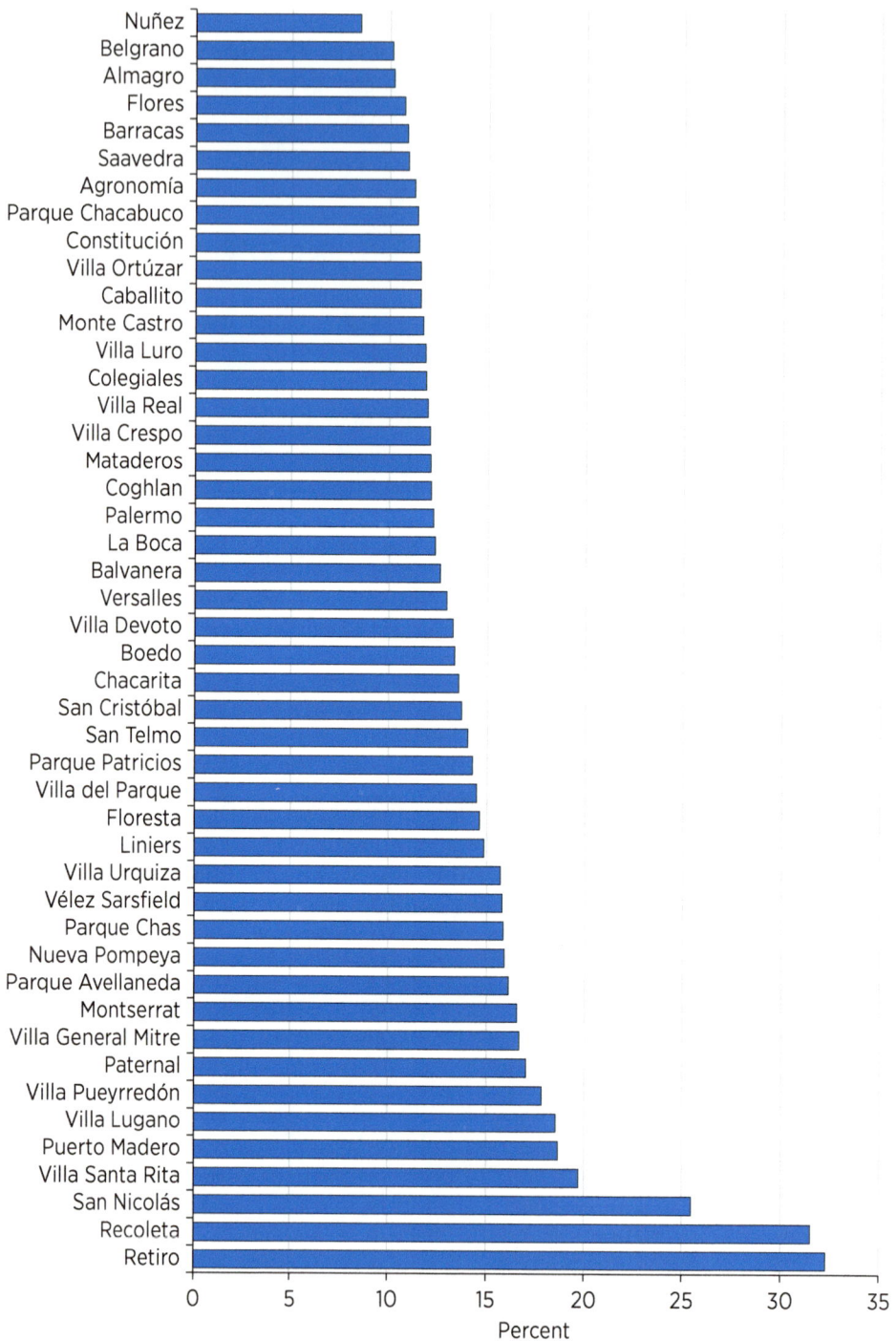

Source: Castano et al. 2024.

Note: The fiscal valuation of the properties was imputed on the basis of the tax code and tax law of the autonomous city of Buenos Aires. Information from Properati publications was used. In the case of missing information in the publications, estimates were built at the neighborhood level with data from the cadastral system of the city of Buenos Aires.

features might be undervalued. Furthermore, what is considered desirable can change over time. A formerly neglected area might become trendy, rendering the initial location-based tax unfair.

- *Type of property.* Presumptive real estate taxes often differentiate between residential and commercial properties, but this simplicity masks complexity. Income generation and societal impact vary widely within both categories. A small, thriving store earns more than a vast warehouse, and residential housing serves a different purpose than commercial spaces that create jobs.

A recent study (Castano et al. 2024) provides a detailed breakdown of some of the most common presumptive taxes used in LAC, EMDEs, and advanced economies. Box 6.2 summarizes this study.

Box 6.2

Unpacking the presumptive tax

The design of real estate taxes in Latin America and the Caribbean (LAC) is quite complex. From a theoretical point of view, the tax should be designed to account for the fiscal valuation of the property and a specific tax rate (Mirrlees 2011), regardless of whether the goal is to tax house consumption or housing as an asset. In any case, the valuation should encompass the flow of consumption or cash involved. Then, if valuations are accurate, all complexity would stem from the tax rate itself. Ultimately, only equity concerns would justify variations among tax rate brackets.

Assuming valuations are accurate, there is no need to deviate from simple tax schedules. In fact, variations from these plans could be associated with some form of government intervention and evidence of favoritism for vested interests. More specifically, industrial or urban policy might be behind the overly complex structures found in the tax design.

Castano et al. (2024) assessed the tax design in Argentina, Brazil, Chile, Colombia, and Mexico. For these LAC countries, the study considered 42 entities from different levels of government (central or federal, regional or state, and local) and found that 10 of them differentiate between urban and rural areas; 6 include land size as a dimension of the design, 29 consider the purpose the property is used for (such as industrial, commercial, or residential), and 9 target duties by zones. One local government in Colombia considers the environmental impact of the properties. The Brazilian national government takes into account the share of the land used for specific activities. Other countries use alternatives in addition to, or as a substitute for, fiscal valuation. However, advanced economies use fewer of these

box continued next page

Box 6.2

Unpacking the presumptive tax *(continued)*

dimensions. Indeed, Castano et al. (2024) find that land use is the only method commonly used in these countries. All the entities reviewed from France, Japan, the Republic of Korea, Spain, and the United Kingdom included land use in their design. So did the Philippines, South Africa, and four of five entities in New Zealand. Nevertheless, other dimensions were rare in these countries. Table B6.2.1. summarizes these stylized facts.

Table B6.2.1 Elements of real estate tax design in LAC and other countries

Country and level of government	Total number of entities	Number of entities considering						
		Urban or rural	Land size	Land use[a]	Impact	Utiliza-tion	Zones	Services available
Latin America and the Caribbean								
Argentina								
Central	—	—	—	—	—	—	—	—
Regional or state	7	6	2	4	0	0	0	0
Local	4	0	0	4	0	0	2	0
Brazil								
Central	1	—[b]	1	0	0	1	0	0
Regional or state	1	—[b]	0	1	0	0	0	0
Local	8	—[b]	0	8	0	0	2	0
Chile								
Central	1	0	0	1	0	0	0	0
Regional or state	—	—	—	—	—	—	—	—
Local	7	0	0	0	0	0	0	0
Colombia								
Central	—	—	—	—	—	—	—	—
Regional or state	—	—	—	—	—	—	—	—
Local	5	2	1	5	1	0	5	0

table continued next page

box continued next page

Box 6.2

Unpacking the presumptive tax *(continued)*

Table B6.2.1   Elements of real estate tax design in LAC countries *(continued)*

Country and level of government	Total number of entities	Number of entities considering						
		Urban or rural	Land size	Land use[a]	Impact	Utiliza-tion	Zones	Services available
Mexico								
Central	—	—	—	—	—	—	—	—
Regional or state	1	0	0	1	0	0	0	0
Local	7	2	2	5	0	0	0	0
Rest of the world								
Egypt, Arab Rep.								
Central	1	1	0	0	0	0	0	0
Regional or state	—	—	—	—	—	—	—	—
Intermediate	—	—	—	—	—	—	—	—
Local	—	—	—	—	—	—	—	—
France								
Central	—	—	—	—	—	—	—	—
Regional or state	1	0	0	1	0	0	0	0
Intermediate	10	0	0	10	0	0	2	0
Local	223	0	0	223	0	0	0	0
Korea, Rep.								
Central	1	0	0	1	0	0	0	0
Regional or state	—	0	0	0	0	0	0	0
Intermediate	—	—	—	—	—	—	—	—
Local	—	0	0	0	0	0	0	0
Japan								
Central	—	—	—	—	—	—	—	—

table continued next page

box continued next page

Box 6.2

Unpacking the presumptive tax *(continued)*

Table B6.2.1   Elements of real estate tax design in LAC countries *(continued)*

Country and level of government	Total number of entities	Number of entities considering						
		Urban or rural	Land size	Land use[a]	Impact	Utiliza-tion	Zones	Services available
Regional or state	1	0	1	1	0	0	1	0
Intermediate	—	—	—	—	—	—	—	—
Local	3	0	3	3	0	0	0	0
New Zealand								
Central	—	—	—	—	—	—	—	—
Regional or state	3	2	0	2	0	0	3	3
Intermediate	—	—	—	—	—	—	—	—
Local	2	1	0	2	0	0	0	2
Philippines								
Central	—	—	—	—	—	—	—	—
Regional or state	1	0	0	1	0	0	0	0
Intermediate	3	0	0	3	0	0	0	0
Local	—	—	—	—	—	—	—	—
South Africa								
Central	—	—	—	—	—	—	—	—
Regional or state	—	—	—	—	—	—	—	—
Intermediate	—	—	—	—	—	—	—	—
Local	5	0	0	5	0	0	0	0
Spain								
Central	—	—	—	—	—	—	—	—
Regional or state	—	—	—	—	—	—	—	—

table continued next page

box continued next page

Box 6.2

Unpacking the presumptive tax *(continued)*

Table B6.2.1   Elements of real estate tax design in LAC countries *(continued)*

Country and level of government	Total number of entities	Number of entities considering						
		Urban or rural	Land size	Land use[a]	Impact	Utiliza-tion	Zones	Services available
Intermediate	—	—	—	—	—	—	—	—
Local	4	4	0	4	0	0	0	0
United Kingdom								
Central	—	—	—	—	—	—	—	—
Regional or state	—	—	—	—	—	—	—	—
Intermediate	3	0	0	3	0	0	0	0
Local	15	0	0	15	0	0	0	0

Source: Based on Castano et al. 2024.

Note: Dashes denote unavailable data.

a. Includes undeveloped land.
b. Urban and rural are divided by level of government.

The lack of robust property price assessment capabilities appears to be the main driver of the complicated nature of property valuation in LAC countries. Some of the tools, such as those targeting the impact of real estate or specific zones, likely represent a form of intervention in private decisions. However, most of the special elements used in taxation seem to be a way to compensate for weak valuations. Because comprehensively updating valuations is a costly endeavor, using alternative data points could be a relatively objective appraisal mechanism (or at least not an overtly arbitrary one).

In any case, improving administrative capabilities to assess valuations regularly and properly is key to a simpler and clearer tax design. Ultimately, this would be central to achieving fairer and more predictable property taxation. Summing up, better valuations would result in avoiding hidden assumptions within the tax system (that is, de facto presumptive taxation).

Source: Based on Castano et al. 2024.

Presumptive property taxes, although useful for increasing government revenue, often lag real estate market trends, leading to significant inaccuracies, inequities, and potential distortions in investment. To address these challenges, enhancing fiscal valuation systems becomes a priority for LAC governments. A study conducted in Buenos Aires (Castano et al. 2024) demonstrated that increasing property tax payments through higher fiscal valuations did not have a significant impact on rents, suggesting that this approach is both effective and neutral for renters (refer to box 6.3).

Box 6.3

Do higher property taxes raise rents? Evidence from Buenos Aires

Anecdotal evidence in the literature on real estate taxes suggests that the tax on immobile properties has few distorting effects on the economy in general. Even quantitative evidence is quite ambiguous regarding its effects on directly related variables, such as the price of the associated properties. For the most part, the empirical literature analyzes cases of cities in developed countries because of the availability of administrative data. Overall, little is known about the impact of the real estate tax in developing countries.

To address this scarcity of evidence, Castano et al. (2024) analyze the effect of real estate taxes on the sales and rental value of properties in the city of Buenos Aires, Argentina. Using a difference-in-differences quasi-experimental approach[a] and unexplored data, they study variations in the effective tax rate that are usual in Argentina because of uneven yearly reassessments of taxes in a context of high inflation.

Their quasi-experimental design relies on the fact that, before each year begins, the city of Buenos Aires passes the yearly tax law, specifying changes in tax rates and other variables that modify the real estate tax base. Castano et al. (2024) leverage a novel database from Properati, a real estate marketplace specializing in listings across Argentina, Colombia, Ecuador, Peru, and Uruguay.[b] The data cover listed properties, both for rent and for sale, between 2018 and 2021. They include the list price, date, location, and property characteristics (such as area and number of rooms). Some listings include more detail. The tax liability is also calculated on the basis of a formula that multiplies the tax base by the tax rate. The tax base is constructed from observable data—such as location and area—with assumptions made about depreciation and construction quality (the latter is based on economic household survey data). Tax rates are obtained from the yearly tax law. On average, the tax rate for residential property in the

box continued next page

Do higher property taxes raise rents? Evidence from Buenos Aires *(continued)*

city of Buenos Aires is about 0.55 percent, ranging between 0.4 percent and 0.7 percent progressively with property values. In Argentina, although rental prices are typically listed in Argentine pesos, sales are usually agreed upon in US dollars.

Using a difference-in-differences approach, Castano et al. (2024) estimate the impact of changes in tax liability on sale prices per square meter. In the first analysis, properties with a tax increase—defined as a percentage increase from the previous year's tax liability—exceeding the median were classified as the treated group. Properties with an increase below the median formed the control group. Additional tests were run using properties exceeding the 75th percentile as the treated group and those below the 25th percentile as the control group. Figure B6.3.1 depicts the results for this initial analysis, showing rental prices before and after the change in tax rate. The horizontal axis is centered on December (0), which is when the tax bill is approved. Data for the three years considered were combined, but additional tests were run analyzing each year separately.

Figure B6.3.1   Evolution of rental prices per square meter in Buenos Aires

Rent prices per square meter (constant Arg$ 2015)

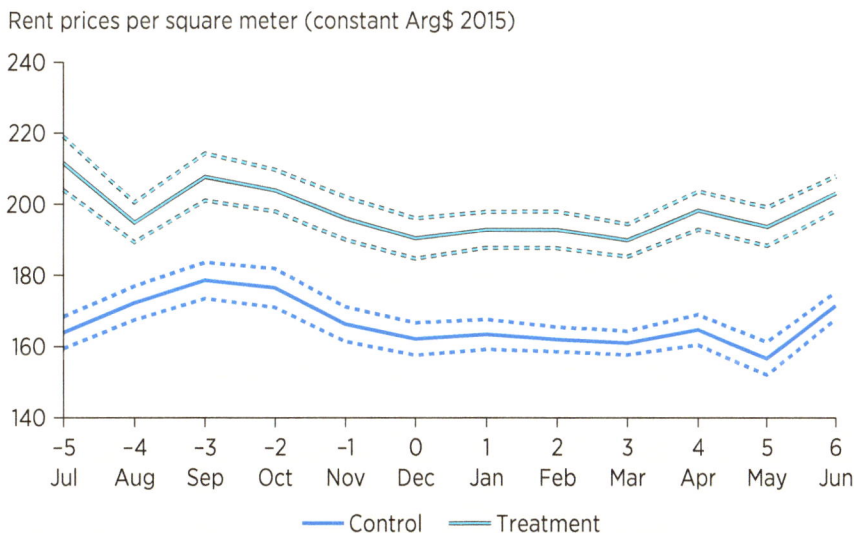

Source: Castano et al. 2024.

Note: The numbers on the *x*-axis are centered on December (0), when the city of Buenos Aires passes a tax law each year. Dashed lines indicate 95% confidence intervals.

box continued next page

Box 6.3

Do higher property taxes raise rents? Evidence from Buenos Aires *(continued)*

Castano et al. (2024) found no direct impact of higher real estate taxes on rental prices. Although one might expect this to translate to lower sale prices because of a decrease in cash flow—resulting from an increase in taxes without an increase in rents—the study also found no significant effect on sale prices. It is important to note that unlike rents, which are often fixed, listing prices typically involve negotiation. This bargaining process might mask a potential impact on sale prices.

The no-effect results are likely a consequence of low effective rates. When property taxes are a small burden on property ownership, any distortions they introduce into the market are likely to be minimal. Imagine a scenario in which property taxes constitute only a small percentage of rental income. Landlords would still have a strong incentive to rent their properties, and tenants would not be significantly deterred by the small increase in rent resulting from taxes. This would minimize any potential dampening effect on rental prices or property values. This evidence suggests that rising property fiscal liabilities, particularly when starting from a low level of taxation, have minimal impact on either sale prices or rents in the real estate market.

Source: This box is based on Castano et al. (2024).

a. As in Elinder and Persson (2017) and Löffler and Siegloch (2021).

b. The data were collected during a small time window when they were available. Nowadays, data are not open.

Using New Technologies for Better Valuation

Traditional methods of property valuation struggle to keep pace with the dynamic nature of real estate markets. Fortunately, technological advancements offer a powerful tool kit to address this challenge. The discussion that follows takes a deeper dive into how leveraging digital platforms and modernizing cadastre systems can unlock the untapped potential of property valuation.

Leveraging Digital Platforms

Real estate websites such as Zillow and Trulia are not simply listing services; they are treasure troves of real-time market data. These platforms aggregate information on property listings, recent sales trends, and neighborhood demographics. By harnessing these data through application programming interfaces or web-scraping techniques, governments can gain valuable insights for several purposes:

- *Comparative analysis.* Digital platforms provide a vast pool of similar properties, allowing for a more accurate assessment of an individual property's value on the basis of comparable features, location, and recent sales. This approach goes beyond simply looking at size and location, leading to a more nuanced and accurate valuation.

- *Identifying discrepancies.* Data integration can reveal properties for which the assessed value significantly deviates from market trends. This can be a red flag for potentially undervalued and undertaxed properties. By analyzing these discrepancies, governments can identify areas in which valuations need to be adjusted, ensuring a fairer and more equitable tax system.

- *Staying on trend.* Real-time data allow governments to track market fluctuations and adjust valuation models accordingly. This ensures valuations remain relevant and reflect current market conditions. For example, if a particular neighborhood experiences a surge in property values because of new development, the valuation model can be adjusted to capture this increase, ensuring property taxes accurately reflect the current market price.

Modernizing Cadastre Systems

Traditionally, cadastre systems have relied on paper records and manual data entry—a recipe for inaccuracies and inefficiencies. But modernizing them with digital tools such as geographic information systems (GIS) is a game changer (Enemark 2010):

- *Digital mapping.* GIS technology can produce a digital map that integrates property boundaries, zoning information, and infrastructure data, enhancing transparency and facilitating property identification and valuation. Officials can easily visualize property locations, zoning restrictions, and nearby amenities, all of which influence a property's value.

- *Boosting data collection.* Mobile data collection tools can streamline the process of gathering property details, ensuring data accuracy and reducing reliance on outdated records. Appraisers can use tablets to capture property features such as square footage, number of bedrooms, and the presence of a garage. This eliminates the need for manual data entry and reduces the risk of errors.

- *Improving data sharing.* Modern cadastre systems can establish secure data-sharing protocols with other government agencies, fostering better coordination and a more holistic view of property information. For example, data can be shared with building departments to ensure property characteristics align with construction permits or with tax departments to streamline the tax assessment process.

The World Bank has been actively involved in helping countries in LAC modernize their cadastre systems. These initiatives have focused on digitizing land records, implementing modern land registration systems, strengthening land administration institutions, and promoting land tenure security. As a result, these efforts have significantly enhanced land governance, reduced land conflicts, fostered economic development, and increased revenue collection, particularly through property taxes (World Bank 2013).

Box 6.4 describes how the determined efforts of local authorities in Bogota and Barranquilla, Colombia, led to significant improvements in the property registry in a remarkably short time. Increased transparency in registration practices enabled these cities to achieve significant increases in local revenues and conduct a more accurate assessment of city developments. This, in turn, has facilitated effective policies related to urban planning, investment, construction, and the purchase and sale of land and real estate in these cities.

Box 6.4

Property registry success stories: Lessons from Bogota and Barranquilla, Colombia

Cadastres in Bogota and Barranquilla, Colombia, represent best-practice examples of cadastral reforms demonstrating the potential for such initiatives to drive significant improvements in property administration systems. Their innovative approaches and significant achievements could serve as a model for other cities and countries in Latin America and the Caribbean seeking to enhance their own cadastral systems and reap the associated benefits.

Bogota's revolution: A map to a brighter future

Bogota Cadastre, established in 1959, was Colombia's first decentralized cadastre. Originally a department of the city's Finance Secretariat, it has since evolved into a vital entity reporting to the tax administration sector.

In 2010, Bogota Cadastre initiated a permanent update process focused on urban areas. This update proved highly successful, expanding the cadastral

box continued next page

Box 6.4

Property registry success stories: Lessons from Bogota and Barranquilla, Colombia *(continued)*

database from 1,279,000 to 2,181,000 plots in just two years. The taxable value for property tax increased by 42 percent during this period, reaching Col$280 trillion.

To enhance data quality and correlation with registry information, Bogota Cadastre underwent a major technological transformation in 2016. This modernization allowed for a shift from intensive fieldwork to a more efficient model relying on secondary sources, including the database of the Superintendence of Notaries and Registry.

This approach has led to significant cost savings and improved accuracy. By leveraging registry data, Bogota Cadastre has been able to identify 75 percent of built areas, particularly new horizontal properties, and to streamline conservation procedures for 60 percent of annual requests.

Bogota Cadastre has evolved from a purely fiscal cadastre to a multipurpose resource. It now provides valuable information to various entities in Bogota, supporting decision-making in areas such as infrastructure management, risk management, and property formalization.

In terms of fiscal performance, property tax revenue in Bogota has increased by 142 percent in the past decade. This growth has made property tax the second most important tax source after the industry and commerce tax, a municipal tax imposed on businesses that operate within the city. The industry and commerce tax, which has seen a 62 percent increase during the same period, remains the city's primary tax revenue source.

Revitalizing Barranquilla: the role of cadastral modernization

Barranquilla, Colombia, has also emerged as a model for effective cadastral management in the country. Before 2017, the city relied on the national cadastral agency, Instituto Geográfico Agustín Codazzi, for these services. However, recognizing the need for greater autonomy and improved efficiency, Barranquilla assumed direct control of its cadastral management.

To modernize its cadastral system, Barranquilla invested heavily in technology. It developed its own proprietary information system, Iguana, which integrates alphanumeric and graphic data, enabling efficient data collection and analysis. The city also prioritized the cross-referencing of

box continued next page

Box 6.4

Property registry success stories: Lessons from Bogota and Barranquilla, Colombia *(continued)*

cadastral and land registry databases, increasing their interconnection from 45 percent in 2018 to 65 percent in 2022.

Barranquilla has focused on making cadastral information accessible to citizens. It launched the Easy Cadaster platform for online inquiries and the Virtual Cadaster tool for requesting and tracking cadastral procedures. Additionally, the city created the Ubibaq Map Portal, offering a comprehensive view of cadastral information, land use plans, and other city services.

By taking control of its cadastral management, Barranquilla achieved significant improvements in efficiency and revenue generation. The city's cadastral update process was accelerated, leading to a 100 percent updated base in 2022. This modernization contributed to a 26 percent increase in property tax collections in 2018 alone.

Barranquilla's cadastral system now serves as a valuable resource for various city departments. It supports decision-making in areas such as urban planning, infrastructure management, and risk assessment. The system also provides data for the Real Estate Observatory, which offers insights into market trends and property values.

Note: This box was developed using original technical contributions provided by the Urban Team at the World Bank, including Dean Cira, Paula Restrepo Cadavid, Ivonne Moreno Horta, and Alvaro Barra.

Prioritizing Property's Substantive Value over Market Whims

Policy makers may overemphasize the concept of accurately assessing property values for tax purposes. Given the inherent medium-term volatility of real estate markets, pinning down an exact market value at any given moment is a challenging, if not futile, exercise. Asset prices, including property values, fluctuate significantly because of factors beyond simple cash flow changes.[4] This suggests that property tax assessments could reasonably focus on capturing a fair approximation of long-term value rather than attempting to mirror short-term market fluctuations. More modest improvements in valuation accuracy, rather than a pursuit of perfect alignment with market prices, could yield substantial benefits for revenue generation without imposing undue burdens on property owners.

How Property Taxes Can Help Reduce Vertical Fiscal Imbalance

LAC exhibits an unusual degree of what is called vertical fiscal imbalance, the mismatch between the revenue-raising capacity of subnational governments and their expenditure responsibilities. The resulting reliance on fiscal transfers from higher levels can create a moral hazard problem: local officials may be less inclined to exercise fiscal restraint because they know that taxpayers in other jurisdictions actually bear the burden of their spending decisions. Moreover, this vertical imbalance can create "rent-seeking" behavior, where local officials prioritize short-term gains and political popularity over long-term fiscal sustainability. For instance, they may engage in excessive spending on populist programs (including excessive public employment) or infrastructure projects that are not financially viable, leading to unsustainable debt levels. The lack of fiscal autonomy can also weaken accountability and incentivize local governments to engage in wasteful spending or corruption, because they may perceive a reduced risk of consequences. These political economy problems can undermine the effectiveness of subnational governance and hinder economic development. This section explores how subnational property taxes can be a tool to address this vertical fiscal imbalance.[5]

Public Spending Decentralization and Vertical Imbalance

Public expenditure is typically distributed across different levels of government, including central or federal, state or provincial, and local levels. The type of expenditures associated with each level varies on the basis of the country's specific governance structure and policy priorities. Central governments typically handle national-level policies such as defense, security, foreign affairs, social security, and sometimes health care and education. State governments frequently oversee regional policies, including transportation, infrastructure, environmental regulations, and sometimes education, health care, and police. Local governments (which include municipalities and cities) often manage local services, such as public safety, waste management, parks, transportation, and other community-based services. Cities may have their own budgets for specific services, such as street maintenance, libraries, and local events.

The degree of public expenditure decentralization—defined as the share of total public expenditure conducted by subnational governments—varies significantly across countries (refer to figure 6.11), including in LAC. Larger economies in the Southern Cone and the Andean region, as well as in Mexico, tend to be more decentralized, which is often attributed to the complexity of managing public services in larger economies, as well as the need to more effectively address diverse regional needs and preferences and the greater capacity of subnational governments in those countries to do so. Smaller countries such as El Salvador, Panama, and Paraguay tend to be less decentralized, potentially because of the economies of scale associated with centralized service. In general, decentralization is greater in more advanced economies, perhaps reflecting a greater confidence in state or provincial and local governance and responsiveness. This is often supported by strong institutions, democratic governance, and a culture of civic participation, which can enhance the capacity and accountability of subnational governments, fostering a more decentralized and responsive system of public service delivery.

Despite the varied levels of public spending decentralization across the LAC region, it exhibits a high degree of vertical fiscal imbalance, unlike advanced economies, as illustrated in figure 6.12. This imbalance, measured as the ratio of a subnational government's own revenue to its total revenue (including transfers from higher levels), indicates that subnational governments in LAC are heavily reliant on transfers.

Figure 6.11   Percentage of public expenditures conducted by subnational governments in LAC countries and other advanced economies

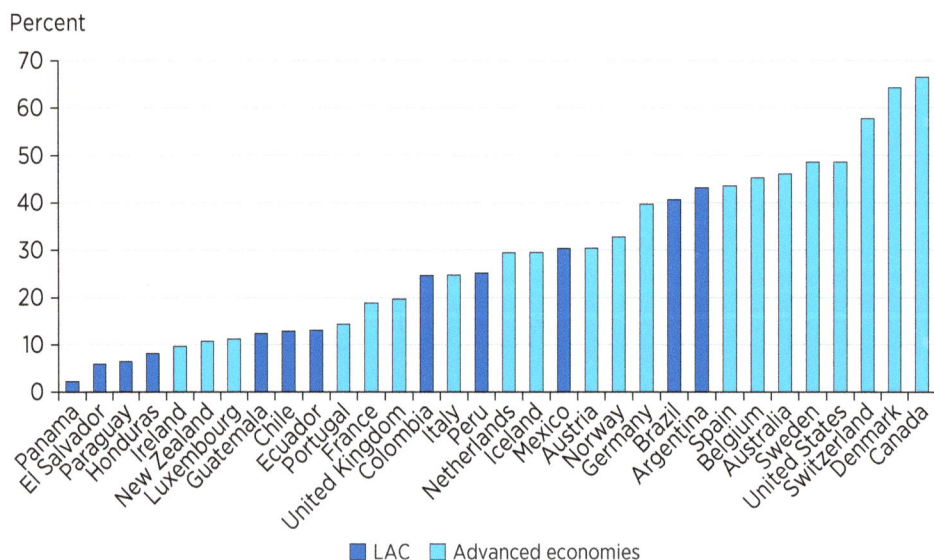

Source: OECD Fiscal Decentralisation Database (most recent year, 2021/22) for OECD countries (excluding LAC) (https://www.oecd.org/en/data/datasets/oecd-fiscal -decentralisation-database.html); IMF Global Finance Statistics, Statement of Operations (most recent year, 2020/22) for Latin America and Caribbean countries.

Note: Fiscal federalism (decentralization) is defined as the total expenditure of state and local governments over the total expenditure of all levels of government. LAC = Latin America and the Caribbean; OECD = Organisation for Economic Co-operation and Development.

Figure 6.12   Fiscal imbalances in LAC countries versus advanced economies

Percent

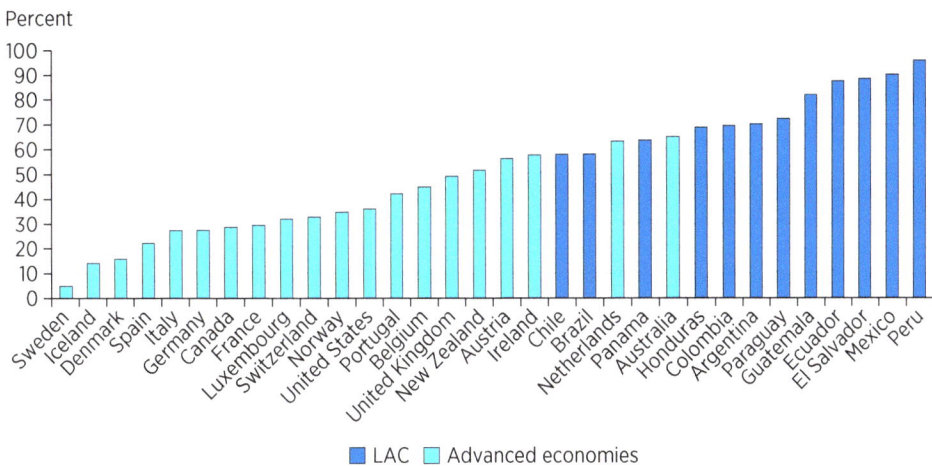

LAC   Advanced economies

Source: OECD Fiscal Decentralisation Database (most recent year, 2021/22) for OECD countries (excluding LAC) (https://www.oecd.org/en/data/datasets/oecd-fiscal -decentralisation-database.html); IMF Global Finance Statistics, Statement of Operations (most recent year, 2020/22) for Latin America and Caribbean countries.

Note: Vertical fiscal imbalance is measured as the ratio of a subnational government's own revenue to its total revenue (including transfers from higher levels). LAC = Latin America and the Caribbean; OECD = Organisation for Economic Co-operation and Development.

The Potential of Subnational Real Estate Taxes

Subnational real estate taxes, levied by local governments on the value of land and property, can be a powerful tool to help mitigate vertical fiscal imbalance, particularly in LAC:

- *Enhanced revenue generation and reduced reliance on transfers.* As discussed, real estate taxes are a reliable source of revenue for local governments. By increasing their own revenue base, subnational governments in LAC can lessen their dependence on national transfers and gain greater autonomy in managing their finances. This can allow them to become more responsive to local needs and priorities, fostering a sense of ownership and accountability.

- *Greater accountability.* When citizens in LAC see a direct link between the value of their property and the level of local services provided, it can foster a sense of accountability between taxpayers and the government. This can encourage responsible spending and efficient service delivery by local authorities.

Although subnational real estate taxes offer potential benefits, there are also considerations and challenges to navigate (refer to Bird 2014; Bird and Slack 2014; Kelly, White, and Anand 2020):

- *Equity concerns.* Real estate taxes can be regressive, meaning they place a higher burden on low-income earners who may own less valuable properties. Careful design and implementation of exemptions or tiered tax rates can help mitigate this concern.

- *Administrative capacity.* Effective administration of property taxes requires a robust system for property valuation and collection. This can be a challenge for local governments in LAC with limited resources. Investments in technology and training for property assessors can improve efficiency and accuracy.

- *Coordination between jurisdictions.* To avoid distortions and ensure fairness, coordination among neighboring localities regarding real estate tax rates and policies may be necessary. This can help prevent residents from moving to areas with lower tax rates, thereby eroding the tax base for all municipalities.

Subnational real estate taxes, when implemented thoughtfully, can be a valuable tool for promoting fiscal decentralization and reducing vertical fiscal imbalance in LAC, by empowering local governments to generate their own revenue and make independent spending decisions. Despite the challenges, subnational real estate taxes hold significant promise for fostering a more equitable and responsive system of public finance in LAC. By addressing equity concerns, strengthening administrative capacity, and fostering coordination between jurisdictions, these taxes can empower local governments to become more effective agents of development and improve the overall well-being of their citizens.

How Rural Land Tax Can Help with Environmental Protection

This chapter has argued that shifting to property taxes could lead to efficiency gains by lightening the burden on entrepreneurs and penalizing inefficiently used wealth such as land. An example is the rural land tax, a levy imposed on the value of unimproved land in rural areas. It can be a promising tool for environmental stewardship by incentivizing sustainable land use practices, which in turn could mitigate deforestation and preserve biodiversity.

Historically, land taxation has deep roots, dating back to ancient civilizations. The Roman Empire, renowned for its administrative prowess, implemented a comprehensive land taxation system. The *tributum soli*, a direct tax on land ownership, formed a cornerstone of Rome's fiscal structure, generating revenue and playing an organizational role in the rural sector (Rostovtzeff 1957). The concept reemerged with vigor during the Enlightenment, when philosophers and economists, grappling with the complexities of industrialization and inequality, explored alternative tax models. Henry George, in particular, became a prominent advocate for land value taxation, arguing that land, as a finite resource, should be the primary object of taxation rather than labor or capital (George 1879). His ideas sparked intense debate and influenced subsequent land tax reforms in various countries.

Contemporary applications of rural land tax vary across countries. South Africa integrates it into broader land reform agendas, whereas in Australia it has been used to fund environmental protection efforts. The efficacy of a rural land tax in this sphere hinges on several core principles. Primarily, it disincentivizes land hoarding, encouraging owners to use their land productively or divest (Turner 2012). By imposing a higher tax burden on idle or degraded land, it incentivizes farmers to adopt methods that improve soil health, reduce erosion, and enhance biodiversity (Pretty 2001). This mechanism can deter large-scale land acquisitions for speculative purposes, often linked to deforestation and habitat loss. Secondarily, the generated tax revenue can be directly channeled into environmental programs, such as reforestation, watershed management, and biodiversity conservation. Hence, land taxes can lead to more sustainable agriculture and bolster ecosystem services while ensuring long-term agricultural productivity.

A unit tax on land can promote sustainable land use because it will prevent the acquisition of any land with a marginal productivity below the tax rate.[6] This is particularly the case if land can be appropriated by clearing and cultivating open-access forest area.

Box 6.5 argues that, with important modifications, Brazil's rural land tax can offer a promising avenue for addressing deforestation and promoting sustainable land use.

Box 6.5

Brazil's land tax: A tool for conservation

The rural land tax currently applied in Brazil, the *Imposto sobre a Propriedade Territorial Rural* (ITR), incentivizes the conversion of forest land to extensive cattle ranching, which is classified as a productive use, resulting in very low tax rates. Changing the parameters of the tax to reward the adoption of sustainable practices and the efficient use of areas

box continued next page

Brazil's land tax: A tool for conservation *(continued)*

that can be farmed or ranched would help foster climate-smart agriculture while reducing incentives for deforestation of additional land.

The rural tax base in Brazil is underused. The current ITR is ineffective as a revenue source. It produces very little revenue: in 2022 federal and municipal governments jointly collected R$3.1 billion (US$0.6 billion, equivalent to 0.03 percent of GDP). Thus, rural land remains an underused tax base, failing to generate meaningful revenue, especially for rural municipalities that lack other significant tax bases.[a] The effective tax rate, using the estimated market value of rural land, is about 0.03 percent, implying that wealth held as rural land is considerably undertaxed compared with other factors of production, especially labor. The average tax per hectare of privately owned rural land is only about R$6.20 (US$1.20), limiting its effectiveness to incentivize efficient and climate-friendly land use.

The current ITR is flawed and counterproductive for incentivizing conservation or efficient land use. It applies to all rural properties above a minimum size and is assessed on the value of unimproved land (not the actual market value), which is self-declared, leading to widespread underdeclaration. The tax rate can vary from 0.03 percent to 20.00 percent, rising with the size of the property and declining with the percentage of property being used productively. For example, a property of between 500 and 1,000 hectares that uses at least 80 percent of usable land (excluding legally mandated conservation areas and other forested areas) is subject to an annual tax of 0.15 percent of the self-assessed value. To be considered in use, pastureland requires a minimum stocking rate. However, these rates, expressed in animals per hectare, are very low, ranging from 0.15 in some Amazonian municipalities to a maximum of 0.9 in much of the south and southeast of Brazil. This implies that extensive cattle ranching, a very inefficient use of land associated with high agricultural emissions and deforestation, is consistent with a low ITR tax rate.

From disincentive to incentive: How reforming the ITR can address deforestation and land productivity

A reform of the ITR should change the assessment of the tax base as well as the rate assessment. The Brazilian Constitution assigns both fiscal and para-fiscal objectives to the ITR, although it does not explicitly name environmental objectives. Several detailed reform proposals have been put

box continued next page

Box 6.5

Brazil's land tax: A tool for conservation *(continued)*

forward to make the tax more effective as a source of revenue as well as for incentivizing efficient land use and conservation.[b] These proposals all include some key features:

- Use an estimate of the market value of land, rather than self-declared unimproved land value. This would provide an important incentive to municipalities to participate in administering the tax, because they would directly benefit from greater tax revenue that would result from more realistic valuations.

- Apply a minimum rate to all land that is not under permanent protection, including forested land. Although applying a minimum tax to standing forest seems counterintuitive, this reduces the incentive to acquire forest land for speculative purposes, with the option to deforest it in the future. To avoid this minimum tax, landowners would need to commit to protecting their forest land permanently (by creating an *área de preservação permanente*).

- Increase the tax rate with the size of the property, although the extent of this progressivity would depend on the policy maker's preferences regarding concentration of land ownership.

- Increase the tax rate on inefficiently used pastures. The criteria for considering a property productive or unproductive, including cattle stocking rates, should be set in line with current agricultural practices.

- Ensure consistency with environmental regulations, especially the forest code and the environmental rural cadastre.

The impacts of a land tax reform on emissions could be significant. A 2014 study by Cohn et al. estimates that a tax linked to intensity of land use for cattle could result in a 61 percent reduction in deforestation as the intensification of cattle ranching reduces the demand for land. Intensification of cattle ranching would also reduce emissions from agriculture—mostly methane—because animals tend not to live as long, and ranchers can supplement feed or switch from grass-fed ranching to using animal feed that reduces bovine methane emissions.

box continued next page

Box 6.5

Brazil's land tax: A tool for conservation *(continued)*

A more effective land tax could reduce rural municipalities' dependence on transfers. Because of the negligible yield of the ITR, municipalities currently have little incentive to cooperate in collection of the tax. A more robust tax could become an attractive own source of revenue for rural municipalities, which currently rely almost exclusively on federal and state transfers. A more effective land tax would also strengthen the case for an environmental fiscal transfer to compensate municipalities for revenue forgone from protected areas.

A general land tax reform could be complemented with a payment for environmental services or a "feebate" scheme to encourage forest protection and restoration. Given the government's pledges to eliminate illegal deforestation by 2030 and restore 12 million hectares of forest and 15 million hectares of degraded pasture, part of the additional revenue from the land tax could be used to provide a subsidy for landowners, especially those at the forest-agriculture frontier, for restoring forests or restoring degraded pastureland (through reforestation; implementation of sustainable productive systems, such as agroforestry and integrated agro-livestock-forest systems; or both). Such a subsidy could be combined with the ability to claim carbon offsets based on carbon sequestration under Brazil's proposed emissions trading system.

Formal and transparent land tenure systems are a prerequisite for effectively levying the land tax and engaging in other land-based policies. Land governance remains a challenge in Brazil, especially in the Amazon biome, with vast territories not formally registered or subject to several disputed claims. Problems stem from the overlapping functions of government agencies and inconsistent regulations. For example, five different federal entities handle the registration of different land tenure categories.[c] They do not coordinate with the multiple state and municipal agencies that have overlapping mandates and manage separate and disconnected databases. The limited interoperability between rural cadastres and urban cadastres and of these with respect to tax administrations at all levels of government undermines the effectiveness of fiscal policies based on land administration—because standardized, updated, and interoperable cadastral information on public and private lands is a basic requirement for consistent land use policies. These complexities, along with antiquated, inefficient, and untransparent (often paper-based) administrative and judicial processes, facilitate illegal land grabbing and encroachment of cattle ranching on

box continued next page

Box 6.5

Brazil's land tax: A tool for conservation *(continued)*

public or undesignated land, which is a key driver of deforestation. Establishing formal and transparent land rights through a land registry has been shown to increase agricultural investments as well as sustainable land use practices. This will require setting up a robust institutional and technical infrastructure to use data from multiple sources effectively.

Source: Based on Fendrich et al. 2022.

a. By contrast, the urban property tax generates about 0.6 percent of gross domestic product in municipal revenue; however, this is highly concentrated in large cities.
b. These proposals are described in detail in Appy (2015), Instituto Escolhas (2019), and Fendrich et al. (2022).
c. The most important land cadastre in Brazil is the Cadastro Nacional de Imóveis Rurais, created by Law 10.267 of 2001 and based on data from the Sistema Nacional de Cadastro Rural (the system used by the Instituto Nacional de Colonização e Reforma Agrária) and from the Cadastro de Imóveis Rurais (the cadastre of rural real estate property administered by the Receita Federal do Brasil). Although Law 10.267 has provisions to strengthen the interconnection among institutions, interconnections remain weak because of use of different concepts, lack of data standardization, and weak law enforcement.

The Billion-Dollar Question: Is Taxing the Ultra-Wealthy the Solution to LAC's Fiscal Shortfalls?

Brazil made headlines as chair of the G-20 in 2024 for, along with France, proposing a "billionaire tax" on the world's richest citizens. Although the equity rationale is clear and the initiative enjoys substantial support, many of the challenges associated with taxing wealth, especially liquid assets, discussed earlier are amplified when targeting billionaires. These individuals often possess access to sophisticated financial advice and have greater mobility, making it difficult to impose and collect taxes effectively. The case of the founder of Mercado Libre, who moved from Argentina to Uruguay, illustrates how high-net-worth individuals can leverage tax differences to reduce their tax liabilities in the Latin American region (refer to box 6.6). In the Latin American context, such a tax, even if perfectly implemented, would not contribute much to reducing the region's fiscal shortfalls.

Box 6.6

Why might Argentine entrepreneurs move to Uruguay? A deep dive into differential taxes on wealth

Tax considerations weighed heavily in the decision of several notable entrepreneurs to relocate from Argentina to Uruguay. A comparative analysis of the tax regimes in both countries provides a clearer picture of the incentives driving this decision.

Argentina's tax environment

Argentina imposes a progressive income tax on both residents and nonresidents for income sourced within the country. Top marginal rates can reach as high as 35 percent. Additionally, Argentina levies a wealth tax, which is a significant burden for high-net-worth individuals. Moreover, the country's complex tax system, frequent changes in tax legislation, and economic instability create an environment of uncertainty for taxpayers.

Uruguay: a tax-friendly jurisdiction

Uruguay has strategically positioned itself as a tax-friendly jurisdiction, particularly for high-net-worth individuals and foreign investors. Key tax incentives include the following:

- *Territorial taxation.* Uruguay primarily taxes income generated within its borders. This means that income from foreign sources is generally exempt from Uruguayan taxation.

- *Nonresident taxation.* Nonresident individuals are subject to a flat income tax rate of 12 percent on income sourced in Uruguay. This rate is significantly lower than the progressive rates in Argentina.

- *Corporate income tax.* Uruguay's corporate income tax rate of 25 percent is competitive compared with those of other countries in the region.

- *Tax treaties.* Uruguay has an extensive network of tax treaties, which help to prevent double taxation and facilitate cross-border investments.

- *Financial secrecy.* Although Uruguay has made strides in tax transparency, it still offers a degree of financial privacy that appeals to some high-net-worth individuals.

All these features amount to strong incentives to relocate to Uruguay.

Global Billionaires

The world has relatively few billionaires. As shown in figure 6.13, the number of billionaires surged from 355 in 2001 to 2,615 in 2023. Given that the global population was approximately 8 billion in 2023, this equates to roughly one billionaire for every 3 million people.

Approximately 75 percent of all billionaires are primarily domiciled in 10 economies: China; Germany; Hong Kong SAR, China; India; Italy; Russian Federation; Switzerland; Singapore; the United Kingdom; and the United States (refer to map 6.1). The United States and China together house half, with 753 and 564 billionaires, respectively.

Figure 6.13   Increase in the number of billionaires around the world, 2001–23

Number of billionaires around the world

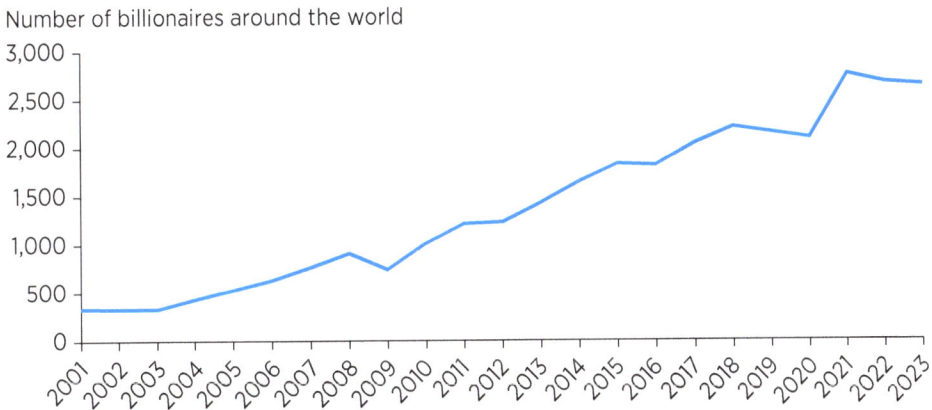

Source: Forbes' World's Billionaires List (https://www.forbes.com/billionaires/).

Map 6.1   Absolute number of billionaires, by country

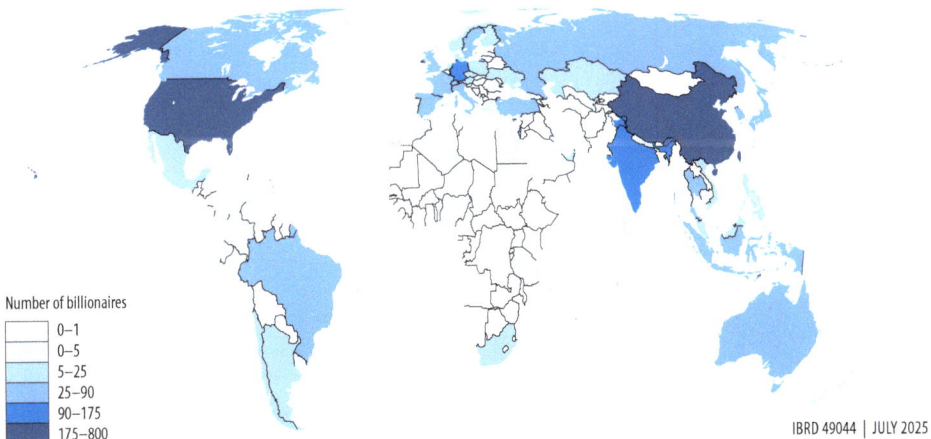

Number of billionaires

0–1
0–5
5–25
25–90
90–175
175–800

IBRD 49044 | JULY 2025

Source: Forbes' World's Billionaires List (https://www.forbes.com/billionaires/).

Although LAC makes up 8.1 percent of the world's population, 7.3 percent of global GDP, and 12.5 percent of the planet's total land area, it is home to only 82 billionaires across 12 countries (refer to figure 6.14), representing a mere 3.1 percent of the global billionaire population. In contrast, the state of California alone hosts 100 billionaires, and the Russian Federation, Switzerland, and United Kingdom have 80, 78, and 83 billionaires, respectively. On a per capita basis (refer to figure 6.15), although there are two billionaires per million inhabitants in North America (excluding Mexico) and one billionaire per million inhabitants in Western Europe, this figure drops dramatically for EMDEs, including LAC, which averages only 0.13 billionaires per million people.

Figure 6.14   Number of billionaires in LAC, by country

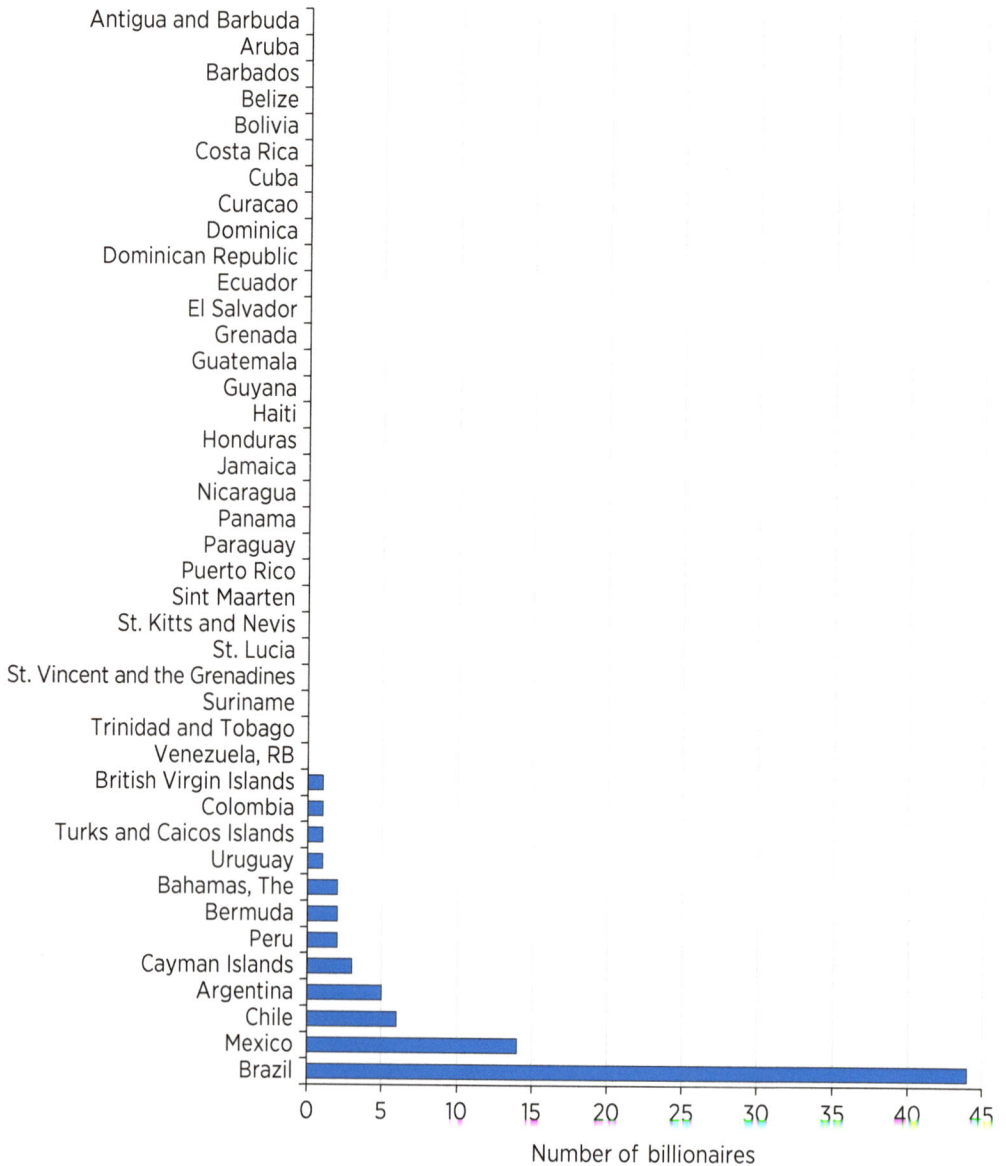

Source: Forbes' World's Billionaires List (https://www.forbes.com/billionaires/).

Figure 6.15   Number of billionaires per million people, by region

Number of billionaires per million people

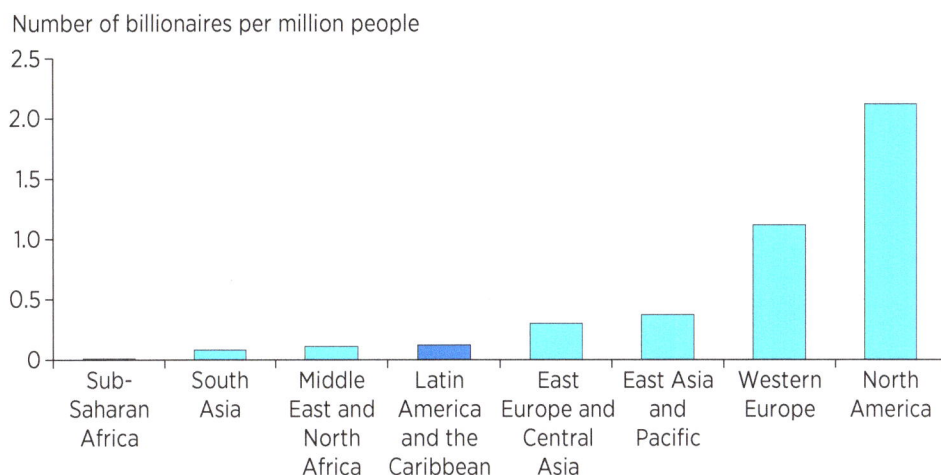

Source: Original calculations for this publication, based on Forbes' World's Billionaires List (https://www.forbes.com/billionaires/) and World Bank World Development Indicators (https://databank.worldbank.org/source/world-development-indicators).

Latin America's Modest Billionaires

In addition, not all billionaires are created equal. LAC's billionaires, although rich, are not spectacularly so by global standards. Elon Musk's net worth hovers around US$225 billion, followed by Jeff Bezos at approximately US$190 billion, Mark Zuckerberg at US$180 billion, and Bernard Arnault at US$175 billion. In fact, the combined wealth of the top 10 billionaires worldwide—nine of whom reside in the United States—totals an astounding US$1.7 trillion, nearly equal to Brazil's GDP and almost triple that of Argentina's GDP. By contrast, the top 10 wealthiest billionaires in LAC together collectively possess about US$250 billion, or just over the wealth of the world's richest person, and the region's billionaires in total account for 5 percent of GDP, far below those of North America, South Asia, and Western Europe at 16 percent, 14 percent, and almost 12 percent, respectively (refer to figure 6.16).

Is Taxing Billionaires the Silver Bullet for LAC's Fiscal Problems?

Again, the point is emphatically not that governments should not ask the best-off in society to contribute their fair share as society determines it. Rather, it is that given the low concentration of billionaires in LAC, combined with the relatively modest amount of wealth held by these highly mobile individuals, it is unclear whether a 2 percent WT—a figure often proposed in policy circles—could generate significant additional government revenue. Figure 6.17 indicates that, even assuming no billionaire migration, the potential revenue collection might reach 0.1 percent of GDP in LAC, which is one-third of the 0.35 percent observed in the United States. That is, it is unlikely to solve LAC's fiscal space problems, and, if star entrepreneurs migrate, the overall economic impacts could be smaller.

Figure 6.16   Total wealth of billionaires by region, expressed as a percentage of regional GDP, and number of billionaires per region

Total wealth of billionaires by region (% of regional GDP)

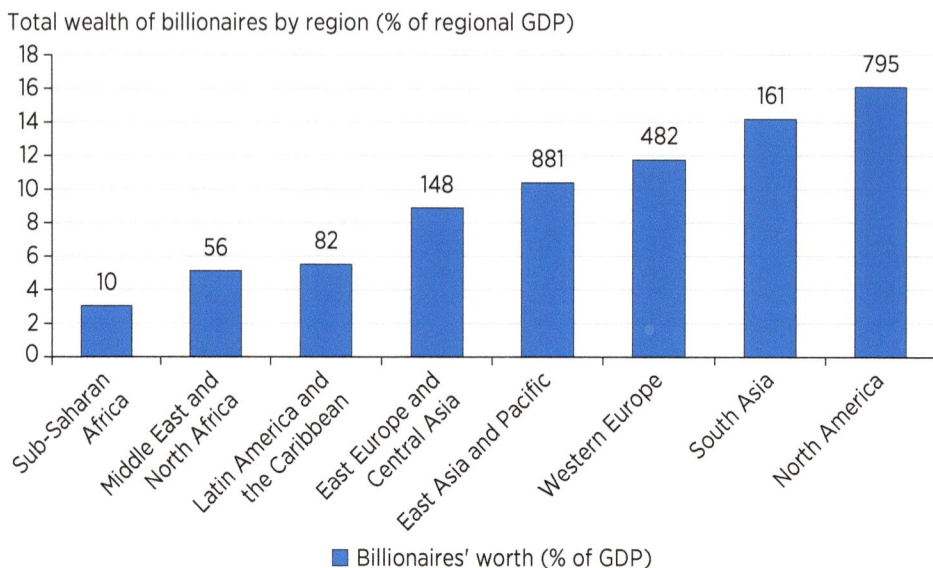

■ Billionaires' worth (% of GDP)

Source: Original calculations for this publication, based on Forbes' World's Billionaires List (https://www.forbes.com/billionaires/) and World Bank World Development Indicators (https://databank.worldbank.org/source/world-development-indicators).

Note: The number of billionaires per region is included above the bar for each region. GDP = gross domestic product.

Figure 6.17   Possible additional revenue resulting from a wealth tax of 2 percent on billionaires, by region

Revenue as a percent of GDP

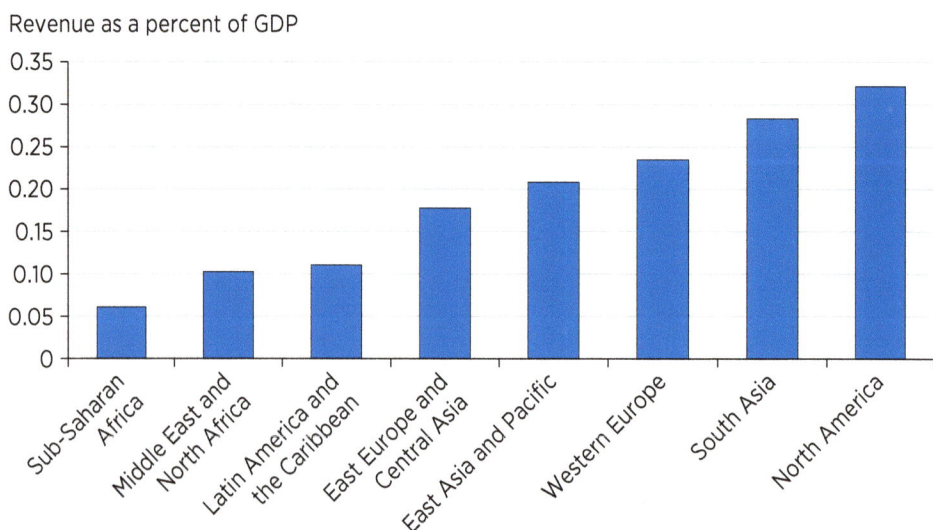

Sources: Original calculations for this publication based on Forbes' World's Billionaires List (https://www.forbes.com/billionaires/) and World Bank World Development Indicators (https://databank.worldbank.org/source/world-development-indicators).

Note: The figure assumes no country mobility response. GDP = gross domestic product.

Conclusion

Although global attention has shifted to WTs, taxing property in particular has the potential to attack the three big fiscal issues facing LAC. Relative to the United States and other advanced economies, property taxes are underused as sources of revenue. They are easy to make progressive and hence contribute to mitigating the persistent inequality in the region. And they have the potential to stimulate growth by shifting the tax burden away from productive investments to less productive types of investment. Property taxes also offer a logical means to redress vertical imbalance when subnational units are dependent on transfers from central governments to cover expenses. The level of imbalances is high in LAC by global standards, and it is accompanied by political economy challenges, such as lack of independence and accountability or even corruption.

Although taxing the wealth of billionaires has moved to center stage in policy debates and has the potential to raise the hoped-for funds for the green transition, it is unlikely to be a magic bullet for the region's broader fiscal shortfalls. LAC has few billionaires, they are less wealthy than those elsewhere, and they are extremely mobile.

Notes

1. See Saez and Zucman (2016). WTs are inherently more progressive than income taxes. Unlike income taxes, which focus on annual earnings, WTs target accumulated assets. Given that a disproportionate amount of wealth is concentrated among a small segment of society, a well-designed WT can more effectively target ultra-wealthy individuals.
2. Specifically, the court found that the tax system, which used a flat-rate return on assets to calculate the taxable amount, did not accurately reflect the actual returns individuals earned on their investments. This was deemed to be discriminatory and to violate property rights because it did not treat all taxpayers equally on the basis of their financial circumstances.
3. *Consolidated government expenditure* refers to the total spending of all levels of government within a country.
4. See discussion in Aguiar, Moll, and Scheuer (2024).
5. Also see discussion in Bird (2014) and Bird and Slack (2014).
6. In this context, a *unit tax on land* refers to a tax levied on the basis of the physical size or unit of land, rather than its value.

References

Aguiar, M., B. Moll, and F. Scheuer. 2024. "Putting the 'Finance' in Public Finance: A Theory of Capital Gain Taxation." Working Paper 32951, National Bureau of Economic Research, Cambridge, MA.

Ahmad, E., G. Brosio, and J. P. Jiménez. 2019. "Options for Retooling Property Taxation in Latin America." Macroeconomics of Development Series 202, United Nations

Economic Commission for Latin America and the Caribbean and Cooperación Española, Santiago, Chile.

Appy, B. 2015. *O Imposto Territorial Rural como forma de induzir boas práticas ambientais.* Instituto de Pesquisa Ambiental da Amazônia, Belém do Pará, Brazil.

Atkinson, A. B., T. Piketty, and E. Saez. 2011. "Top Incomes in the Long Run of History." *Journal of Economic Literature* 49 (1): 3–71.

Bahl, R. W., and J. Martinez-Vazquez. 2008. "The Determinants of Revenue Performance." In *Making the Property Tax Work: Experiences in Developing and Transitional Countries,* edited by R. W. Bahl, J. Martinez-Vazquez, and J. M. Youngman, 35–57. Cambridge, MA: Lincoln Institute of Land Policy.

Bailyn, B. 1967. *Ideological Origins of the American Revolution.* Cambridge, MA: Harvard University Press.

Bird, R. M. 2014. "A Better Local Business Tax: The BVT." IMFG Papers on Municipal Finance and Governance 18, Institute on Municipal Finance and Governance, University of Toronto, Toronto.

Bird, R. M., and E. Slack. 2014. "Local Taxes and Local Expenditures in Developing Countries: Strengthening the Wicksellian Connection." *Public Administration and Development* 34 (5): 359–69.

Bouillon, C. P., ed. 2012. *Room for Development: Housing Markets in Latin America and the Caribbean.* Development in the Americas. Washington, DC: Inter-American Development Bank.

Brondolo, J. D. 2011. "Taxing Financial Transactions: An Assessment of Administrative Feasibility." Working Paper WP/11/185, International Monetary Fund, Washington, DC.

Castano, F., P. Garriga, I. Guardarucci, and G. Vuletin. 2024. *Real Estate Tax: Toward a Practical Wealth Tax in LAC.* Washington, DC: World Bank.

Cavallo, E., and T. Serebrisky, eds. 2016. *Saving for Development: How Latin America and the Caribbean Can Save More and Better.* Development in the Americas. Washington, DC: Inter-American Development Bank.

Cheysson-Kaplan, N. 2024a. "Impôt sur la fortune immobilière: ce qu'il faut savoir pour la declaration." *Le Monde,* May 23, 2019, https://www.lemonde.fr/argent/article/2019/05/23/impot-sur-la-fortune-immobilere-ce-qu-il-faut-savoir-pour-la-declaration_5465799_1657007.html.

Cheysson-Kaplan, N. 2024b. "Impôt sur la fortune immobilière : comment estimer ses biens à leur juste Valeur." *Le Monde,* May 28, 2024. https://www.lemonde.fr/argent/article/2024/05/28/impot-sur-la-fortune-immobiliere-comment-estimer-ses-biens-a-leur-juste-valeur_6235973_1657007.html.

Cohn, A. S., A. Mosnier, P. Havlík, H. Valin, M. Herrero, E. Schmid, M. O'Hare, and M. Obersteiner. 2014. "Cattle Ranching Intensification in Brazil Can Reduce Global Greenhouse Gas Emissions by Sparing Land from Deforestation." *Proceedings of the National Academy of Sciences* 111 (20): 7236–41.

Elinder, M., and L. Persson. 2017. "House Price Responses to a National Property Tax Reform." *Journal of Economic Behavior & Organization* 144 (December): 18–39.

Enache, Cristina. 2024. "The High Cost of Wealth Taxes." Tax Foundation Europe, Brussels.

Enemark, S. 2010. "From Cadastre to Land Governance in Support of the Global Agenda—The Role of Land Professionals and FIG." FIG Article of the Month, International Federation of Surveyors, Copenhagen.

Esping-Andersen, G. 1990. *The Three Worlds of Welfare Capitalism.* Princeton, NJ: Princeton University Press.

Fendrich, A. N., A. Barretto, G. Sparovek, G. W. Gianetti, J. da Luz Ferreira, C. F. Marés de Souza Filho, B. Appy, C. M. Guedes de Guedes, and S. Leitão. 2022. "Taxation Aiming at Environmental Protection: The Case of Brazilian Rural Land Tax." *Land Use Policy* 119 (August): 106164.

George, H. 1879. *Progress and Poverty: An Inquiry into the Cause of Industrial Depressions and the Increase of Want with Increase of Wealth*. New York: D. Appleton.

Grace, M., and A. J. Yale. 2024. "Property Taxes by State: Guide to Understanding Rates and Exemptions." *Business Insider,* November 26, 2024. https://www.businessinsider.com /personal-finance/mortgages/property-tax-by-state#:~:text=For%20the%20US%20 as%20a,each%20year%20in%20property%20taxes.

Guvenen, F., G. Kambourov, B. Kuruscu, S. Ocampo, and D. Chen. 2023. "Use It or Lose It: Efficiency and Redistributional Effects of Wealth Taxation." *Quarterly Journal of Economics* 138 (2): 835–94.

Instituto Escolhas. 2019. *Imposto Territorial Rural: justiça tributária e incentivos ambientais.* São Paulo, Brazil: Instituto Escolhas.

Kelly, R., R. White, and A. Anand. 2020. *Property Tax Diagnostic Manual*. Washington, DC: World Bank.

Klapper, L., A. Lusardi, and P. van Oudheusden. 2015. *Financial Literacy around the World: Insights from the Standard and Poor's Ratings Services Global Financial Literacy Survey.* Stanford, CA: Global Financial Literacy Excellence Center.

Leali, G. 2024. "Macron Joins Brazil's Lula to Tax Billionaires—But Is It All It's Made Out to Be?" *Politico,* June 23, 2024. https://www.politico.eu/article/emmanuel-macron-brazil -lula-da-silva-global-minimum-tax-billionaires-wealthiest-people/.

Le Guern Herry, S. 2024. "Wealth Taxation and Portfolio Allocation." SSRN, April 23, 2024. https://doi.org/10.2139/ssrn.4911583.

Löffler, M., and S. Siegloch. 2021. "Welfare Effects of Property Taxation." Discussion Paper 21-026, Centre for European Economic Research, Mannheim, Germany.

Londoño-Vélez, J., and J. Ávila-Mahecha. 2021. "Enforcing Wealth Taxes in the Developing World: Quasi-Experimental Evidence from Colombia." *American Economic Review: Insights* 3 (2): 131–48.

Mirrlees, J., ed. 2011. *Tax by Design: The Mirrlees Review.* Oxford: Oxford University Press /Institute for Fiscal Studies.

Norregaard, J. 2015. "Taxing Immovable Property: Revenue Potential and Implementation Challenges." In *Inequality and Fiscal Policy,* edited by B. Clements, R. de Mooij, S. Gupta, and M. Keen, chapter 11, 191–221. Washington, DC: International Monetary Fund.

OECD (Organisation for Economic Co-operation and Development). 2018. "The Role and Design of Net Wealth Taxes in the OECD." OECD Tax Policy Studies 26, OECD Publishing, Paris.

OECD (Organisation for Economic Co-operation and Development). 2022. "Housing Taxation in OECD Countries." OECD Tax Policy Studies 29, OECD Publishing, Paris.

OECD (Organisation for Economic Co-operation and Development). 2023. "Base Erosion and Profit Shifting (BEPS)." OECD. https://www.oecd.org/tax/beps/.

Piketty, T. 2014. *Capital in the Twenty-First Century.* Cambridge, MA: Belknap Press.

Pretty, J. 2001. "Social Capital and the Environment." *World Development* 29 (2): 209–27.

Rostovtzeff, M. 1957. *The Social and Economic History of the Roman Empire.* Oxford: Oxford University Press.

Rudnick, R. S., and R. K. Gordon. 1996. "Taxation of Wealth." In *Tax Law Design and Drafting,* Vol. 1, edited by V. Thuronyi, 1–46. Washington, DC: International Monetary Fund.

Saez, E., and G. Zucman. 2016. "Wealth Inequality in the United States since 1913: Evidence from Capitalized Income Tax Data." *Quarterly Journal of Economics* 131 (2): 519–78.

Turner, B. L. 2012. *The Earth as Transformed by Human Action: Global and Local Ecological Change.* Cambridge: Cambridge University Press.

World Bank. 2013. *Land Governance Assessment Framework Implementation Manual.* Washington, DC: World Bank.

7

Conclusion: A New Blueprint for Taxation in Latin America and the Caribbean

Summary

This report undertakes a critical reevaluation of taxation in Latin America and the Caribbean (LAC), both introducing new considerations into the conventional discussions of trade-offs in optimal taxation and broadening the scope of instruments and objectives considered. The report has explicitly incorporated and documented the importance of behavioral responses from taxpayers and firms to tax changes, highlighted the transformative potential of technological advancements in considerations of collection efficiency, and raised fostering sustained economic growth as an objective when considering the optimal tax mix.

Such insights advocate for a promising recalibration of LAC's tax systems. Rather than solely relying on potentially distortionary high rates on narrow bases or unrealistically difficult-to-tax assets, a more strategic blend emerges to simultaneously enhance revenue, promote equity, and foster growth. This involves the following:

- *Maximizing the potential of the value added tax's (VAT's) broad base and strategically reducing excessively high standard rates.* The traditional argument of VAT regressivity is mitigated by evidence focusing on consumption (including informal transactions) rather than income, as well as by the superior redistributional efficiency of targeted cash transfers (TCTs).

- *Moderately expanding the reach of the personal income tax, focusing on upper-middle-income earners among whom behavioral responses are less pronounced.* By doing so, this strategic tax approach effectively enhances revenue and avoids increasing disincentives for entrepreneurship and evasion while simultaneously protecting vulnerable populations.

- *Implementing intelligent property taxation, capitalizing on its immobility, revenue underuse, significant regional wealth share, and improved valuation technologies.* Although taxing highly mobile financial assets and billionaires holds popular appeal, its practical implementation is challenging and often necessitates near-perfect international coordination.

- *Fostering corporate dynamism through a more competitive corporate income tax (CIT) regime that attracts investment and creates jobs.* Currently, LAC's exceptionally high CIT rates hinder growth and prompt firms to evade taxes and "evade the region," exacerbating an already challenging business environment.

- *Strategically pairing TCTs with the tax system to redefine the traditional trade-off between tax collection efficiency and redistribution, liberating tax policy to focus on simpler, more efficient revenue generation and even mitigating behavioral responses linked to aggressive progressive taxation.* Beyond supporting vulnerable populations, TCTs also address low- to middle-income needs through mechanisms such as negative income tax and personalized VAT.

Crucially, the central goal of this report is not to advocate for simply taxing more. Instead, it is about finding the right blend of taxation instruments. In practice, implementing these recommendations might imply increasing some taxes that are more inelastic and easier to collect while simultaneously reducing others that are more distortive, antigrowth, anti-investment, or anti-entrepreneurial.

This holistic and dynamic perspective extends beyond tax policy in isolation. Although this report focuses specifically on taxation, a nation's overall fiscal health is profoundly influenced by the efficiency and growth-friendly composition of its public spending. Inefficient spending can erode tax morale and public trust (Izquierdo, Pessino, and Vuletin 2018). Furthermore, spending rigidities often lead to fiscal imbalances that crowd out crucial public investment, seriously hindering long-term growth (Riera-Crichton and Vuletin 2024). Therefore, efforts to enhance spending efficiency and ensure a growth-supportive expenditure mix across LAC are not merely complementary but paramount to building a truly resilient fiscal system in harmony with a pro-growth taxation agenda.

Ultimately, by embracing these evolving realities and adopting a truly dynamic and holistic approach to both revenue and expenditure, LAC can strategically harness the power of taxation. This is not merely about fiscal stability; it is about transforming taxation into a robust engine for sustainable development and improving lives across the region. This report aims to contribute valuable perspectives to that complex and vital challenge.

References

Izquierdo, A., C. Pessino, and G. Vuletin. 2018. *Better Spending for Better Lives: How Latin America and the Caribbean Can Do More with Less*. Washington, DC: Inter-American Development Bank.

Riera-Crichton, D., and G. Vuletin. 2024. *Public Spending Policies in Latin America and the Caribbean: When Cyclicality Meets Rigidities*. Latin American Development Forum. Washington, DC: World Bank. http://hdl.handle.net/10986/42022.

* 9 7 8 1 4 6 4 8 2 2 5 3 7 *